At Home

IN UPPER CANADA

At Home
IN UPPER CANADA

Jeanne Minhinnik

*Illustration design and drawings
by John Richmond*

A BOSTON MILLS PRESS BOOK

© 1970 by Clarke, Irwin & Company Limited

ISBN 1-55046-156-7

Published in 1994 by Stoddart Publishing Co. Ltd
34 Lesmill Road
Toronto, Ontario
M3B 2T6
(416) 445-3333

A BOSTON MILLS PRESS BOOK
The Boston Mills Press
132 Main Street
Erin, Ontario
N0B 1T0

The publisher gratefully acknowledges the support of the Canada Council,
Ministry of Culture, Tourism and Recreation, the Ontario Arts Council and
Ontario Publishing Centre in the development of writing and publishing in Canada.

Printed in China
By Book Art Inc., Toronto

Acknowledgements

Two organizations have helped to make this book possible. The Canada Council in its wisdom and discretion dispenses not only money but recognition, confidence, and patience; recognition that its beneficiaries exist, confidence that their plans and hopes are capable of realization, and patience with the length of time it takes to produce results. For all these gifts I am very grateful to this excellent institution.

The Province of Ontario's Department of Tourism and Information lent me one of their outstanding photographers, M. W. Wormley, to take pictures at Upper Canada Village. The singularly happy result of this generosity is evident throughout the book.

Philip Shackleton who was responsible for more than a hundred pictures was especially helpful since he had expert knowledge of the subjects he covered and shared my enthusiasm for them. His advice on all aspects of the book was valuable. Other photographers have contributed pictures of quality. Page Toles and Peter Varley of Toronto, Tom Boschler of Hamilton, Mary Kinney of Picton and Pat Hodgson of Kingston all worked with great interest and care.

I am indebted to the Niagara Parks Commission, the Metropolitan Toronto and Region Conservation Authority, the Toronto Historical Board, the City of Hamilton and the St. Lawrence Parks Commission for permission to use pictures of their historic preservation and restoration projects.

For hundreds of reference sketches, including one for every finished drawing in the book, I am exceedingly grateful to my husband who patiently produced them on request. On my publisher's staff I should like to thank my very able editor Ruth DonCarlos for encouragement and guidance, and Isobel Walker whose creative pictorial planning included engaging John Richmond to design and illustrate the pages. With these people I have had a very happy association.

My lifelong experience with librarians has given me an affectionate, grateful respect for them all. To name those to whom I am indebted would be impossible. I shall always be thankful to A. J. H. Richardson, Head, Architectural History Section, National Historic Sites Service, and to V. B. Blake, Ontario Department of Public Records and Archives, who for many years encouraged my research and answered my questions. I have had great help from two former associates, Margery Dissette, Curator of Furnishings, Upper Canada Village, and Peter John Stokes, Consulting Restoration Architect at Niagara-on-the-Lake.

Miss Louise Heringa, formerly of the staff at the Department of Horticulture, University of Guelph, and Mr. Leslie Laking, Director, Royal Botanical Gardens, Hamilton, have been kind enough to encourage my efforts to make a list of garden plants grown in Upper Canada. Answers to perplexing questions have been sought at the Textile Department of the Royal Ontario Museum and have been kindly answered by Mrs. K. B. Brett and Mr. Harold Burnham. Donald McLeish of Toronto, Leslie Donaldson of Galt, and John Russell of Montreal have generously shared their knowledge of Canadian furniture.

I should like to thank my relatives, friends and neighbours in Prince Edward County for indulgently allowing me access to their gardens, their houses, their family histories, their opinions, and their memories. I have been learning from them for as long as I can remember about the old ways of living in Ontario.

J.M.

Foreword

"We are born at home, we live at home, and we must die at home, so that the comforts and economy of home are of more deep, heartfelt and personal interest to us than the public affairs of all the nations of the world."

This editorial creed was printed on the title page of every issue of "The Magazine of Domestic Economy" published in Edinburgh from 1836 and once familiar reading in Upper Canada. Such an assumption of the importance of protecting and improving the family and home was general among the people who lived in nineteenth-century Upper Canada.

This feeling is reflected in many written records of early life which provide us with our chief knowledge of the way people lived. The houses they occupied and the goods and chattels which furnished them are described in advertisements and inventories of the day. Until lately people were still alive who could recall the domestic economy and practices of their Loyalist or immigrant grandparents. A considerable quantity of house furnishings have survived the depredations of indifferent owners over the last hundred and fifty years. From all of these sources I have derived much valuable information in piecing together the background of family life.

This subject has been of great interest to me since my childhood, and I have been fortunate in having opportunities to research and reassemble furnishings and equipment in some old houses in Ontario to create a picture of early domesticity for the interest and pleasure of a new generation of Canadians. The intention of furnishing a house so that it appeared to be lived in required that everything it contained—furniture, heating, cooking and washing apparatus— must be in its customary place and be usable, so that every household task could be satisfactorily carried out. This kind of practical research provided a clearer understanding of what everyday life was like at home in Upper Canada. The knowledge (still to be augmented) which informed such projects is contained in this book.

More recollections of early days and ways than may be thought possible for one born in 1903 are the result of intimate association with an older generation. My mother died when I was born. I lived for the first years of my life with my maternal grandparents in Toronto. Both had been born well before 1850 and were the grandchildren of Loyalists who had left Poughkeepsie on the Hudson River and the city of Philadelphia about 1783 and made homes for themselves on the north and south shores of Prince Edward County. Each summer we went visiting in the County where my grandparents had been born and where they knew almost everyone. Both had taught school there, and in the 1870s my grandfather had owned and edited the *Picton Times*. He was interested in local history and had as friends several of the writers from whom I have quoted in this book. We stayed in old houses and on farms where the furnishings, customs, speech and manners were those of the nineteenth century.

On my father's remarriage, I joined a much more modern household. However, his nostalgia for his Scottish background took us all to stay regularly with families in the Ottawa valley where the soft speech and broad dialect were often unintelligible to me. (My father's grandparents had left the royal burgh of Rutherglen in Scotland in 1822 to take the old settler's road out of Brockville to Perth and eventually to settle in Carleton County.) In their homes the domesticity—particularly the food—was different from the Yankee-influenced atmosphere to which I was used, but the customs and the family intimacy were just as old-fashioned.

None of these people made any special effort to impart a picture of the past. But all their tales of births and deaths, storms and mishaps, travels, the building of a house, and never-to-be-forgotten parties and shivarees inevitably described details of houses and streets and towns. Best of all I loved their stories of "characters." They had a tolerance, indeed a warm appreciation, of eccentric taste and behaviour. They would say, "Once a daft old man came into the dooryard. He had been travelling clear across the country and we bade him stay a while. . . ." Then followed the old man's stories of what he had seen. Or, "They lived in the big house on the hill. They were gentry, I suppose, but they couldn't farm and couldn't learn. They were lonely and hungry. We had to be very clever, when we took food, not to offend them." Then there would be a description of that house.

As I remember my people and their friends, they were confident, indedependent and democratic. They loved Canada and believed wholeheartedly in its future. They were content though not complacent. They were not acquisitive. Their houses and furniture changed scarcely at all during my childhood but within most households the atmosphere was busy, lively and stimulating. As it happened, they had a great respect for education and actively supported all measures which put it in reach of everyone. But we also knew and liked many people in the countryside who had no education, who had never read a newspaper, yet were sharp and observant, practical and resourceful. We were used to a variance of speech and accent which added flavour to encounters and evoked no disrespect, for were we not all of different origins? Now we were *all* Canadians.

Memories are not always completely accurate. Perhaps my parents and grandparents and I have not always remembered correctly; nor, perhaps, have those writers whom I have quoted. I have been too anxious to know what it was really like and what truly happened, to make any knowing misrepresentations, but I am as subject to error as anyone else, and so make apology for unwitting fallacies. While describing domestic life from 1783 to 1867, I have included many of my own later memories. The years from 1903 to 1970 cover a period of such extraordinary change in family life that I have felt a desire to record scenes which may soon be forgotten.

JEANNE MINHINNICK

South Bay, Prince Edward County
August 1970

To my daughter, Alix Gronau, with love

Contents

Gardens, dooryards & verandahs

It was a splendid landscape to which the first settlers came. The forest presented an overwhelming spectacle of teeming fresh beauty in the spring and flaming glory in the fall. But to those whose hopes and plans were based on its eventual destruction it was a formidable and frightening sight. The making of a small domestic garden in a clearing was a gesture of defiance. Little clumps of marigolds, a doorway-shading vine, and wispy wands of roses grown from treasured roots and seeds were promises that someday here would be a home.

When people speak sentimentally of old-time gardens in Ontario they are talking of the gardens they remember. For the pioneers there was little time for growing flowers. In fact there was practically no extensive gardening or garden designing until the middle of the nineteenth century. John Howison, a critical English traveller, complained in 1821 that not even kitchen gardens were to be seen. He added,

> This is a convenience which few Canadian farmers care to possess. They in general suppose that it requires a great deal of time and attention, but most erroneously, for the soil is so productive that all useful vegetables grow without much culture. . . The peasantry evince the utmost indifference about everything that is not absolutely necessary to support existence. They raise wheat, Indian corn and potatoes enough to place themselves beyond the reach of want, but rarely endeavour to increase their comforts by making gardens or adorning the sites of their rude abodes with those rural improvements that so often grace the cottages of the British peasantry.

Ten years later, Adam Fergusson, who subsequently founded the town of Fergus, remarked in his *Practical Notes Made During a Tour in Canada*, "In general, Canadians and Americans are deficient in what we call 'dressing up their doors'; they are, in fact, so much engaged in heavier and more important work that the period for training roses and honeysuckles has not yet arrived." Even in 1860 the Board of Agriculture reported, "There are evident symptoms of a taste for horticultural pursuits springing up amongst our population, yet they are too limited to elicit anything more than this passing remark."

That the pleasure and pride in gardening developed rapidly in the 1860s is shown in *Eighty Years Progress of British North America* by H. Y. Hind and Others, published in 1864:

> The progress of horticulture in Canada may be inferred from what has taken place at and near Toronto since 1836. In that year, with a population of about 6000, there were two small greenhouses in the town, where common plants only were cultivated. In 1862, there exist many thousand square feet of glass-roofed structures, most of them built upon the most approved modern principles, and adapted to the growth of foreign grapes, greenhouse and exotic plants. Orchard houses are already numerous, and a taste for the delightful pursuit of horticulture is rapidly spreading.

This was gardening for towns, and for the rich. Newly founded horticultural societies encouraged, with their exhibitions and awards, the growing of potted plants and greenhouse specialties. Exhibits came mostly from gentlemen's

R. Shirreff's house on the Ottawa River in the 1830s, shown in a romantic drawing by W. H. Bartlett. The verandah, or stoop, was considered an essential addition to a Canadian house, affording protection from winter's storms and summer sun and rain. / From "Canadian Scenery" by N. P. Willis

Opposite page: A front dooryard garden of the 1820s recreated at Upper Canada Village. In the foreground are plantings of peonies, love-in-a-mist, mignonette, Flora's paint-brush, nicotine, bachelor's buttons, four o'clocks, morning glories, violas and cypress spurge. / U.C.V.

I

estates and from those few people who in all places and at all times have a compulsion to grow flowers with great interest and care. There were still very few domestic gardens throughout the province, however. This did not mean that no one was growing flowers but that few people who had any knowledge of botany, horticulture or design were making flower gardens. Most people simply planted where there was a convenient space. And though flower seeds were for sale in all towns from the 1830s on and a number of nurseries were able to supply plant material, the common practice was to save seeds from year to year and to share divided shrubs and perennials with one's neighbours.

The early flower gardens of the farmhouses were not gardens at all, but small, casual groups of shrubs and flowers which were planted in clumps, usually within the confines of the dooryard, a small enclosure around the house.

The descriptions of the rapidly growing towns give us a picture of yards studded with tree stumps, piled with raw lumber, and cluttered with garbage. There were few tidy lawns with flowers in pioneer towns. Cattle, dogs, pigs and poultry roamed at will.

The fact that most pioneer communities were called "clearings" implies that uprooting, not planting, was a universal endeavour. The forest, in all its virgin magnificence, had been the enemy, and shade was considered a fearful thing. It is interesting to see, in early sketches of settlements, that practically the only planted tree is the poplar—straight, tall and ornamental; not shade-giving. Susanna Moodie, one of the most informative of the author-settlers, writing in 1834, commented, "The total absence of trees about the doors in all new settlements had always puzzled me, in a country where the intense heat of summer seems to demand all the shade that can be procured."

In all communities there were doubtless some people who attempted to make a domestic flower garden, for whom the beautiful wild flowers that abounded in the countryside were not enough. Indeed, interest and delight in the native plants seem to have been shown only by travellers and settlers with some botanical education, a few of whom, like Mrs. Moodie's sister, Catherine Parr Traill, a fine amateur botanist, have left us records of their observations.

The practice of planting in clumps that began with settlement has continued ever since around small houses in the country. It resulted in a style of garden that reached its best expression in the years just before the First World War when the general rural prosperity brought some leisure that could be spent in gardening.

The remnants of these old gardens that are still to be found along rural Ontario roads are our chief source of information about the flowers that were once commonly grown. A little distance back from the road's edge one can often see a lilac, the first evidence of an old house site. Closer search will often reveal, half-smothered in hay, a bush rose and a climbing rose gone to brier.

Many farmhouses in Upper Canada had verandahs similar to the vine-shrouded stoop shown in this 1920 photograph of an early nineteenth-century house just east of Cornwall. / Ontario Archives

The fenced dooryard garden of Wallbridge farm, Prince Edward County, still flourishing when this photo was taken fifty years ago. / Public Archives

Plumes of rhubarb in seed may show above the grass. Sometimes a stunted old peony survives, and always there is a tight growth of day lilies. In midsummer one may see the dim pink of bouncing Bet, the joyful riot of butter-and-eggs, and the neat, dense growth of the blue chimney bellflower—all originally garden flowers of the settlers that now grace our roadsides everywhere. We can look hopefully in the long grass for other plants which might once have been there but few of them will have survived the long neglect.

I have seen and can remember many gardens which exemplify the clump-planting pattern, all quite similar although they were planted many years apart. On a farm which borders my own garden there is a stone foundation and cellar hole of a house which was there long before anyone can remember. A lilac hedge forms a stockade around it. The gnarled old apple tree which stood before the front door bears a drift of pink blossoms in spring and small, wormy, sweet apples in September. Close to what was the front doorway is a single yellow rose bush and a few crowded roots of pale mauve and white columbine. The thicket at the back of the foundation is carpeted with wild Canadian phlox, a favourite flower for transplanting from the woods to the home. Mingled with the phlox are purple violets with particularly long stems and sweet fragrance. A group of orange lilies blooms there in July, and August covers the old stones with the pink and rose blossoms of bouncing Bet. Elecampane stands in tall, important-looking clumps here and there, as do those valued medicinal plants, Joe Pye weed and boneset. This house-site planting is typical of many old abandoned gardens to be found throughout the province.

From my early childhood I remember the garden of the hired man's house on my uncle's farm, which was built about 1860. By the time I knew it the house was deeply shaded with elms in front and its half-acre dooryard was surrounded by a rail fence. A yellow rose completely covered the parlour window. An enormous old clump of early-flowering red peonies stood in the small, roughly-scythed lawn, as did a clump of yellow day lilies and one of iris. Below the lawn a small hayfield stretched to the road. On the south wall of the house there was a massive honeysuckle bush and when the kitchen window was open in June the scent of the flowers and the hum of the bees were a delight to the senses. Close around the house on three sides were tall ferns, plantain lilies, and both white and magenta phlox. Around the front step was a carpet of lily of the valley.

The back stoop was a delightful place to sit. It was shaded with lilac and scented with overgrown plants of sweet Mary. Pots and pots of great, leggy house geraniums spent the summer on the ground just below the floor of the stoop. And there was an old wooden washtub filled with earth from which small variegated morning glories climbed up a piece of chicken wire.

In the back yard were two small plots of garden, one with lettuces, radishes, a couple of tomato plants and parsley. ("Never give parsley away;

The Hughes farmhouse, North Marysburg, Prince Edward County, built 1845, as it appeared in 1923. Mature trees and simple planting remained unchanged over many years. / Public Archives

An old homestead in the Niagara district, built in 1810, photographed nearly a hundred years later but showing a characteristic early country garden. / From "Pen Pictures of Early Life . . ." by M. Scherck

3

Bridge Street, Picton, in 1847, as drawn by Capt. J. P. Downes. Some flowers were usually grown in the narrow fenced areas in front of houses on town streets. / Mrs. Gordon Walmsley, Picton

Back garden fence of Judge John Powell's house, Spadina Avenue, Toronto, 1842. / Ontario Archives

it brings bad luck," said the hired man's wife.) The other plot had nasturtiums, bachelor's buttons, pot marigolds, sweet Williams and mignonette. They grew so tightly that they spilled over onto the grass. Currant bushes lined the back fence, and near the privy were sunflowers much taller than I was.

At the side gate the fence was so blanketed with wild cucumber that the latch used to disappear in its tangled vines overnight. Here the rhubarb grew, as always in a clump by itself. (I was given the job of weeding out the dock roots which inevitably infested it.) Outside, on the lane side of the fence, were the hollyhocks. They lined the path to the drive shed—a glorious sight when the sun was behind them in the evening. Chimney bellflower was everywhere in the lane and bouncing Bet grew thickly.

These two gardens belonged to humble homes. They were doubtless loved but no special amount of time and certainly no money was spent on them. Seeds and roots were traded from farm to farm. To this day one is apt to find the same varieties of coleus and impatiens—those two great stand-bys for farmhouse windows—in all the houses of one area, while ten miles away different varieties will flourish. The ordinary country garden of today, if one adds the ubiquitous petunia, still bears a close resemblance to the gardens I have described.

Nowadays one scarcely ever finds a well-tended burial plot on the old farms. What was once a place of veneration and care has become a thick mass of weeds, still respectfully fenced but standing lonely and neglected, often in the midlde of a cultivated field. The roots of trees have toppled the gravestones and leaf-mould has buried them. Remainders of the old plantings, when they exist, almost always include lily of the valley, myrtle, southernwood, a white iris with a faint blue tinge (perhaps the old Florentina), and a rose or two, often ramblers. Although there are records of the tombstones in these old graveyards there are none of the flowers, and the burial grounds that survive are worthy of exploration.

Although there were some traditional customs regarding the place where particular flowers should be planted—such as peonies always in the front yard and marigolds always in the back—there was rarely any formal design in farm gardens. The exception to this was the traditional dooryard garden, sometimes called the parlour garden, a design which came to America from the cottage

4

gardens of England and which was surely one of the loveliest forms of planting ever seen.

In older parts of Ontario the enclosure around the house is still called the dooryard. It is simply the fenced area immediately surrounding the house, as contrasted with the barnyard, also an enclosure. It was always fenced to keep out straying and grazing animals, and in towns the fence on the street was usually a picket fence with a gate.

In the front of the dooryard only flowers were grown, bisected by grass, pebble, or tanbark paths. Annuals and perennials of all colours and heights were massed together without plan. Daffodils, poet's narcissus, tulips, grape hyacinths, and star of Bethlehem bloomed in spring among the slowly rising green shoots of perennials. Predominant among the early summer dooryard flowers was the iris, which used to be called flower de luce, a corruption of the French name. There were always day lilies, Canterbury bells, sweet Williams, mignonette, Oswego tea, and feverfew. Aconite, lupins and honesty were there. Amaranthus—the old name for prince's feathers—was often grown, and four o'clocks were sometimes used as a border. Ageratum, lobelia, verbena, dwarf morning glories, sneezewort and filependula were favourites. The great days of these gardens, however, were the twenty days of peony bloom. (They were called "pinys" then and the country people still call them so.) Martagon and Madonna lilies and crowds of tall phlox followed the peonies.

At the corners of the fence, a few old-fashioned shrubs were always seen. Inevitably there was the lilac ("laylock" in those days) and the snowball and the high bush cranberry. Virgin's bower often tumbled over the fence, or showers of matrimony vine. The viola tricolour, called ladies' delights, and periwinkle, or myrtle, grew under the bushes and often crept through the palings. At the sides of the dooryard were often specially prized fruit trees and currant bushes.

Some vegetables for the table were grown at the back of the house. A clump of rhubarb, invariably called pie-plant, and one of horseradish, were usually located in a back corner of the fence; here too was often found the Jerusalem artichoke, sometimes called the Canadian potato. Crowding everything were thickets of the fragrant currant known in rural Ontario as Missouri currant, with its sickly-sweet yellow blossoms and dark fruit.

Though it was unusual for vegetables to be grown in the front dooryard, one author, Michael Scherck, in *Pen Pictures of Early Pioneer Life in Upper Canada* has described early gardens in the Niagara Peninsula where that was done:

Among the Pennsylvania Dutch settled in Canada, the garden plot stood close by the house and was surrounded by a picket or board fence to keep out the poultry, pigs and other animals that would soon have made havoc of the flower and vegetable beds, if accidentally allowed to enter. A path ran round

Town fence of the 1860s, Wellington St., Ottawa

Fenced dooryards and gardens in the village of Wellington, Canada West, 1847, as drawn by Captain J. P. Downes. / Mrs. Gordon Walmsley, Picton

the sides of the garden and one or two paths through the centre. The bed enclosed by the centre was usually devoted to flowers and the rest of the garden to vegetables, herbs, etc. One could not help wondering how our busy grandmothers found time to devote to such work, but their gardens were apparently their pride, and they spent a good deal of time working in them. It was the custom always to take visitors out and show them through the garden before leaving. We can see the women now, with perhaps a white handkerchief or an apron tied over their heads, strolling through the garden and yard interested in looking at the flowers. In the spring of the year our grandmothers would bring out the boxes in which were stored the seeds collected the previous fall, each kind of seed being wrapped up in a separate parcel, some in folds of newspaper, some in pieces of brown paper, some in cloth, some in paper bags, all carefully marked and pinned up or tied with a piece of string or tape. Together with the flower seeds there were also all the common vegetable seeds, as lettuce, cabbage, onions, beets, beans and cucumbers.

In the flower-beds, plants were to be seen blooming the whole summer through, commencing early in the spring with the crocuses, tulips, and daffodils, and ending in the fall with the dahlias, phlox and asters. There was generally a border of daisies and amaranthus (called in German *Schussel Blume*, because the shape of a dish, or rather a cup and saucer) and in the centre hyacinths, marigolds, Caesar's crowns, bachelor's buttons, carnations (called pinks in the early days), primroses, sweet Williams, four o'clocks, pansies, sweet peas, mignonette, a choice rose bush here and there, peony,

"The Homestead," Goderich, about 1890—a fine house and garden representative of the one or two "mansions" usually found in towns of Upper Canada during the mid-nineteenth century. / Public Archives

white-scented and red (called *Gichter Rose* by the Germans, because its roots were supposed to be a cure for fits), and a tomato stalk with its red fruit, called love apples sixty years ago [i.e. 1840], and cultivated only as an ornament, as its fruit was not thought to be fit to eat.

(It is very curious that many people say tomatoes were not eaten in their grandparents' day. Yet many early cookbooks in America gave recipes for their use. Mrs. Child in *The Frugal Housewife* in 1835 said that tomatoes should be skinned by pouring boiling water over them, and suggested that they be stewed with salt and a little water and butter. She added, "This is a delicious vegetable." *The Improved Housewife* by "A Married Lady" in 1843 recommended stewing and gave a recipe for escalloped tomatoes. All later recipe books enlarge on the use of tomatoes.)

In a corner of the garden [Scherck continued] was to be found a bush of old man and one of live-forever, used in bouquets. A grape arbor or trellis was to be seen in the garden or yard and a hop-pole or two in one of the corners. Then there were beds for vegetables of all kinds and a bed for the herbs used for medicinal and culinary purposes, such as rue, thyme, sage (German *solvein*), sweet savory, fennel, carraway, loveage (German *liebsteckley*), wormwood, pennyroyal and catnip. In the fall of the year these herbs were collected and dried for winter use. Along the garden fence, on the inside, were to be seen hollyhocks and gooseberry and currant bushes, and in the yard or lawn a few beds of daffodils (smoke pipes), peony and fleur de lis. Scattered

Family gathering on the verandah at "Clark Hill," Niagara Falls, in the late 1860s. / Ontario Archives

through the yard were to be found a variety of shrubbery such as rose bushes, lilacs, or syringias [sic] and snowballs; against a lattice near the house a honeysuckle vine and around the back door the familiar sunflower.

No one sat in these gardens, and few people even walked up the centre path to the front door. The casual visitor who, driving up the lane, would naturally come to the side gate and the back door, would be taken "through" and out the front door for a short, admiring stroll among the flowers. This was the women's sphere; it was they who traded the seeds, the roots and the cuttings of their treasures.

Although the dooryard garden was chiefly planted between 1820 and 1840, its form lingers in many small towns in Ontario. It is not often found now in front of the house but between houses. Here flowers and vegetables are planted thickly in a great colourful mass rather than in beds. If you look for dooryards you can find them, but only on the older streets, and even these may soon disappear. Such old-fashioned gardens are often made by people who have retired to the town from the farm and unconsciously carry the old traditions with them.

The pioneer housewife grew, or gathered, both herbs used in cooking and those for medicinal use (which were called simples). A tradition of the use of herbs in Upper Canada has remained till now in the memories of old people, but no tradition or record seems to show that a special part of the garden was reserved for them. Even in the United States where herb gardens were planted from the earliest times the practice of making special gardens for them had begun to disappear by about 1850 when the general cultivation of gardens was just developing here.

The most common culinary herbs grown in Upper Canada were sage, summer savory (used for soups, stews and sausages), dill and marigold. (Marigold flowers were also used in soups and were rubbed on wasp or bee stings to alleviate the pain.) Dandelions made a bitters used as a liver tonic.

The old tradition of a scythed lawn with clump plantings and a few shrubs is evident in this 1905 photograph of a typical small farmhouse.

Wintergreen was steeped for rheumatism, and the various mints were stewed as a tea for indigestion. Sage was used as a tea for curing headaches. Fevers were abated with catnip tea, and thoroughwort tea was taken for dyspepsia. A cure for a cough which appears in an 1835 household guide used in Ontario calls for lungwort, maidenhair, hyssop, elecampane and hoarhound steeped together.

An immigrant, John McDonald, writing about the New Lanark district in 1823, listed wintergreen, maidenhair fern and the inner bark of maple as substitutes for tea. Michael Scherck recorded that herbs and barks such as sage, thyme, chocolate roots (?), spice wood, hemlock boughs and sassafras were used, and that peas and barley, acorns and dandelion roots, rye and carrots were roasted as a substitute for coffee.

In 1851, Asa Parker, who called himself "gardener and seedsman," published a small book called *The Canadian Gardener* which contained "practical directions for the kitchen and fruit garden," and in it he gave a list of suitable herbs for Canadian gardens, with their medicinal and culinary uses. The herbs were: "balm [his name for Oswego tea], sweet basil, garden burnet, chamomile, comfrey, coriander, catnip, celendine [*sic*], dill, feverfew, hoarhound, hyssop, house leek, ground ivy, sweet marjoram, winter marjoram, marigold, mint, peppermint, spearmint and pennyroyal, opium poppy, rue, saffron, sage, savory, scurvy-grass, southernwood, thyme, and wormwood."

A solidly planted forecourt or dooryard garden before an old Ontario house as it looked in 1900.

Chicory and molasses made a good general physic for all. Dried burdock leaves, with the tough parts cut out, were warmed in vinegar and applied to sore feet. Wormwood, both green and dried, the latter softened in warm vinegar, was used as treatment for fresh wounds of all kinds. Bunches of tansy were hung in the kitchen to discourage flies. All of these uses are culled from household manuals published prior to the 1860s and from the recollections of old people.

Herbs were gathered when they were beginning to blossom. Those used as medicine were dried and put away in paper. The cooking herbs were pounded in a mortar, sifted, and then put in boxes or bottles. The warmth of the oven a few hours after the bread was taken out was reputed to be the best heat for drying, but I can remember an attic which was once festooned with strings of drying apples and great bunches of sage.

In most old Ontario communities there are legendary stories of splendid gardens that once flourished there—gardens which, we are told, were enclosed by walls. But we have no written records of their flowers, no descriptions of their walls. Few writers have remarked on them.

When the English author Anna Jameson visited Stamford Park, built and landscaped by a former Lieutenant-Governor, Sir Peregrine Maitland at Stamford, she simply commented, "It is the only place I saw in Upper Canada combining our ideas of an elegant, well-furnished English villa and ornamented grounds with some of the grandest and wildest features of the forest scene." Beyond describing an "open glade" in front of the house she had nothing more to say about what must have been one of the outstanding gardens of the 1830s.

Verandah on "The Hall," Bathurst Street, Toronto. "The Hall" was the residence of Colonel Sir Casimir Gzowski from 1855-1860. / Ontario Archives

Since no exact description remains, one can only conjecture about the nature and use of early garden walls. They were probably chiefly built to contain kitchen gardens, as is shown on the 1860 plan of the grounds of Dundurn Castle in Hamilton. And it is likely that they were simply built, of rough stone or vertical boards, for the sole purpose of keeping out marauding animals.

The earliest Canadian fencing for flower gardens, as seen in old pictures, was either a pile of small stumps or an interwoven thicket of dead branches, probably thorn. Picket fences were used from the early nineteenth century on and many old photographs show houses in villages, towns and cities with only the few feet of ground in front fenced in from the street with painted pickets.

9

Afternoon tea in the garden, Toronto, 1890. Gardens of this type were numerous in towns and cities of Upper Canada from 1850. / Public Archives

An 1870 photograph of the extensive gardens at "Rodman Hall," home of Thomas Rodman Merritt, St. Catharines, Ontario. The gardens were established around the year 1855. / Ontario Archives

On farms the rail fence (sometimes set on stone) was usual.

In 1802, the annual town meeting of York decreed, "[A legal fence] shall be the height of five feet, and there shall be no space through the fence of more than four inches." Such fences served as a protection against thieves and roaming animals, chiefly hogs, but also as protection for the garden. Over a hundred years later, in my childhood, I remember pleasant Toronto back gardens surrounded by just such high vertical board fences with gates giving on to the stable lanes which bisected all the old city properties.

Wooden fences of this kind were to be found in most Ontario towns. In places like Kingston, Belleville, Brockville, Guelph and Galt, where stone was abundant, some houses had—and still have—tall stone walls around the rear of their lots. Through arches and gateways the passer-by may catch glimpses of lawns and flowers, although many of these gardens were once only stable yards. It was not until the 1850s that the large open lawn became common in towns.

"Formal garden" is a modern term. Until the eighteenth century no other type of planned garden existed. The natural garden, sometimes called the picturesque or poetic garden, which developed in England in the eighteenth century, imitated the most grandiose of landscape painting, so that what appeared natural was the result of meticulously careful planning and planting. In early Victorian days in England and America there was a revolution from the natural design and a studied form became popular. This type of gardening was known as bedding-out or carpet gardening, or as mosaic culture. The formal arrangement of flower beds and shrubbery was reflected in the gardens of well-to-do houses in Upper Canada towns in the years between 1850 and 1900. The Canadian version of the formal style provided for a much more open planting than in England, and front gardens here were scarcely ever closed from public view. The introduction of an enormous number of half-

hardy plants made it possible to spread before the passer-by small geometric beds of lobelias, calceolarias, geraniums, antirrhinums, and all the other bright-coloured low-growing flowers of the period. Fascinating varieties of geraniums were bedded out, centred with plume poppy or celosia, and bordered with pansies, lobelia and alyssum. Bleeding heart, when it was introduced, was an immediate success for these beds. Zinnias were available, rather small in size, and dahlias (for which the growers issued special catalogues) were the pride of all such gardens. The double petunia came in during the 1850s and from then till now has probably been one of the most popular annuals ever grown. These gardens were showpieces where only the gardener or hired man stooped to pick a dead flower or pull a weed. The front garden became a public rather than a private place.

There was usually a semi-circular drive, or at least a walk, from street to front entrance door, and some space was left in grass before the house so that it could be seen to advantage. Then began the round, crescent, diamond, and other fancifully shaped beds of flowers imprisoned by arched iron hoops. Vines were much grown; Virginia creeper and ivy clung to the house walls. Clematis, cobea and honeysuckle were grown for show and shade on the verandah posts, and Dutchman's pipe grew in strangling profusion on the side porches.

Tall posts, bark-covered, were used to support roses and flowering vines at intervals around the house. Grape arbours bearing the popular Isabella or catawba vines were thought to be both beautiful and economical. Privet and hawthorn were favourite hedges, and the much-admired Norway spruce, hemlock and weeping willow were planted in groups on the lawns, in preference to the orchard trees, Lombardy poplars and catalpas favoured earlier.

Garden approach to a house on Queen Street North in Hamilton, Ontario. The house was built in 1841 by Thomas Stinson. / Hamilton Public Library

Though the front garden was formal, the back retained many of the characteristics of the farm dooryard. Round the kitchen door sweet Mary, summer savory, mint, dill and pepper grass were planted where dishwater could easily be emptied on them, and plentifully sprinkled through this green were the orange heads of the pot marigolds. Plantain lilies and chimney bellflower grew beside the rain barrel. Small violas, myrtle, or the dwarf morning glories often carpeted the ground around the pump. Lilac grew beside the woodshed and trumpet vines grew over it. Here, too, tumbled one of the loveliest of vines, the virgin's bower, a vine of many names—climbing fumitory, Alleghany vine and mountain fringe—both flowers and seeds of which are delicately beautiful.

Some of the old flowers were planted close to the sides of the house. Always there were ferns and lily of the valley and mignonette but as well there would often be Oswego tea, phlox, sweet William, bachelor's buttons, rose campion, oriental poppies, and the little self-sowing pink poppies. Lupins, foxgloves, rose of Sharon and hollyhocks lined the back fence. There was usually a small kitchen garden as well.

Many of the houses for which late formal gardens were created are still here. Vestigial remains of bedding-out gardens are sometimes to be seen in smaller towns, although perennial borders have usually replaced the mosaic beds. Antique dealers have swept away most of the cast-iron elegancies which ornamented lawns.

It seems strange that many popular flowers of the early days, flowers which are both hardy and lovely, are now almost forgotten by most flower growers. The old single peony is not generally grown now. Achillea Ptarmica which used to fill in the spaces between tall perennials, is seldom seen. The self-seeding feverfew, whose greeny-yellow foliage and white button flowers softened and enhanced all the other plants, is also rare. Is it because of their noxious smell that the lovely crown imperials are not seen in modern gardens? They always used to be grown at a distance from the house, on a fence or in the lawn, where they could be seen and not smelled. The globe thistle which lent a haze of cool blue in August, and the rose campion which often grew as tall and as thick beside it, seem to appear only in old gardens; the magenta colouring of the rose campion is out of favour. So neglected is the purple,

The house, on Main Street West, Hamilton, where the family of Dr. Henry Thomas Ridley lived from 1856 to 1896. Many town houses had narrow enclosures in front and large gardens in the rear and were located on beautifully shaded residential streets. / Hamilton Public Library.

mauve and white sweet rocket that now it appears chiefly as a roadside flower. Yet from the days of Elizabeth I till about fifty years ago its tall, long-lasting flowers and sweet scent made it a favourite in all country gardens. I remember it growing in great beauty with the tall white valerian.

The varieties of silene, or catch-fly, including the wild bladder campion, were once much cultivated, and around the doorstep there used to be a special place for star of Bethlehem which I have known to bloom for twenty or more years without care. The hardy annuals tri-colour gilia and Flora's paint brush also deserve a place in every garden but they, too, are seldom grown today.

The yellow brier rose that continues to bloom on abandoned house sites and still blankets the walls of old houses where cultivating may have been indifferent or non-existent is usually Harrison's Yellow, widely sold from about 1830. The English sweetbrier Eglantine brought by Old-Country settlers in the '30s and '40s, also persists. Its foliage smells of apples and it has small single pink flowers in spring. Sometimes it runs out into hedgerows where it meets the native low pasture rose.

There were not many roses around houses in the country but those that were grown were all sweetly scented. There was the lemony smell of the single and double yellow rose, the ineffable delicacy of the old damask, and the heady fragrance of the cabbage, or Provence rose. The cinnamon rose was so called for its faint spicy odour. The varieties of old roses, cuttings of which were exchanged throughout the countryside, are now usually botanically nameless to their owners, though they are often called by the name of the persons who contributed the cuttings perhaps two or three generations ago. Most of the surviving farm roses are what used to be called summer roses and bloom only in June.

Varieties of summer roses recommended by a rural manual of 1859 are: Coupe d'Hébé, Perle de Panche, Persian Yellow and Madame Plantier. The pale pink roses on four- or five-foot bushes (with plenty of suckers), frequently seen around farmhouses, are probably Maiden's Blush. This rose, introduced in 1797, was for many years a favourite on the North American continent. The foliage is a bluish-green and the stems are tall and arching. The scent from the Maiden's Blush is the essence of all roses.

The cup-shaped La Reine, one of the most beautiful of the late-nineteenth-century roses, is rarely seen today. Madame Hardy (1832), a white damask which blooms so profusely in June that the bush is weighted to the ground, belonged in all fine gardens in Upper Canada and is, happily, still to be had.

All gardeners with pretensions to a cultivated taste grew moss roses after 1850. Salet was the favourite everywhere, and the crested moss rose called Chapeau de Napoleon (first sold in 1827) was the pride of good town gardens. Its buds were even more beautiful than the blown flower. There are few surviving old moss rose bushes. "We used to have a really pretty rose with green all around the buds, but it just disappeared," people say.

There was a great deal of trading of rose cuttings, seeds, and the roots of shrubs and plants. Many Loyalist families visited their relatives and friends in the United States for years after the Revolution and no doubt brought back some of the new and less familiar flowers to Canada. Several American nurserymen had agents in Canadian towns and orders could be quickly filled since daily shipments were made across Lake Ontario during the season. The Prince Nursery on Long Island, which was opened in 1730, was responsible for the introduction of the Lombardy poplar and was for many years a source of supply of these trees as well as of fruit trees and ornamental plants. The firm was still advertising in Brockville in 1835. The Rochester Nurseries were favoured as suppliers to the Niagara and Toronto districts. Grant Thorburn of New York, an eccentric itinerant preacher and seedsman, had agents in Upper Canada. An advertisement in *The Traveller or Prince Edward Gazette,*

Advertisement for nursery stock, 1856. / Ont. Arch.

A typical county atlas depiction of a farmhouse, garden and grounds in 1862. The house may be seen today, with trees grown to maturity but otherwise scarcely changed. / Mr. & Mrs. K. Wright, Dundas

published in Picton in 1836, carried the announcement of a stationer and fancy-goods dealer: "Cecil Mortimer having made arrangements with G. C. Thorburn, Seedsman and Florist of New York, is now prepared to receive orders for all kinds of flowers and garden seeds, roots, and plants."

William Custead of York, who had an orchard nursery from 1811, issued a remarkably interesting catalogue in 1827 listing "fruit and ornamental trees, flowering shrubs, garden seeds, green-house plants, and bulbous roots." In a list of twelve ornamental trees at one shilling each he featured the catalpa, for many years a favourite lawn tree in Eastern Ontario. He could supply thirty-six varieties of flowering shrubs, six of honeysuckle, twenty-five of tulips, and twelve of hyacinths. Twenty-two rose varieties were listed at a shilling each and the very desirable moss rose at five shillings. His catalogue of green-house plants includes China ever-blooming roses, six varieties of geraniums, Jerusalem cherry, and Chinese "changeable" hydrangea, all of which he said would "thrive in a comfortable sitting room during winter."

Twenty years later there were nurserymen in Toronto like George Leslie and Joseph Pape whose names have been given to the streets that once bordered their premises. There were early nurseries in Niagara and a notable one, Chapmans, in Bytown. Kingston had Belonge's Royal Saloon and Conservatory which in 1838 advertised "upwards of 3000 thriving plants, among them . . . many rare exotics, great variety of superb carnations, seventy varieties of geraniums and sixty of roses." Advertisements for Dutch flower roots did not appear till the '50s.

Flower seeds were quite frequently advertised from the 1830s on and were designated as English, French or German seeds. The *Kingston Chronicle* for 1818 advertised garden seeds "raised by the Shakers" which were being sold by a doctor. Seeds were sometimes sold by milliners as a sideline, which reinforces the view that flower gardening was a feminine pursuit. Both fancy-goods stores and general merchants also carried seeds.

Names of flower seeds were rarely given in advertisements but occasionally vegetable seeds were named. The enterprising general merchant Quetton St. George advertised a notable list from his store at York in February of 1808: "Red onion, white onion, green marrowfat peas, blood beet, early cabbage, winter cabbage, savoy cabbage, red cabbage, scarcity [sic], lettuce, cucumber, early cucumber, turnip, sage, carrot, parsnip, radish, French turnips, summer squash, winter squash, watermelon, muskmelon, early beans, cranberry beans, early purple beans, asparagus, summer savory, celery, parsley, pepper grass, burnet, carraway, pink."

Old established seed houses such as Carters in England, Landreth of Philadelphia (1784) (who sold seeds to George Washington for Mount Vernon), and Peter Henderson (1845) of New York (who introduced the double zinnia) were all in the mail-order business and must have sent seeds to Upper Canada.

The few really devoted gardeners followed the inexhaustible writings of J. C. Loudon in his *Gardener's Magazine* and books—material which was often pirated by American magazines. The classified catalogue of the Free Reference Library (Toronto Mechanic's Institute) in 1861 included five entries on gardening:

Downing: *Treatise on the Theory and Practice of Landscape Gardening Adapted to North America*, 1860.
Gilpin: *Practical Hints on Landscape Gardening with Remarks on Domestic Architecture*, 1835.
Loudon: *Landscape Gardening and Landscape Architecture of the Late Humphrey Repton*, 1840.
Thomas: Volume of *Rural Affairs* for 1855, which included several house plans and plot layouts.
Watson: *American Home Garden*, 1860.

1857 advertisement for nursery stock. / Ont. Arch.

Geraniums, coleus, celosia, begonias and cannas were surrounded, in nineteenth-century urns, by lobelia, ageratum, alyssum, myrtle, oxalis, verbena and violas. / After an old engraving

The Toronto Horticultural Society was founded in 1834, with the Lieutenant-Governor, Sir John Colborne, as patron. The annual subscription was ten shillings, which was paid by thirty-six members in Toronto as well as by eighteen corresponding members and fourteen members abroad. Other towns such as Kingston, Guelph, Brantford, London, Paris, Elora, Goderich, Picton, Bowmanville, Cobourg and Lindsay organized societies in the '50s and '60s. By this time some of the grand houses in Upper Canada—*Alwington* in Kingston, for example—had greenhouses and, occasionally, gardeners to tend them. The horticultural society shows gave these growers an opportunity to display some of their prized flowers. During the first half of the nineteenth century Canadians interested in competition flower-growing shared the English craze for multitudinous varieties of pinks, carnations, dahlias and pelargoniums.

By the middle of the nineteenth century the American garden architects Andrew Jackson Downing, F. L. Olmsted and Calvert Vaux were well known to serious Canadian gardeners and their influence was strong. Downing said, in the 1839 edition of his *Treatise on the Theory and Practice of Landscape Gardening Adapted to North America*, that André Parmentier, a Belgian exponent of landscape gardening, was responsible for laying out two or three places in Upper Canada (probably in the 1820s). (But since Downing went on to say "especially near Montreal" one feels that he suffered from a common American confusion about our geography.) Frederick Law Olmsted is also believed to have planned some gardens in Ontario. In the 1850s Canadian nurserymen and architects were drawing plans for gardens, and gardening manuals showed patterns for laying out flower beds.

Cemeteries were the first landscaped areas to be enjoyed by the public which was, in any case, predisposed to spending holiday occasions in these sorrowful places. One of the first alternatives to cemetery visiting in the province came with the opening of the Horticultural Gardens in Toronto. The Gardens were given as a park by the Hon. George W. Allan in 1860 and opened by the young Edward VII when he was Prince of Wales. In my childhood it was still a beautiful, much-frequented spot to walk and meet one's friends after Sunday morning church services.

Calvert Vaux wrote in 1857, "The verandah is perhaps the most specially American feature in a country house, and nothing can compensate for its absence." Downing thought that no country house in America was tolerable without a verandah. These opinions were shared by most house builders in Upper Canada at that time. Direct exposure to the sun was regarded by everyone as dangerous, which is why people wore a large straw hat or a sunbonnet when they gardened.

The old Dutch *stoep* was the first type of verandah, although the double galleries common to inns were sometimes so used. (This was the case in the 1794 Fairfield house near Bath to which galleries were added about 1825.) The covered farmhouse stoop was level with the ground or only slightly above it. It was usually built on the wing of a house at both front and rear but sometimes stretched across the entire front. As Michael Scherck says, "Very often the roof projected over, giving an elliptical shape to one side, and the projection of about six feet formed a cover of what was then called 'the long stoop'." (Canadians to this day have ignored Miss Leslie's dictum in her *Behaviour Book*, published in 1853: "Do not call the doorstep or porch the 'stoop' even if you are a provincial New Yorker.") Mrs. Traill called it a "stoup" and remarked that few houses, either log or frame, were without one. She added, "The pillars look extremely pretty wreathed with a luxuriant hop vine mixed with the scarlet creeper and morning-glory." From this shady shelter vines, bushes, flowers in pots and clumps, and the prospect of fields and

Cast-iron chairs, benches and urns were popular garden furnishings from the 1840s on. The chair pictured here was sold, in the 1850s, by the J. L. Mott Iron Works, and the urn was sold by Hutchinson and Wickersham, both of New York

woods could be enjoyed. Old Windsor and ladder-back chairs and rockers offered well-cushioned summer ease amid the drowsy hum of bees.

Downing called the verandah "the resting place, lounging spot, and place of social resort of the whole family" in writing of those elaborate appendages at the front of mid-century houses, with their surprisingly varied and interesting posts and vergeboards or their magnificent cast-iron trellisages. Cast-iron furniture and some "rustic" and wicker pieces began to replace the old-fashioned house furniture of the stoop about this time and the townspeople "dressed" for the verandah, to be seen as part of the impressive street-front. Comparatively inexpensive cast-iron furnishings in the shape of chairs, benches, tables, hitching posts, deer, birdhouses, urns and ornaments, all in the baroque and rococo styles, appeared on the market in the late 1850s and dotted the lawns. This ornamental furniture coincided with the growth of seed houses and the introduction of new flowers. Both inspired the development of those absurdly spotty formal gardens with lawns, shrubbery, rigidly planted flower beds, and carefully arranged iron furniture which were still being pictured in our county atlases of the 1870s.

I remember summer afternoons on the verandah of a "county atlas" sort of house in the early twentieth century. There were two rocking chairs, some side chairs, a hammock and a table. On the edge of the verandah was a regiment of house plants. Japanese wind harps tinkled from the sky-blue verandah ceiling. Palm-leaf fans lay on the table. At half-past three a tray with a jug and glasses was brought out and we sipped lemonade or raspberry vinegar made with cold well-water. Beyond the clematis vines, over the "bedded-out" lawn we looked to the wooden sidewalk where ladies with long white dresses and parasols strolled by on their way to pay calls. We speculated as to their destinations. An occasional buggy drove past and we always knew the occupant. But most people were home enjoying the peace and pleasure of their own verandahs and gardens.

A list of flowers, shrubs, herbs and some vegetables grown in Upper Canada before 1860 is contained in the Appendix.

The remains of a garden around an abandoned early house in Prince Edward County. The double briar rose and Virginia creeper, once carefully planted, have almost smothered a few remaining roots of lemon lilies, lily of the valley and "wild" ferns.

Opposite page: Parlours of the 1820s were elegantly furnished but informally used. The wallpaper here is English, pre-1825. The late Regency mahogany sofa was imported from England for a Dundas county family in the 1820s. The Pembroke table and small candlestand are Canadian. William Stodart in London made the upright piano around 1825. / The French-Robertson residence, U.C.V.

Parlours & sitting-rooms

The mid-nineteenth-century parlour, in all its glory, with coal fires burning and lamps lighting up floral carpets, rich draperies, polished mahogany, and glittering lustres, was a brilliant background for crinolines and curls. In ordinary houses, though, its hours of luminosity were brief and infrequent. Weeks and months passed when its door was never opened.

By custom, the parlour presented a social face to the world; there judgments were made on comparative prosperity and standards of housekeeping. Consequently, dreams and sacrifices went into its furnishing. And since, in many families, the requisites for furnishing the parlour could be afforded only once in a lifetime, the compulsion to preserve the room forbade any easy family use of it. Carpets, wallpapers and fabrics faded quickly, polished surfaces scratched easily, gilt tarnished, and embroideries became soiled. So the blinds were kept down, the curtains were drawn, dust covers were laid over the furniture, gauze was tied on the pictures, and the door was closed. Even the parlours of wealthy houses were not in everyday use.

Parlours of all classes from 1860 on were overfurnished; a mixture of accumulated furniture and objects surrounded the best that could be afforded in the way of a parlour suite. The harvest of many years of gift-giving, souvenir collecting, and handiwork was collected there. Black horsehair upholstery, deep-coloured fabric and wallpapers, and grained brown woodwork all contributed to the gloom of the décor.

The mid-Victorian taste in parlour furnishings survived in thousands of town and country houses until the First World War, but most young Canadians have never seen such a room. Those who have remember draped tables holding photograph albums, stereopticon viewers, and waxed flowers under a bell glass. They recall what-nots laden with small china and shells, lace antimacassars, and tasselled velvet skirts on the mantel shelves. The parlour, opened only for christenings, weddings, funerals, clerical calls, and first visits of courtship, had by 1914 become a dead room, but it took two more generations to bury it completely.

Early parlours, unlike their Victorian successors, were meant to be used constantly. Whether rich or poor, they were the rooms where the family and their friends sat, talked, took tea, played cards, did sewing and drawing, and occasionally ate meals. Children and their toys were not excluded. Chairs and tables were moved about as needed—drawn close to the fireplace or stove in winter, set near open windows in summer. In spring and fall screens were moved about to control draughts. Only when the room was cleaned and tidied were chairs placed around the walls against the chair rail. The atmosphere was one of light and spaciousness.

Even the first small houses that succeeded the log cabin had a parlour. By 1820 advertisements of houses for sale specifically mentioned parlours, and plans of the 1830s and 1840s always included, even in a workman's cottage, a room called a parlour. More elaborate plans showed both a drawing room and a parlour. In such cases the parlour often became a family sitting room or dining room, and the drawing room was used for entertaining.

The parlour was a significant room for families who had been confined to kitchen and bedrooms for a long time. People were at home a great deal more then than they are today and spent much time together as a family. Even in houses which had been divided to afford separate quarters for the elderly, or for a young married son and his family, the parlour in warm weather was generally the common sitting room.

Though the kitchen was still the natural gathering place of the family, the parlour became the projection of their ambitions or claims to social position. It contained the best furniture, the family relics and valued objects. Even its window curtains proclaimed to the world the respectability of the family within. In old Ontario houses that have not been altered the importance of the

An 1820s baluster-framed mirror, with reverse-painted frieze. It is unusual in that the frame is white with gilt trim; most were black or imitation mahogany. All such mirrors were intended for the parlour. / Upper Canada Village

parlour is clearly evident in the carefully selected knot-free floor boards and wood-trim, the good wainscot or chair rail, and the wooden cornice at the ceiling. Many houses had built-in china cupboards and the nailing boards which stretched between window frames show where the long case clock was once screwed against the wall.

In summer the parlour was a place to relax, away from the eternal heat of the cooking fireplace, but in many early houses the parlour in winter was too draughty for comfort. The doors and windows had to be sealed with long strips of putty or lath wound with strips of cloth, and a bolster made of a stocking filled with sand had to be placed at the bottom of the door to keep the chill air of the parlour out of the cosy kitchen where the family retired till the warmth of May.

There was a prevailing tendency always to use the room on the left of the front door as a parlour and, from about 1800 to 1835, to use white or light-coloured paint on all wood-trim. Windows were sometimes left uncurtained or had light swags attached to the window frame. Short muslin curtains, called "blinds," were often strung on the lower sash and moved with it as it was raised or lowered. Floors were either sanded or painted, usually grey or grey-green, and were made lovely with several coats of shellac which imparted a glittering, glassy surface. The evidence of stencilled floors in the province has largely disappeared, but there may have been many, as there were in New England. Walls, for the most part, were washed with white or coloured lime and were sometimes stencilled in tones of blue, pink and green, or gold, green and terra-cotta.

Exceptionally grand houses boasted London-made furniture, wallpaper, carpets, silver candelabra and fine porcelain in the china cabinet. In garrison towns many of these imported luxuries eventually came up for auction, and everywhere in the province changing fortunes brought fine furnishings under the hammer, thus enabling many families to acquire things they could not ordinarily afford. Andrew Hurd, a householder in Augusta, in an inventory of 1838 valued "a carpet for the parlour" at 8/13/-, and "three window curtains for the parlour" at 2/3/-. Moreen curtains for four windows in John Turnbull's house in Belleville in 1827 were valued at 9/10/-. These were prices no average person could afford but at auction the prices were much lower. An advertisement in a Kingston newspaper in 1811 stated that tables, chairs, stoves, and carpets, "the property of a gentleman about to leave the Province," would be sold. "Leaving" was a typical reason for sales and the bargains from such sales must have enhanced many a parlour in Upper Canada.

Some of this beautiful imported furniture is still treasured in Ontario. Regency tables, chairs, small writing desks with brass inlay or ormolu mounts,

tripod candlestands and fire screens, fine engravings, silver and porcelain, all come to light when the contents of old family houses are sold.

"Fashionable" chairs were advertised for sale in 1811 in Kingston, and since the adjective was intended to distinguish them from everybody's Windsors and slat-back chairs, they were presumably either provincial renditions of Sheraton and Hepplewhite designs, or of the more up-to-date Regency style. The prevailing colour scheme of the parlour was often echoed in the squabs (thin loose cushions with ties) which were used for comfort and protection on the cane and rush seats of many of these early chairs. Fancy chairs with imitation mahogany or black finishes, heavily decorated with gilt and colour, were an obvious choice for the parlour, and even rocking chairs were made worthy of the "best" room by an excess of gilded and painted decoration. An upholstered wing chair was a luxury, as was a fine "chimney glass," which was often a vertical mirror in a mahogany or gilded frame.

Sofas in the Sheraton-Hepplewhite tradition were thin and elegant, upholstered in black haircloth, silk, plush, velvet or wool. A light bright blue or soft orange were favourite upholstery colours. The Empire or Late Regency sofa which followed them was often upholstered in chintz. Mahogany, both solid and veneered, rosewood and walnut were the woods ordinarily used for sofas. Springs were not used for many years; instead the seats, backs and arms were stuffed with wool or hair. The first covering under the upholstery fabric was often linen. Most sofa legs had castors, as the furniture was intended to be moved about frequently. Cushions were rarely used on early sofas but round, tightly-stuffed bolsters were often placed at either end of the seat.

Footstools, large and small, were either upholstered to match chairs and sofa, or their covers were worked in cross-stitch or embroidery. Painted or embroidered satin was framed for tall fire screens, and embroidered pictures were hung on the wall. Silhouettes and portraits in oil and water colour were used as the family purse permitted. Engravings were considered very desirable but were rather expensive. (The number of surviving engraved portraits of George III and George IV indicate that they must have been popular subjects.) Carpets were rare till after 1830, but hearth rugs and other mats, including animal skins, were used. The china cabinet, whether part of the architecture of the room or a fine piece of mahogany furniture, contained the porcelain treasures of the family that were never intended for ordinary use. The "chimney ornaments," as they were called in advertisements, consisted of vases, candlesticks, china figures, clocks, lustres and face screens (used to protect the faces of ladies from the glow of candle or firelight).

In houses where women had leisure, both embroidery frames and drawing boards or tables were also part of the parlour furnishings. Embroidery silks and satins were obtainable very early and even in 1802 in York one store advertised drawing and writing materials: "black lead pencils, common ditto, red and black sealing wax, India ink and India rubber, sands, pewter inks with tops, and blotting paper." All these things were requisites of parlour life. From 1831, the subscription of $3 per year brought *Godey's Lady's Book* every month, with its voluminous advice on sketching and patterns for needlework, to say nothing of fashions and entertaining or improving articles and stories.

In the 1830s a small piece of furniture was introduced for the well-appointed parlour and was called, alternatively, a chiffonière or an étagère. In the eighteenth century this was a small bookcase with one drawer, but in the nineteenth it became a little cupboard, the lower half with a solid or glazed door concealing shelves for music or books. Above the top surface were one or two shelves on which ornaments were displayed. Often made of mahogany (later of rosewood), étagères were also made in soft woods, painted and grained. In sparsely furnished rooms they were an important addition, and although not particularly useful, they gave a fashionable note much desired by their feminine owners.

Cardplaying, in all but strict Methodist circles, was a passion in early days.

An English-style mahogany card table topped with bright blue baize, c. 1840. / Upper Canada Village

Opposite page: The small parlour-sitting room of Mrs. Sophia MacNab, sister-in-law of Sir Allan MacNab at Dundurn Castle, Hamilton. The dark red ceiling cornice with black and gold moulding is restored from the original. The parlour suite in bird's-eye maple was made by a cabinetmaker in the area for William Bates about 1850. Gas lighting was used in Hamilton in 1851 and the centre fixture is typical of the period. / Dundurn Castle

Parlour in the William Lyon Mackenzie house, Bond Street, Toronto. / Toronto Historical Board

"The Bridal Prayer," an 1845 engraving showing a fashionable parlour of the day. / Author's coll.

Playing cards were advertised as early as 1803, and the card table was a necessity in the parlour. Most card tables had a folding, hinged leaf supported either by a swing-out leg or a bracket, and all were approximately the same size. It is astonishing, then, that such an endless variety of these tables remains. In mahogany, maple, cherry, walnut and rosewood, with tapered or delicately turned legs, with or without blue or green felt-covered playing surfaces, they are seen everywhere, with never an exact duplicate. When not in use they stood against a wall with the extra leaf up, forming an excellent background for silver or brass candlesticks and snuffers, or a Solar lamp.

The other tables that furnished a parlour were likely to have been a Pembroke, a candlestand, and a sewing table, all of which were commonly made by Canadian cabinetmakers. "Pembroke" is a carry-over name from the eighteenth century when such tables were first made. Their general usefulness is so great that they are still made today. Characteristically, the table has two short drop leaves hinged to a rectangular top usually twice the width of the leaves. The leaves frequently had rounded corners. There is a drawer set in the apron, and sometimes a false drawer front appears at the opposite end. Candlestands often had a round top on a tripod pedestal, but they also appeared as small, square-topped tables with one or two drawers. Maple or cherry were the preferred woods for candlestands. Sewing tables were variously fashioned with one or two ordinary drawers with locks, and a bag drawer, made like a pouch, of silk or wool mounted on a wooden frame, where the sewing was kept. These were often gifts from parents or husband to the lady of the house and were regarded as her personal property. In this table, old letters, a book of devotions or poetry, pieces of treasured lace, and even jewellery mingled with the threads and thimbles amid the scent of potpourri.

Papier-mâché chairs reached the height of their popularity about 1850. Made of pressed paper, decoratively painted and inlaid with mother-of-pearl, they were relatively inexpensive. / U.C.V.

Mahogany parlour chair, one of a set made by the cabinetmaker James Reid of Hamilton around the year 1860. / Dr. & Mrs. J. F. Houston, Hamilton

The desk in the parlour, on the other hand, was the property of the man of the house. Stand-up desks, now called schoolmaster's desks, were to be found anywhere in a house according to the convenience of the man who used them. They were used chiefly for writing accounts and for keeping them locked in the pigeon-holed space beneath the sloping writing surface. A flat ledge at the top-rear held a pewter inkwell, quill pens, a sander, sealing wax and wafers. When made of good woods with handsome brass pulls and escutcheons, these desks were fit for the parlour. The painted ones were considered suitable for hall, kitchen or even bedroom.

Sit-down desks were also slope-fronted in the early period and had one or two drawers or a whole section of them beneath the writing surface. They were rarely seen without locks, and were as much part of a man's privacy as the sewing table was of a woman's. Most houses had a portable writing desk or two, and these unfolded to reveal a sloped writing surface, an ink bottle, drawers for pens and penknife and sealing wax and the small candle to melt the wax.

Many men looked forward to owning a tall secretary bookcase with glazed shelves above, desk in the middle, and cupboards or drawers below. The use of these great heavy pieces of furniture extended throughout the nineteenth century. Many were made to order. The one I own has its history written on the side of a secret drawer—a typical history, for it says that the wood was cut from the farm wood lot, taken to a local cabinetmaker and finished to order.

Pianofortes appear in the inventories of quite a few houses, but were rarely advertised for sale except at auctions. The following are typical descriptions of pianofortes: in 1811 at York, "fine-toned, double-keyed harpsichord and pianoforte inlaid with sattinwood [*sic*] and of beautiful mechanism"; in 1834 in Brockville, "a circular end pianoforte with additional and extra keys, six octaves, pedal . . . on four large pillar legs in a French-polished mahogany case, finished expressly for a cold climate." It is interesting to note that, also in Brockville in 1834, Mr. William Newell taught "pianoforte, flute, clarionette [*sic*], flageolette, etc." Jews harps, guitars and fiddles, the musical accompaniments to country conviviality, were offered for sale from the earliest times.

23

Middle-class town parlours at that time were often much cluttered with family living; the many basement kitchens were not as agreeable places in which to sit as were those in the country. The assortment of furniture in these parlours was the same as that in the best houses but there were fewer pieces and they were well below the style and finish of the more expensive kinds. The early farm parlour contained a collection of Windsor-type chairs, a settle of the same type made comfortable with a thick woollen pad, a rocking chair, a fall-leaf table with candlesticks and a Bible, and stools by the fire. Often the big old storage chests containing the family papers and other valuables were kept here.

Books were scarce in farmhouses and were read over and over again. An interesting advertisement in the *Kingston Gazette* in 1810 shows one source of reading. The advertiser, signing himself "A friend of the poor," says, "Bibles and Testaments and a large number and great variety of small books and entertaining tracts can be exchanged for cotton and linen rags of the type suitable for paper-making." And in 1817, both books and engravings were advertised in Kingston as the "property of a gentleman about to leave this place." Even today there are eighteenth- and early nineteenth-century books in farmhouses which are described as "some that grandpa bought once at a sale." What few books there were usually sat on a small wall shelf or were kept on the top shelf in a cupboard.

There was nearly always a cupboard in the farm parlour. Its solid doors shut away miscellaneous collections of linen, china, books and letters. If there was a clock in the house other than the usual long-case one, it sometimes graced the parlour mantel along with some of the cheap ornaments from Staffordshire or Bennington. Small coloured engravings which could be bought for pennies, and the lithographs of Messrs. Currier and Ives provided cheerful colour on the walls. A length or two of handwoven rag carpet or a braided rug made from old clothing completed a pleasant picture.

By 1840 the furnishing of ordinary parlours was beginning to have a "fixed" look and the use of the room became more formal in the town and country. The word "living room" as the name for an additional room appeared on a few building plans around this time, though "sitting room" was still preferred to designate informal parlours. Miss Beecher, writing in 1841, complained, "Multitudes of persons will cramp their bedrooms, kitchens, and closets to secure a large parlour—to be shut up most of the time." In many houses there was a dining-sitting room, or "breakfast-parlour," as it was first called, where small families took informal meals and generally relaxed. This left the parlour inviolate, a practice which is not yet quite obsolete in rural Ontario.

In the 1840s wood-trim, instead of being white, was often painted and grained in imitation of mahogany or walnut or of a gloriously grained wood of the painter's imagination. Most parlours were wallpapered, as papers were then to be had in much greater and more tempting variety and cost much less than before. Carpeting was cheaper. Scotch Ingrain and Kidderminster carpeting by the yard was offered in gorgeous combinations of colour. Strips could be sewn together at home and laid over newspapers and straw. An article in *The Canadian Journal of Fabrics* in 1906 gives us a clue to early prices: "In 1845 I had in use in my own house carpets manufactured in Georgetown by Barber Bros. prior to their removal to Streetsville. They were all wool, good weight, and retailed at 75¢ per yard, and for personal use I doubt if more serviceable goods can today, sixty years later, be purchased for the money." It is extraordinary how many early parlour carpets are to be found in old country houses today where closed doors and drawn blinds have preserved their fine textures and colours.

Mirrors for the mantel, long horizontal glasses divided into three sections by mouldings and framed in gilt, in gilt and black, or in mahogany, were sold

Parlours, halls and photographers' studios often contained an "antique" chair, called alternatively a prie-dieu or a slipper chair, similar to that shown in this 1867 carte de visite. / Author's coll.

Opposite page: An affluent Victorian farmhouse parlour. Gilt mirror, red glass lustres, portrait, armchair, covered centre table, kerosene lamp, keepsake annuals, photograph album, and fancy box with parian figure of a tumbling child are all of the 1860s. The sofa is earlier. / U.C.V.

everywhere. The ornaments that had been accumulated over the years were stiffly arranged on the mantel shelf. At either end were coloured glass lustres with crystal prisms, a clock or a glass of wax flowers was in the middle, and pairs of cased glass or Parian vases were delightfully reflected in the mirror.

The centre table was now left stationary (though often cleared off for playing loo). It held the best lamp, which probably still burned whale or lard oil, though some new and dangerous lamps burned camphene. Chairs of a new kind, with back-splats in the shapes of lyres or urns, and others called "gondola chairs," were the correct thing to buy. Later in the '40s, balloon-back chairs made their appearance and in their great variety became the most popular parlour and dining chair for the rest of the century. Sofas had serpentine backs and outward-curved arms, or were made with deep back-rail and heavily scrolled feet. The scroll form was used on much furniture of this period: as armchair arms, as feet and side trim on cupboards, and as supports for the overhanging top drawer of chests, the writing surface of desks, or the keyboard of pianos. A Bytown advertiser of the period lists "sophas [*sic*] covered in haircloth and common framed chairs with hair seats." Haircloth was the most prevalent upholstery material. Slipcovers of chintz or linen were not uncommon for both sofas and chairs. They were generally made loosely and were intended only to protect the furniture, not to add to the decoration of a room. In 1839 Anne Langton, a settler, wrote, "Aunt Alice has manufactured a complete set of chair covers, sofa covers, etc. and a second cover for each of the great chairs." Helen Macaulay, wife of the Surveyor-General, wrote to her mother-in-law in 1838 that she could find nothing in Toronto with which to cover the drawing room furniture but brown linen and asked her to find something for her in Kingston. She said, "I should prefer a furniture stripe, there must be blue in it—it ought to be what would not require washing for a long time, but what would bear washing. I cannot think of waiting till new goods come out." (This last complaint was against local stocks depleted between the shipping seasons from England.)

Papier-mâché furniture, usually chairs, sewing tables, tilt-top tables, workboxes and writing cases, were imported from England and added delightful colour to the parlours. One of the most popular items for furnishing parlours of all classes was what is now called a tabernacle mirror. This was inspired by Sheraton and other early designers and at first was very fine and expensive. Gradually, more reasonably priced mirrors were made, and eventually smaller sizes and cheaper finishes brought them within everyone's reach. The frames were gilt, black enamelled with gilt trim, or mahogany. An overhanging cornice and finely moulded classic pilasters distinguish the early mirrors but the later and cheaper mirrors had vase-and-ring, or vase-and-cylinder turnings for frames. In all cases, however, the upper third of the mirror frame enclosed a moulded frieze or reverse painting on glass. The best of these mirrors are of extremely good design and workmanship and even the poorest have a great deal of naïve charm.

A foreign flavour was introduced into the parlours of the post-1840 period by the French and Italian furnishing available by that time. In 1848 William Wakefield in Toronto advertised "four cases of handsome ornaments just received from Italy consisting of superb mosaic marble tables, vases of handsome patterns, marble bowls, various marble watch holders, various alabaster and marble candlesticks and a collection of oil paintings." Window shades were everywhere advertised, both plain and with painted scenes, and the practice of drawing the shades began.

It was not until the 1850s that the parlour began to take on all the characteristics which people ordinarily associate with the word "Victorian." Both travellers and newcomers to the country were impressed with the opulence that was displayed. In *Pictures of Canadian Life*, edited by the Rev. H. Christmas in 1850, there is a description of houses on Yonge Street north of

The curtains in the impressive drawing room at Dundurn Castle were copied exactly from the chapter on Grecian and Modern Villa Furniture in J. C. Loudon's "Encyclopaedia of Cottage, Farm, and Villa Architecture," London, 1833. They are of velvet, silk damask and mull. Linen blinds were an 1840s addition. / Dundurn Castle

Toronto "occupied by gentlemen of the highest standing and respectability": "Such abodes as these of course are replete with every comfort which would be presented by a similar residence in England, such as pianofortes, carpets, mirrors, handsome tables and chairs, etc." And Mrs. Moodie in 1853 said, "In large cities, like Montreal and Toronto, the higher classes are as refined and intellectual as ladies and gentlemen at home, and spend their lives in much the same manner. Their houses abound in all the elegancies and luxuries of life, and to step into their drawing-rooms you would imagine yourself still in England. . . ." From then on, through the '60s the parlour flowered as it never had before and never would again. Some new types of furniture were available, such as "mahogany rocking chairs with haircloth seats and backs," and bookcases which were separate pieces of furniture unrelated to desks. Large ottomans and tables were now placed in the centre of the room; in fact cabinetmakers designated "centre tables" in their advertisements, and no parlour was complete without one. Very frequently they had marble tops. Tombstone makers enlarged their trade to include "marble mantelpieces, centre table, and stand tops," as they were advertised in Chatham in 1847. Cabinet organs priced anywhere from $70 to $500, and melodeons which cost from $60 to $170 were now available on easy terms "packed and shipped free of charge."

The Gothic style of furnishings reminiscent of Sir Walter Scott's *Abbotsford*, left its influence on parlour furniture in the '60s. One type of chair in particular was often added to existing furniture in the parlour. Its common designation now is "prie-dieu," whether it is a prayer chair or not. The popularity of prie-dieus was partly due to the fact that they made a perfect frame for the elaborate Berlin wool or bead work then being produced in such quantities. These chairs now haunt antique stores where they seem lonely and unassimilated. Other Gothic shapes invaded the parlour in stoves, what-nots, and photograph frames, while neo-Gothic shapes and motifs appeared on book covers, vases, picture-frame mats, and writing and sewing boxes. All exhibited the pointed arch, crocketed finial and tracery.

In 1851, reports and pictures of the furnishings and ornaments displayed at the Great Exhibition in the Crystal Palace at London were widely distributed on this continent and influenced all furnishing, establishing new styles as fashionable and correct. Much furniture was sold under the label of "Elizabethan" and the chairs so often seen as photographers' props in *carte de visite* photographs best illustrate this very adaptable style. Some furniture-makers used Elizabethan-type strap-work in their designs, but more often employed the kind of spiral turning which was first popular in the period of Charles II. This style was responsible for the welter of furniture loosely called "spool-turned." What-nots and tables, chairs and hanging shelves were all made with spool turning and appeared in fashionable parlours.

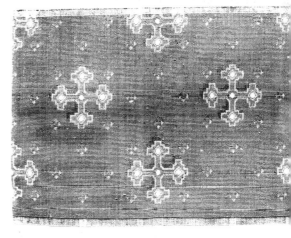

The most completely acceptable style, however, was that heralded as modern, rococo, French or New French, Louis XIV or Louis XV. Most furniture commonly labelled "Victorian" today can be placed in this category. Such furniture as the upholstered chairs (now often called "ladies' and gentlemen's chairs"), the sofas that matched them, centre tables and desks all expressed this style which has yet to find an agreed-upon name. They were made of mahogany, walnut and rosewood. Most outlines were curved; legs were cabriole; high-relief carving was usual, particularly in scroll, grape or rose forms. Most of the new parlour furniture was made in this rather French style. "Sets" of this furniture were sold for the parlour, and included sofa, two armchairs (one with only vestigial arms), at least four side chairs, a centre table and an ottoman. Sometimes there was a matching étagère or what-not. Some parlour sets were produced by cabinetmakers and were very fine, but many pieces that are found today were the popularly priced products of early factories. There was a certain gaiety about this style which, along with the

English carpets of the mid-nineteenth century. From top: (1) Kidderminster—yellow ground with grass-green scrolls and strapwork and dark red accents. (2) Kidderminster, with off-white ground, alternating bands of varying reds and green; broad stripes of grey, and narrow stripes of yellow. (3) Brussels, with brown and gold crosses on a deep green ground. (4) Brussels, with red and orange flowers and green and brown leaves on a beige background. / Courtesy Victoria and Albert Museum, London

The making of the embroidered or beaded face screens used to protect the eyes and face from the glow of firelight or candles was a lady's occupation. Elaborate stands of brass and other metals were sold as mounts for this handiwork which graced parlour tables from 1850. / Dundurn

Ornamental glass vases such as this fine ruby-coated one were made by Bohemian and English factories and by the New England Glass Company in Massachusetts in the mid-nineteenth century. They were favourite mantel ornaments. / Dundurn

change in taste from horsehair upholstery to brocade, damask, and velvet, lent a light opulence to the parlour.

Window drapery, too, was changing from muslin to lace for undercurtains, and to larger patterns in heavier brocades of silk and wool for overcurtains. These last were sometimes held back with large stamped brass hooks, which often matched brass cornices mounted on wood concealing the curtain poles. Or they might be held back by very heavy multicoloured silk cords and tassels.

Carpets such as Ingrain and three-ply Kidderminster were used in the average house; Velvets, Wiltons and Brussels carpets appeared in more pretentious parlours in extraordinarily beautiful colours. Laid over straw or straw matting, or often another old carpet, they made walking in the parlour soundless.

I remember so well a spring-housecleaning practice, observed for many years, which involved taking up the tacks and heaving the carpets to the back garden where, on the ground or the clothesline, they were thwacked with wooden-handled wire beaters. The floor was washed and the straw matting was taken outside, washed and dried. When it was put back it was well sprinkled with pepper to discourage both moths and a scourge with the dreadful name of Buffalo bugs. When the carpet was relaid it had to be pulled and stretched to fit and no one seemed sure that it was not turned the wrong way round. In the meantime the whole room had been scoured and everything at least wiped and polished. When it was all over the air still smelt of dust, but the room looked rich and handsome.

"Rich" was the most significant adjective that could be applied to any parlour furnishings. Even in my childhood, to say that anything was "parlour quality" meant that it was unrestrainedly handsome. All things in the parlour shone with satiny French polishing, the lustre of silk, the glitter of glass or the brightness of gilt. Everything was seen in the endless reflections of the largest over-mantel mirror that could be afforded.

It was in the parlour of an old house in the country that I saw my first corpse. An elderly relative had died and we travelled what seemed a very long distance in the train through a February blizzard to attend her funeral. We arrived at a hushed house. Voices were only raised in the kitchen where an enormous amount of baking was going on. Cakes were going into the oven, cakes were cooling, and cakes were being iced. A large ham sat steaming on a platter. In the pantry someone was wiping off jars of pickles just brought from the cellar and sorting out pickle dishes. We ate in the kitchen since the dining room was being cleaned and polished for the next day's funeral feast.

After supper, we children were washed and brushed and mentally prepared for the fact that we were going to "say good-bye" to Aunt Cassie. Feeling solemn and scared, we waited in the hall until the parlour door was opened and then were taken by the hand and led to the coffin which stood on trestles at the far end of the room amid the heavy scent of flowers. No rose-coloured lights softened the face of death. Only a shaded oil lamp burned whitely on a nearby table. Fright disappeared in the surprise at feeling nothing at all. We tiptoed out over the heavy carpet, aware of long curtains pulled over drawn blinds and a paralyzing air of stillness.

In the course of time I attended other funerals in that house but by then I knew the parlour well. The woodwork was finished as walnut. The paper on the wall was the original, put on when the house was built in the '60s. The pattern was a giant scroll-and-leaf design in shades of bronze and bottle green. My aunts had said, "A good wallpaper should last at least twenty years and, if you take care, longer." This paper had proved their contention. It was only when the pictures came down for housecleaning that there was any sign of fading, and that was one of the few times when the blinds were raised. The carpet, which they used to sweep weekly with wet shredded newspaper or tea leaves, was tacked from wall to wall and represented innumerable garlands of white and yellow roses just tinged with pink on a green ground.

28

An elegant, slippery, medallion-backed sofa and its matching chairs were upholstered and buttoned in plum-coloured brocatelle. The sofa, which stood against the wall, now had embroidered and lace-covered cushions arranged precariously along the top and in the corners—a new fashion. A marble-topped centre table held an oil lamp, the shade and font painted with full-blown pink roses on a dusky rose background. It stood on a doily whose frills had been stiffened in sugar and water. When lit, it shed an aura of romance. A large, but obviously miserable palm tree sat in a hand-painted jardiniere on the floor in one bay window, and in the other was a rococo lady's desk, which was never equipped with ink or writing paper but instead displayed a group of framed photographs and daguerreotypes portraying the family, from crinolined ladies and side-whiskered gentlemen to those of my generation who coyly smiled in their infant nakedness as they reclined on bearskin rugs.

The melodeon was never played except by experimenting children who endeavoured to make "Chopsticks" sound reasonably true. The thing we liked best was a long gilt mirror between two windows which had a shelf beneath it holding an alabaster urn full of peacock feathers. In front of this we assumed attitudes and poses by the hour. We admired the ornaments on the marble mantelpiece, particularly a coloured one called, even by the aunts, "Boy Picking Toe." The prisms on the lustres glittered and twinkled at a touch. The clock with a gilt lady reclining on top of it had long since stopped, but we always moved the hands to the witching hour of twelve and never knew who moved them (or for what reason) to other hours. The room was so dark that we were reflected in the glass of the large engravings.

The double room occupied a large space in the house, but it was only used on the occasions of marriage, christening, death, and the annual tea of the Ladies' Guild. It was forbidden ground for children and yet in fascinated disobedience we spent a great deal of time looking at it and posturing through its mysterious depths.

After 1860 the furnishing of the parlour offered great scope for the house-proud, even in rural districts. During the American Civil War farmers sold their produce at high prices. New houses (with bigger parlours) were built and many undreamed-of luxuries in the way of ornaments for the home were bought. By now "sending away" for furnishings and ornaments was beginning to lend more prestige than confining purchases to the local town. Newspaper and directory advertisers addressed themselves to would-be customers with cheap prices and free deliveries.

Fine old wooden mantelpieces could now be exchanged for marble ones in white, grey, green or black, and most new house owners regarded them as essential. A good painter could reproduce the appearance of any kind of wood on windows, doors, and other trim. Carpets and rugs were easily available, and curtaining from England, the United States and France was for sale. The old chintzes were relegated to bedrooms, and new and sumptuous fabrics took their place. If a new "set" of furniture could not be purchased, at least a modern sofa could be added and Berlin needlework could be used to recover many old chairs. Skirts, called lambrequins, were attached to mantelshelves and to many fretwork or carved small shelves on the wall. Lambrequins were often worked with gilt thread and colours and had fringe or baubles hanging from their edges. The old green table covers were discarded for elaborately embroidered and fringed ones, the bright colours of which set a dominating note in the parlour. Parlour tablecloths could be bought in great variety or made at home.

Wallpaper was advertised, from the 1850s on, as being English, French, or American. Roller printing and new chemical dyes had rendered it cheaper and marvellously varied in colours. And art, in the form of large-sized black and gold framed lithographs, brightened the walls. It was the fashion to design and make all sorts of wall adornments, such as painted velvet panels, beadwork,

Popularly called lustres, coloured glass vases with pendant crystal prisms were parlour mantel decorations from the 1840s through the rest of the nineteenth century. / Upper Canada Village

The best wax flower arrangements were made by craftswomen for fancy goods stores and sold encased in bell glasses (called shades), but they could be lovingly and laboriously put together at home for display in the parlour. / Dundurn Castle

feather-and-tinsel pictures, hair wreaths, and wool-worked Biblical illustrations. These too, went on the walls, along with the older engravings.

Photograph albums, books and magazines lay on parlour tables. *Keepsakes* and *Young Lady's Annuals* were the favourites. These were issued each year and contained fine engravings protected by coloured tissue paper, poems, and short articles of great sentiment. Improving literature was eagerly sought and easy to find. In 1852, S. Hewson, a stationer in Hamilton, "supplied at publishing prices, and punctually delivered, free of charge, *Harper's New Monthly, Sartain's Magazine, Godey's Lady's Book, Graham's Magazine, Knickerbocker, Blackwoods, London Quarterly Review, Edinburgh Review, Westminster Review, Chambers Papers for the People, Putnam's Semi-Monthly Library, Appleton's Popular Library*, etc." The illustrations in many of these magazines showed furnishings in vogue in the British Isles and the United States, and consequently rendered Canadian taste less provincial. *The Illustrated London News* was sold by many stationers at this time and old bound copies turn up every now and then.

In 1861, while giving an estimate for the furnishing of a modest house, Mrs. Copleston, author of *Canada: Why We Live In It, and Why We Like It*, remarked, "In giving an estimate of our own expenses it must not be supposed that where there is plenty of money at command, furniture and internal house decorations, with all the lustre of pier glasses and ornaments, cannot be obtained. In the houses of the wealthy an air of luxury and sumptuousness is more indulged in, in proportion to the means and condition of the owner, than is the case at home." (By "home" she meant England.) Certainly, if we can judge by the advertisements of the time, and to some extent by the remaining heirlooms, luxurious ornaments were held in great esteem.

Candelabra of a particular type, called at the time "girandoles," were used in great variety on mantelshelves and tables. They had marble bases and gilded iron holders, well strung with prisms, and were advertised for sale in shapes like Jenny Lind, Queen's Page, Romeo and Juliet, Metamora and many others. The fonts and shades of the parlour kerosene lamps added still more pictorial interest to the parlour. The depiction on these of every sort of flower that grows, singly and in groups and garlands; landscapes and animals, such as stags seen on craggy hillsides, was considered legitimate decoration. Alabaster figures and vases, heavy and funereal in appearance, were greatly admired. Flower vases were advertised as of English, Bohemian and New England glass; they and Parian ornaments and vases were the most elegant of parlour accessories. Etched glass and painted china depicted the most popular Victorian motifs: floral designs featuring the rose, morning glory, fern and fuchsia.

The American Photograph Porcelain Company of 781 Broadway, New York, advertised in Canada in 1861 a delightful kind of ornament still found in old homes. This was the reproduction, on porcelain, of portrait photographs in full colour. The prices ran as follows: "Breakfast cup and saucer, $5.00; handsome French vase or toilet article, $10.00; pair of rich Sèvres vases, $15.00; vases of every quality, ranging from $20.00 to $100.00 the pair." The practice continued for quite a few years and the vases and other articles we find today show ladies in costumes ranging from crinolines to bustles. The directions for ordering required the customer to send photograph, daguerreotype or ambrotype.

There were plenty of rich bibelots in the shops in Canada, however, that did not have to be ordered from the United States or England. W. H. G. Kingston, writing in *Eastern Wanderings* in 1856, said, "The shops . . . in size, elegance, and the value of their contents . . . vie with any city in England, except perhaps London and Liverpool."

The styles of parlour furnishings which began in Upper Canada in classic simplicity ended in a welter of romantic shapes and sentimental motifs, not because of any indigenous feeling, but because Canada was now completely linked with the fashions and foibles of the English-speaking world and reflected its taste with great rapidity.

Leather-covered armchair, a typical "father's easy chair," bought in Prince Edward County. Labelled "James McRobie, 1846." / Author's coll.

Opposite: An 1860s sitting room where reading, writing and sewing were done, and an atmosphere of ease prevailed. When there was a sitting room in a house the parlour was reserved for great occasions and special visitors. / U.C.V.

Dining rooms

In the first quarter of the nineteenth century, while backwoods settlers in Upper Canada were cooking, eating and sleeping all in one room, there were town and country houses with elegant dining rooms, well equipped to offer generous hospitality. And on the *voyageur* routes from Montreal to the North-West, remote from the mainstream of immigrant settlers, fur traders often entertained at mahogany tables glittering with silver candelabra, china dinner services and crystal decanters and glasses. Their elaborate hospitality was legendary.

With the flow of settlers from the United States and abroad came government administrators, land developers, army and navy officers, professional people and merchants whose houses, principally in the towns, became the focal points of political and social life in the province. Many of these houses had dining rooms with furniture and appointments equal to the best to be found in the cities from which their owners came. The new citizens prided themselves on the extravagance of their dinner parties.

The dining rooms and their furnishings were impressive enough to have been described in memoirs, travellers' accounts and inventories, so that we know how richly the tables were set and how lavish was the food and drink. In remote districts across the province, from Glengarry where the Frasers of *Fraserfield* made welcome all their army and fur-trading friends as well as their kin from Scotland, to the Huron Tract where the wealthy Hyndmans at *Lunderston Hall* and William Dunlop at *Gairbraid* kept open house, the dining room offered hospitality in the wilderness.

Some of the furnishings for the dining rooms of fine town houses were brought over from England or Scotland, other pieces were acquired in Montreal and the local towns. This was the case in the home of William Dickson at Niagara and in two early York houses, D. W. Smith's *Maryville Lodge* and William Firth's *Holyrood House*. The variety and quality of these furnishings may be judged by items listed in William Firth's auction at York in 1811: "Dining tables, dinner service of plate, epergne, salver, blue and white English china—complete set, dessert service, decanter of the best Gloucester shape, cut glasses, hock glasses, green and white finger glasses, table linen, jelly glasses, tumblers, West India cooler, wines, liquors." Among the articles for which William Dickson claimed damages after the War of 1812 were: "Full set of India table china, guilt [*sic*] set of tea china, cherry tea table, three small tea tables—walnut, nine water plates, one large brass-clamped liquor case (contents whiskeys, wine and shrub), walnut sideboard, two walnut knife boxes, china cups and saucers, salad and punch bowls, very fine knives and forks in a mahogany case." In Kingston in 1818 an interesting sale of the household furnishings of Robert Hall, Esq., included "elegant table service of stone china including dessert and breakfast services; side dishes of metal plated with silver edges; a canteen containing an elegant table service for 24 persons, including breakfast service purchased in London in 1816—for five hundred guineas." Other inventories and war claims list similar articles.

Even before 1815, furnishings such as these—luxuries in a pioneer society—were beginning to be available in towns like York and Kingston.

A mahogany sideboard in the English style of Sheraton and Hepplewhite, with brass posts and a splash-curtain rail. It formerly belonged to a military family in Kingston. / Upper Canada Village

Opposite page: A dining room in the modest house of a country doctor in 1845-50. Sideboard, table and chairs are Canadian. A handwoven tablecloth is laid for tea, over a dark red wool cover. / U.C.V.

Cabinetmakers there advertised dining tables, chairs and sideboards. Auction lists included "[sets of tables] consisting of two large dining and two ends; large plated candlesticks, china punch bowl, elegant mahogany liquor case containing twelve crystals—three quarts each." Stores advertised "damask tablecloths, table and dessert knives and forks, table knives with ivory, stag and black horn handles, plated candlesticks, elegant sets of china, plated sugar tongs, tea caddies with locks, japanned sugar cannisters, toast racks, chafing dishes, gravy strainers, nutcrackers, cut-glass water decanters and silver wine funnels."

Fancy foodstuffs as well as staples were also available. Provisioners offered "sugar loaves and lump sugar, spices, chestnuts, hickory and black walnuts, cranberries, coffee, chocolate, Hyson, Souchong, green and Bohea teas of first quality, and assorted pickles." They carried large stocks of rum, brandy, Geneva wine, Madeira, sherry, claret, port and Burgundy. Whisky was sold everywhere. But while, as this shows, a great deal of fastidious eating and drinking was being done in fine dining rooms, the majority of settlers were thankfully dining on "hog meat" and "corn meal mush."

A country-style solid cherry sideboard based on the Sheraton tradition, c. 1830. / U.C.V.

In most houses built during the early period the dining room was usually to the left or right of the front entrance hall and was close to the kitchen. Although the dining rooms almost always contained dish cupboards and sometimes sideboards, they were just as likely to include a bed and a writing desk. The dish cupboard that was part of the architecture was a feature of these rooms and was incorporated in many houses, large or small, till the middle of the century. Some were corner cupboards, others flanked the fireplace. In formal dining rooms the sideboards were often set in specially-built alcoves with keystoned arches. Most dining rooms, like the parlours, had moulded chair rails against which the chairs were placed when not in use.

Profits from the fur trade furnished many early dining rooms. The 1814 stone house built by Charles Oakes Ermatinger in the wilderness at Sault Ste Marie and the Macdonnell house of about 1820 at Point Fortune in Prescott County had dining parlours as formal in trim and furnishings as those in the houses of London, Montreal, or Philadelphia. The Campbell house near Williamstown in Glengarry, which had an elegant formal parlour, also had a handsome dining room which contained cooking fireplace and ovens.

Landowner-farmers such as William Fairfield, who built the *White House* in 1794 near Collins Bay, dined mostly in the huge kitchen with their families but reserved a small, well-furnished room adjoining it as a dining parlour for entertaining friends and business associates.

Merchants and tradesmen in the towns, who enjoyed a temporary prosperity due to the War of 1812, built houses with separate dining rooms or with double parlours, the rear of which could be closed with sliding or folding doors to serve as a dining parlour. In many such houses the kitchen was in the basement and was adjoined by a sitting-dining room for servants. A creaking elevator called a dumbwaiter, that worked with ropes and pulleys, was often used in town houses so that food could be sent up by the cook from the basement kitchen and placed directly on the table.

Inventories give us pictures of early dining rooms. The dining-room furniture of John Turnbull, the Belleville agent for the Commercial Bank of the Midland District, was recorded on inventory in 1827 as "a set of cherry dining tables, 2 breakfast tables, a china tea set, 1½ doz. tumblers, 2 doz. glasses, 1 doz. custard glasses, 5 flint decanters and a cruet," as well as "20 painted chairs and 8 rush-bottomed chairs" some of which could have served as dining chairs. The inventory of John Walden Myers, also at Belleville, in the twenties lists the unassuming furnishings used by a prosperous yeoman-merchant: "Cherry table, ten Windsor chairs, silver teaspoons, sugar tongs, wine glasses, and a set of china." John Macaulay, the Surveyor-General, who rented

Top left: An early Empire maple sideboard made in the Niagara area. / Mrs. Hazel L. Sheridan, Hamilton
Top right: Another version of an Empire-style sideboard, made in maple for Asa Weller at The Carrying Place, Prince Edward County, c. 1825. / R.O.M.
Lower right: A painted pine and maple sideboard said to have been made for Philip Dorland in Prince Edward Co. by cabinetmaker P. Macdonald. / U.C.V.

a house "in the College Avenue" (now University Avenue, Toronto) in 1837, brought to it for his dining room:

    dining room table, cost £25
    marble top sideboard, 27/10/-
    1 doz. hair-bottomed chairs, £18
    2 armchairs covered crimson damask, £18
    1 imperial carpet, 32½ yds., 12/18/4
    crimson damask window curtain and pole, £10
    fender, fire irons, shovel & tongs, 3/5/-
    large walnut bookcase, 20/10/-
    small walnut bookcase, 12/10/-
    plate warmer, 45s.
    walnut woodbox, 15s.
    child's mahogany chair on table, 35s.
    1 hearth rug, 2/5/-
    cloth table cover and 2 hearth brushes, 1/5/-
    rosewood writing desk, inlaid with brass, £5
    mahogany piano, £90, and stool, 3/15/-

It is evident that when there was no "company dinner" the dining room was a pleasant place to spend the evening. We can picture Mr. Macaulay at his

Following page: Even in large houses the dining room often doubled as a sitting room, as indicated in this 1890 photo of "Whitehern," Hamilton home of the McQuesten family, now a museum. Sideboard, table and chairs are in the Victorian style of 1850-1860. Doors flanking the sideboard conceal china cupboards. The room was gas lit. / Hamilton Parks

writing desk, Mrs. Macaulay in an armchair sewing by the fire and little Annie Macaulay in the highchair which was provided by the "chair on a table."

By the 1830s social entertaining was on the increase throughout the province among the élite, the military, and the middle class, and there was a consequent increase in store goods required for this purpose. Sideboards, hair-bottom chairs (which might be chairs upholstered in the then-popular haircloth or chairs with seats stuffed with horsehair), Grecian and Trafalgar chairs, dining and breakfast tables, and all kinds of silver, china and napery were advertised in newspapers.

Strong, well-made Windsor chairs, most of them conservatively painted green or black, were as commonly used in dining rooms as they were elsewhere in a house. Upholstered-seat chairs with pierced back-slats, in styles reminiscent of Chippendale, Sheraton and Hepplewhite, were also interchangeable parlour-dining-room chairs. Another commonly used dining chair was the "Grecian" which was based on the shape of the ancient Greek "klismos," having a concave curved back rail and curved legs which splayed out front and back. These were made in great numbers in mahogany, maple and walnut and were widely advertised. Many people call chairs of the Grecian style Canadian Regency today for they have a close resemblance to many English Regency chairs. Early "Fancy" chairs with rush or caned seats and charmingly painted or stencilled decoration were also based on the Grecian form and were used in both parlour and dining room.

Dining tables were frequently referred to as being in "sets"—which usually meant that there was one table with deep drop-leaves supported by swing-out legs, and two semi-circular table "ends" with which the centre table could be extended. Or there might be two pedestal-supported narrow tables which could be joined at either end to a large two-pedestal centre table. English tables were usually mahogany but there are many references to Canadian walnut, black walnut, and more particularly to cherry dining tables.

There were more advertisements between 1820 and 1840 for "breakfast tables" (a purely Old-Country and Canadian term) than for dining tables. The breakfast table was simply a small dining table somewhat larger than either a Pembroke or a tea table. It was commonly used in morning rooms or breakfast parlours in town houses. In farmhouses where there was no dining room a table of this kind was sometimes used in the parlour for entertaining. Canniff Haight, author of *Country Life in Canada*, writing of Prince Edward County as it was in the 1830s, remarked, "When there was company . . . the cherry table with its folding leaves was brought out and the pure white linen cloth was spread on it." The centre table of a dining-room set was also used alone for a small family.

Sideboards, which were important acquisitions for the dining room, were expensive to buy. Adam Fergusson, writing in 1833, suggested that £15 was an average price for one. John Macaulay, writing to his mother in 1839 from Toronto, said, "I could get a sideboard made of plain solid walnut for about £12 if you would prefer it to the beautiful one at £18. Of course it cannot be so handsome."

Most surviving early sideboards (1800 to 1840) are of one of two types. The first style, based on Sheraton-Hepplewhite designs, was often veneered with fine crotch-grained wood, had six narrow tapering or turned legs, two or three drawers, cupboards below, and possibly a back gallery or a brass rod for a short curtain. The second style, which is the more commonly found, is often called Regency or Empire in the nomenclature of books and collectors. In this type, the top and the drawers beneath it frequently overhang the rest of the piece and are supported by free-standing pilasters or attached half-columns which end in a base with ring-and-ball-turned, or paw, feet. An interesting variant of these sideboards was the rather formal and handsome style which had two cupboards on bases joined across an open space by drawers,

An Eastern Ontario dish cupboard of unusual design, built in the 1840s of butternut. The cabinet contains blue and white china, including some "sprigged ware" with small raised decoration in blue, which was once very popular. / U.C.V.

Opposite page: China cupboards were usually part of the architectural trim of a room in early Upper Canada. This one contains part of a Nankin pattern dinner service made by Mason about 1825. The top shelf contains a New Hall tea set. / U.C.V.

38

A china cabinet in the Gothic style, one of a pair made to order for "Brockton," Sulphur Springs Rd., Ancaster, about 1850. The china is Derby, brought from England in 1834. / Mrs. Thomas Leith, Ancaster

Mahogany dining chair with vase splat, a style greatly favoured between 1835 and 1845. It formerly belonged to the Crysler family. / U.C.V.

top and backboard. Sometimes the side cupboards were higher than the serving top and had hinged lids which covered storage space for cutlery and wine.

The Regency or Empire sideboard began as a mahogany, walnut, cherry or maple piece, but was endlessly copied in lesser woods, then stained or painted in imitation of the prototype. A well-furnished dining room had, as well as a dish cupboard and sideboard, a serving table or two and perhaps a "butler's tray" on which soiled dishes were placed before being removed to pantry or kitchen.

Rounding out the dining-room furniture there was probably a small table for informal meals, which with its leaves down doubled as a serving table. There might also be a console, or pier, table on which decanters were kept, and a liquor cabinet, usually in the shape of an antique sarcophagus. In addition, beds, desks, armchairs, a washstand, chests of drawers and wardrobes have all appeared on dining-room inventories.

The dining room was a quiet, usually tidy room where the family could read or business could be discussed. An easy chair by the sunny window was an inviting spot from which to enjoy a view of the garden. The dining table offered an excellent surface for writing and painting, cutting out materials, playing cards, and for sorting freshly ironed linen. A green baize cover customarily protected the surface of the table in early days, and "green table covers" were sold and used from about 1810 on. Oilcloth was also used, but it was imported from England and expensive. The surface of early table-oilcloth was oil-painted and block-printed with designs in colour, and the underside was covered with wool flock.

To have a dining room at all presumed some formality in living, and carpets and curtains were important items in the furnishing of the room. The early houses might have had nothing more than animal skins used as hearth rugs, but by the '30s carpeting was available by the yard and considered very desirable. It was used to cover the entire floor, and much thought was given to the subtle relationships of colour between wall paint or paper and the curtains and carpet. Wool damask, serge, velvet, silk and moreen were used for curtains; Kidderminster and Brussels carpets were usual; and haircloth, leather, and wool or silk damask were the popular coverings for chair seats.

Chief among those who could pride themselves on having a dining room were the officers of the garrisons and the ladies and gentlemen of means who had come directly from England. As had been their custom, they rose early, walked, rode, wrote letters, and then breakfasted at ten or eleven o'clock. They dined at three or four o'clock in the afternoon, and had tea—or supper, which was an informal family meal—any time from seven o'clock on. This was the pattern followed by the gentry for many years. Even in the 1830s breakfast was still late, though a very light luncheon was sometimes served between breakfast and dinner which by now was postponed till five or six o'clock. American household manuals, right up until the 1850s, pointed out that for most people luncheon was quite unnecessary and that four o'clock was still the most suitable hour for dinner. It is quite possible that old-fashioned townspeople who did not work for a living may have continued with the custom for some time here.

Merchants, clerks and other people who worked in towns breakfasted at seven, dined at noon, and had supper between seven and eight. Those who worked on the land rose at five and Joseph Pickering, author of *Inquiries of an Immigrant*, reported in 1831 that they breakfasted at eight, dined at twelve, and supped at sunset in the summer and at six o'clock in the winter. These town and country mealtimes remained unchanged for the next thirty years. As long as a man worked within easy walking or riding distance from his home he ate dinner at noon. Among the gentry, though, formal dining moved firmly into the older tea and supper hour and evening tea parties declined.

When it *was* in the height of fashion, however, "tea" was a social evening occasion, elaborate and formal. One or two tables were set up on which there were tea urns, tea services and a coffee pot, cups and saucers and teaspoons. The hostess or other ladies of the household poured tea of two kinds, and coffee. According to Miss Leslie's *House Book* "large cakes of the best sort" were passed by servants or gentlemen to the ladies who sat on chairs and sofas about the room, or drew up to the various tables. Dresses for these occasions were light-coloured and of delicate fabrics, and gloves were worn, so the hostess was warned never to serve buttered or greasy dishes. There was a great deal of walking about and greeting of friends, and a second repast of lemonade, and baskets of "small mixed cakes, macaroons and kisses" were circulated "less than an hour" after the tea. Afterward "the blanc mange, jellies, sweetmeats, ice creams, wines and liquors" were handed round. This was a popular method of entertaining from 1820 to the mid-1840s, and though the description given is of a fashionable affair, it is a matter of record that refreshments were generally served in three stages and that there was often dancing.

Tea as a quite different sort of formal occasion was resurrected as "five o'clock tea" in the late 1870s. Only sandwiches and cake were served. Fashionable versions of afternoon tea, held in house or garden in the 1880s, were called kettledrums. In the late nineteenth century Old-Country immigrants brought with them the custom of a supper-tea at which, as I remember, Canadian children sampled such exotic fare as steak-and-kidney pie, potted meats, treacle tarts and trifle. A late-evening tea consisting of sandwiches, cakes, jelly, tea and coffee has, for some years, been served at gatherings in farmhouses and is inexplicably called lunch.

Dining chair, one of a set formerly belonging to an old family in Eastern Ontario. It is quite typical of the most popular "good" dining chairs of the 1850-60 period. / Upper Canada Village

From earliest times those who could afford it found no difficulty in finding suitable china for the dining room. That it was available in the province is evidenced by its appearance on inventories, auction lists, and in advertisements where the goods for sale are often prefaced by the words "elegant" and "fashionable." Messrs. Ridout and Mercer of York in 1810 listed earthenware and china in patterns no longer familiar to us but probably readily recognizable at the time: "Yellow, brown, orange pattern, flowerwork, spring pattern, Star and Lace border, enamelled tea ware, plain, lined-handled, and fluted, with or without coffees, etc., Red and Leaf china with coffees, gilt-enamelled ditto complete, together with a variety of glassware." Other merchants listed "meat dishes, vegetable dishes, dessert dishes, soup dishes, egg cups, dinner services, breakfast plates, tea sets, cream cups, tea pots, salad bowls, tureens and sauce boats."

"China" has been an all-embracing word since the first fine tableware was brought to Europe from the Orient. "Real china," as it was often advertised, was porcelain, translucent rather than opaque, and was more expensive than earthenware. Earthenware, which was then being produced in improved forms, was very popular, however, and fine dinner tables were as frequently set with it as they were with porcelain.

Before 1820, the names of types and kinds of earthenware and china were used sparsely in written records and advertisements. We read of Queensware, which was a beautifully designed and glazed earthenware of a light cream colour made by Wedgwood and other English potters. We read of "Wedgwood candlesticks, cream pots, sugar pots, and egg cups," some of which may have been black basaltes. Cream-coloured ware was generally well designed and glazed and was favoured as dinner ware. Some of it was decorated or edged with colour. (It was often designated by the initials "C.C." on invoices and inventories.) India china was a name used in Canada for Chinese export china which was brought by clipper ships in large quantities to New England. However, this label might also have referred to Samuel Alcock's Indian Ironstone made at Burslem in 1839, or to the Indian Stone China pro-

Slip-seated walnut dining chair, made between 1825 and 1840. Chairs of this style were sometimes advertised as "Grecian" chairs. / Upper Canada Village

duced by Charles Meigh of Hanley between 1835 and 1849. Printed ware and blue ware describe the transfer-printed earthenware in blue on white which appeared in brilliant dark blues or in lighter tones.

Stone China, first marketed by Josiah Spode in England in 1805, copied very successfully the coloured designs which had made Chinese wares so popular. By the 1820s, in Canada, both Spode's Stone China and Mason's Ironstone China (patented 1813) were among the tablewares offered for sale. They were sold in sets of prodigious size. The singularly attractive colours and comparatively low prices of these wares must have sold quantities of them, but only odd pieces are to be found today in the possessions of old Ontario families. Thomas Benson's stock record for his shop in Port Hope in 1835 lists a "set of imitation china," which may have been one way of describing Stone China.

Once a home was established, most people could afford some silver, if only teaspoons, and the dining rooms of the wealthy contained silver equipment for every purpose. Silver plate was advertised at an early date and until about the mid-1830s it meant pure silver and not "silver-plated." Among articles listed before 1840 were silver tea, dessert, toddy, gravy and tureen spoons; sugar tongs; forks, fish and butter knives; tooth picks; fruit knives; plated branches (branched candlesticks); epergnes; candlesticks and snuffers; silver-edged stands with cut-glass bottles; cruet stands; saltcellars; pickle forks; silver and German silver spoons and forks; elegant plated candlesticks with patent slides."

Elaborate tea and coffee services with trays were sold in all towns of any importance. Prices were rarely given in advertisements but sometimes values are shown in inventories. Two dozen silver teaspoons were valued at £7. American teaspoons which, at the same period were worth about $1 each, are often found in Canadian family treasure troves. They are unmistakable because they do not carry the English hallmark nor the simulated hallmark of Canadian spoons—only the name of the maker. Jewellers and silver-

Cutlery in common use in Upper Canada. Such pieces were frequently made with solid horn handles or split bone handles, riveted.

Typical dining tables. Top left: stretcher
table, pine and assorted woods, c. 1800-30.
Top right: pedestal table, walnut or maple,
c. 1850. Lower left: circular table, walnut
or butternut, sold with extra leaves, c. 1865.
Lower middle: drop-leaf table, walnut, maple
or cherry. c. 1850-60. Lower right: common
dining tables with drop leaves and swing-out
extra legs, all woods, c. 1845. / After Upper
Canada Village or Prince Edward County tables

smiths such as S. C. Frey and Company in Brockville were advertising in 1833: "Silver spoons on hand and made to any pattern on short notice." Buckhorn-handled knives and forks were commonly used and ivory-handled cutlery, sometimes finished with silver cap and collar, was much admired.

For those who could not afford silver the ever-popular Britannia ware was sold, in the same shops which stocked silverware and in many general stores. Britannia metal was an alloy of tin, antimony, and a small amount of zinc and copper which could be given a polish brighter than pewter, less bright than silver. The designs of Britannia jugs and tea and coffee pots were often copied from traditional shapes and were extremely handsome. A great many of these remain in Ontario and often carry the incised name of the English firm James Dixon and Son who were prolific makers of Britannia hollowware. There were also American makers of Britannia, many of whom copied English patterns. Their ware may have been brought here by pedlars.

Linen tablecloths and napkins in both damask and diapered patterns were advertised for sale from 1810, but neither early housewives nor the ordinarily observant travellers have much to say about their use. It is likely that for formal dining the English custom of removing the cloth before the dessert and wine was observed. The creases and folds of the tablecloth never lay quite flat owing to the pressure of the mangle which smoothed them. When still clean, they were sometimes refolded and kept in a linen press (that looked like a mangle) in the dining room or pantry. In good houses white linen table-cloths were used for breakfast, tea and supper.

Decanters, tumblers and wine glasses of all sorts were always found in the inventories of gentlemen's houses. Most of these were English and were often advertised as "richly cut" or of "finest crystal." Various shapes were required to serve the Madeira, sherry, claret, port, champagne, brandy, cognac, Jamaica shrub, Holland gin, peppermint, Blackburn's best Madeira wine, Benecarlo, Sicilian port, and Teneriffe, all advertised before 1835. Burton's ale, London porter and "Guinness" porter were also sold. (H. Billings and Company of Brockville advertised in 1832 that they had "just received 20,000

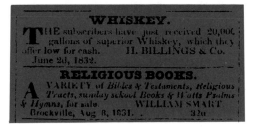

43

Teaspoons made by Joseph Robinson and Co., of Sheffield House, 15 King Street West, Toronto, about 1860. Robinson made and sold silverware. He also dealt in clocks, watches, soaps and perfumery from France and Germany, fishing tackle, and archery and cricket supplies. / Author's coll.

gallons of superior whisky"—a typical advertisement of the time.)

The 1830s saw the rise of the temperance movement which first suggested that its adherents give up drinking spirits and confine their refreshment to wines and ales and eventually asked for total abstinence. There were only 252 members in the York Temperance Society when it was founded in 1830 but they were influential people like Egerton Ryerson and Jesse Ketchum whose concern for the abuse of alcohol was intense. Small temperance societies sprang up throughout the country and succeeded in making excessive drinking a social misdemeanor. The fact that all members of the rapidly growing Methodist Church automatically became abstainers meant that decanters and wine glasses, if they were not destroyed, were packed away or put on the topmost shelf of the china cupboard. It is interesting today to find old wine glasses in houses where three or four generations of teetotallers have lived and ignored them.

Other glass tableware, according to advertisements, could have come from the United States. In the 1830s Horace Billings and Company announced, "Just received, 75 casks of American glassware consisting of creams, sugar bowls, salts, preserve dishes, fruit and stand dishes." English glass sweetmeat dishes, custard cups, preserve dishes and fruit bowls were also easily obtainable.

Early tables were set on the assumption that all food would be served by the master or mistress of the house and either passed around by servants or, from hand to hand, by the guests. For the first course, tureens of soup were at either end of the table, and soup plates and spoons in front of each guest. Castor or cruet stands were at the right of the host and hostess. If there was only one tureen of soup it was served by the hostess. Plates were passed to the tureen, filled and returned and, when empty, were removed from the table. Then fish and a roast replaced the tureens and side dishes were deposited all down the table in front of the guests. When the main courses had been eaten and the dishes taken off, the tablecloth was quickly rolled up or folded from end to end. Then the dessert service with its accompanying fruit, nuts, cheese and wine, were put on the polished table.

Considering the extremely varied conditions under which people lived, it is to be expected that all sorts of compromises were made in methods of service. Former customs, as well as sporadic efforts to achieve the latest fashions, dictated some of the styles of dining.

Ordinary middle-class table setting, by the 1840s, was a matter of rule and people long resident in Upper Canada observed the American customs. This was so general that querulous travellers and writers from England felt that the whole British tradition was being debased. It was about this time that many people began to lay down their knives when they had cut their meat and eat it with the fork held in the right hand, and in British eyes this was vulgar.

Generally speaking, though, American customs included many "niceties": A small table-rug was sometimes used on the carpet under the table, and after dinner the crumbs were shaken off it, and any stains from sloppy eating sponged away. Table covers of red or pink were laid under the white linen cloth to give it a pleasant hue. Table mats for hot dishes, doilies for others, and tray-cloths at the serving ends of the table were all used to protect the tablecloth. This was a habit which grew, till in later years every pickle dish and butter-pat had its own doily, embroidered and fringed, knitted or crocheted. Small plates or mats protected the cloth from the inevitable drip that occurred when the tea was poured from cup to saucer for drinking. This was such a common problem that scarcely any American book on etiquette neglected to mention what to do about it.

Decanters, water carafe and wine glasses as pictured in advertisements of 1853. / Author's coll.

The use of the saucer or the handleless tea bowl for sipping tea, a practice which seems so unfamiliar to us today, had survived from the earliest days of tea-drinking. The custom persisted with people who liked it right up to the beginning of the twentieth century and after.

Canadians and Americans sometimes observed the English custom of laying a roll or a chunk of bread at the side of the plate, but more commonly they sliced it, wrapped it in a napkin, and served it in a bread basket or tray. Beautiful japanned bread trays imported from England at an early date were used for this purpose. Only for informal meals was bread on a board at the table and no advice on table settings ever recommended it. The crumb tray and brush were introduced about 1850, as were tall goblets for celery and fancy biscuit jars.

Waiting on table was as correct and efficient as the servants who could be obtained to do it. C. Stuart, writing in *The Emigrant's Guide to Upper Canada* published in London in 1820, said, "The want of servants in Upper Canada is perhaps the greatest inconvenience to which persons of property are exposed. There is such a general independence and provision that persons of that description, especially female servants, are very rare." His words are echoed throughout the first half of the nineteenth century and in 1861 Mrs. Copleston recorded in her book entitled, *Canada: Why We Live In It, and Why We Like It*, that she had "fallen into another egregious error, viz; that of taking a 'bush girl'; it having been represented to me that Toronto servants were anything but desirable beings to admit within your doors." She was forced to teach herself to keep house and cook, and to instruct a completely ignorant girl at the same time. Mrs. Copleston, like many other Old-Country women, resorted to the cookery guides, and since most of these were American, she may have modified some of the English customs she had brought with her. To the girls from "the bush" the complexities of English table service must have seemed overwhelming and absurd.

Tableware commonly used in early Upper Canada. Fish drainer, platter 15" x 21", cream jug, sugar basin marked "Clewes Stone China," tea bowl, saucer, are all English underglaze blue transfer-printed earthenware, c. 1820. Dish in foreground is "Canton," c. 1840, typical of inexpensive Chinese wares which were imported from the port of Canton to the Atlantic coast of America from about 1790. / Author's coll.

Lustre and lustre-trimmed wares. Back row, left to right: copper lustre jug with floral decoration in bright pink and green; cream jug with broad band of pink lustre, red and blue flowers; platter, deep blue embossed design tipped with copper lustre; small jug, embossed coloured figures of horses, cows and cottage on copper lustre with bands of pink lustre; copper lustre jug with deep blue band. Front row: tea bowl and saucer, pink and gold lustre; cake plate, pink lustre; bowl, purple design with copper lustre, impressed Wedgwood. All 1800-50, all from old Ontario houses.

Silver-plated tea urn decorated with ram's head masks, formerly property of the Lesslie family in Dundas, c. 1810-25. / Dundas Historical Society

The large towns attracted unskilled people from the crowded cities of Britain and from these many servants were recruited. According to their general characters and adaptability they were trained for house and stable work. Some of the well-to-do families like the John Beverley Robinsons in Toronto managed to find a full complement of servants. At *Beverley House* in January 1854 the servants were: "footman, coachman, Hannah, cook, housemaid, boy, gardener, waiters, needlewoman, charwoman and scrubbing woman." In lesser houses "my Irish girl" was a common phrase in housewifely conclaves. In both town and country wages were very low. A satisfactory servant girl in Kingston in 1840 who was also a good seamstress was paid $2.50 a month, and a cook received $5 to $7. There were too many other and more promising ways of earning a living for the men, and too many opportunities of marriage for the women, to make remaining in service attractive.

Few people boasted of their cooks, and the mouth-watering reminiscences that have come down to us are mostly of food that was cooked by the people at home. The accomplished housewife was capable of turning out many fancy dishes and a great deal of substantial and appetizing everyday cooking. The addition of home-baked bread to most meals was a satisfying thing in itself, and the extra pancakes, tea biscuits, rolls and waffles that made for variety were things which most Canadian women produced with some pride. Elaborate puddings were a common dessert and the variety of pies and cakes that were served in well-to-do homes far outshines that of the average household today.

A great deal of trouble was taken to preserve fruits in special ways to provide delicious desserts for the long winters. I remember very clearly how my grandmother made one of the finest of preserves, sun-berries. The berries were washed and hulled into a colander where they drained for an hour or so. Then to every pound of strawberries three-quarters of a pound of sugar was added. The berries were gently pushed around in a kettle until each was covered with sugar; they were then put on the stove and brought to a boil for no more than three minutes. Next they were turned out on to old platters and taken to a table in the garden where they were covered with very clean polished panes of glass. If the sun was shining brightly, the platters stayed out for about three days. (They were brought in at night or if clouds came up.) The underside of the glass had to be wiped occasionally as drops of moisture gathered, and the berries were then shoved around with a spoon from the outer edges to the middle. They were eventually ladled with a silver spoon ("Be careful not to mash them!") into shining glass jars which were placed in rows on a stone shelf in the cellar. They were something between a jam and a preserve and were generally regarded as a "company" dessert.

46

Meat, game and fish were plentiful and smoked Canadian fish was sold everywhere. Every cookbook gave recipes for using oysters which were a favourite dish throughout Upper Canada. Even when I was a child we bought oysters by the barrel and never thought of them as expensive luxuries. The bacon and the pork side meat of those days, when properly smoked, had a succulence which seems to have been lost forever.

Tea and coffee were available at an early date and chocolate was mentioned as early as 1800. The historian William Canniff, writing in 1869, said, "Tea, now considered an indispensable luxury of every family, was quite beyond the reach of all for a long time because of its scarcity and high price." The earliest tea in the province was China tea. There was no other till the first Indian tea was sold in London in 1839. As Indian tea for some time cost just as much as China tea and as people were used to the latter it had a small sale at first. Eventually it became the custom to mix the two. The lady of the house did her own blending in a little glass bowl which nested between two compartments in her tea caddy. The small porcelain tea bowl covers which came to Europe with the first tea things imported from China at the beginning of the eighteenth century became saucers in Western usage. When tea bowls and small, handleless cups were used there was a prescribed method for holding them in the hand. The thumb was kept under the bowl, the middle finger kept on the rim, and the fourth finger moved about for support and balance. Later and larger bowls, the use of which was not confined to the drawing room, were often encircled with both hands. Bohea was the most popular tea and one of the least expensive. It was sold in Upper Canada in 1799 for 9s. a pound when the more fashionable Souchong cost 14s. and Hyson 19s. Gunpowder tea, which consisted of small pellets made from broken leaves, was 12/6 in 1816. In later years Twankey and Imperial tea were very frequently mentioned.

In the 1840s and '50s all tea was much cheaper and became the usual beverage in middle-class houses. So much tea was drunk as a pick-me-up that tea-drinking was referred to as a vice. Country people preferred green tea and village stores still stock at least half as much green tea as black because for older farm people black tea is just not tea as they were brought up to enjoy it. Most people preferred their tea hot and weak and took it with milk and sugar. The cream or milk jug was part of every tea service.

From 1830 to 1865, the coffees named in advertisements were: Java, Brazil, St. Domingo, Mocha, Old Government Java, Green Rio, Languayra or Laguira, and Wild African. In the earliest years more coffee than tea was advertised and coffee grinders were stocked in every general merchant's store.

47

Top: decorated tin tea caddy shaped like silver tea caddies of early 1800s. Centre: Victorian painted tin tray, c. 1860. Bottom: tin tea tray stencilled in colour, c. 1830. / All U.C.V.

Coffee cups were often sold without saucers and were used with tea saucers.

Pickles and conserves, though produced in almost every house, could be supplemented with "boughten" luxuries such as "bottled West Indian preserves, Tamarinds, and Guava Jelly" which were sold in Niagara in 1832. "Pica Lila" pickle was also advertised. In another twenty years there were all kinds of delicacies to be had; French and English pickles, and fancy biscuits like ratafia and macaroons were advertised in grocery stores.

The housekeeping account book of Mrs. John Beverley Robinson, wife of the Chief Justice, shows her dealings with her grocer W. Monaghan in Toronto in the years between 1853 and 1857. Among the ordinary supplies listed for *Beverley House* were some rather interesting items:

1 bottle essence of coffee	3/9
2 lemons [very frequent]	−/9
matches	1/4
2 lbs. Chestnuts	1/8
1 mint tea [very frequent]	4/9
3 lbs. wax candles	10/6
1 pot Anchovy Paste	2/6
Citron (one-half)	1/6
1 lb. Vermicelli	1/6
Bottle Mustard	−
Wax tapers	/7
1 bottle jelly	4/6
1 bottle pickles	1/10
1 pkt. Starch	−
1 pkt. Gelatine	1/3
1 lb. macaroni	1/6
B & H Anchovy sauce	1/10½
1 bottle Marmalade	1/6
1 lb. Tapioca	1/10½
Egg Powder	2d
1 box herrings	5/−
1 pkt. gas lighters	5/−
1 box dates	1/−/−
½ doz. oranges	1/6
1 drum figs	6/3

A recipe in a manuscript *Receipt Book*, used from about 1820 to 1840 in the household of the Reverend Robert Blakey at Prescott, shows how many imported ingredients were counted on as being readily available. The recipe for "Carrack; or Indian sauce for cold meats," requires:

2	heads garlic sliced
5	spoonfuls of Soy
5	spoonfuls Mushroom Catsup
8	spoonfuls of walnut pickle
15	anchovies or 5 spoonfuls of essence of anchovies
3	spoonfuls mango pickle
1	quart of vinegar

The directions are to mix it in a bottle and set it in the chimney corner and shake daily for a month. (The mango called for might have been the common muskmelon or even a citron, rather than the tropical fruit, as many American recipes called their native melons mangoes.)

Critical observers of the Upper Canadian scene remarked on the fact that people ate too quickly, that many of the fine points of traditional English table manners were neglected, and that the backwoodsman was frequently boorish in the way he attacked his food. Since we cannot see our ancestors at table we can only judge that if they were frequently cautioned by the etiquette books of the time not to do various things, they probably did them.

It was wrong to ask for a second helping of soup or even to accept it if one's host was vulgar enough to offer it; wrong to put the knife in the mouth, wipe the mouth on the tablecloth, pull the serving dishes askew when taking food from them; wrong to use one's own knife or fork to take any food from a serving dish, lean one's arms on the table, tilt one's chair back, or rinse the mouth with water from the finger bowl.

The question of fork versus knife for conveying food to the mouth had quite a few champions on the knife side. Mrs. Farrar, in *The Young Ladies' Friend* (1838), said:

> If you wish to imitate the French or English, you will put everything in your mouth with your fork, but if you think as I do that Americans have as good a right to their own fashions as the inhabitants of any other country, you may choose the convenience of feeding yourself with your right hand armed with a steel blade; and provided you do it neatly, and do not put in large mouthfuls or close your lips tight over the blade, you ought not to be considered as eating ungenteely [*sic*].

It must be remembered that the two- or three-pronged fork which many people used was not curved and was really more suitable for holding meat while cutting it than for lifting anything but chunks of food to the mouth. The custom of putting the knife in the mouth was so general that for many years men who did otherwise were considered effeminate. The backwoods settler used his own knife from pocket or sheath, plus a pewter spoon, and it was hardly likely that his children would grow up thinking that forks were essential. One wonders, however, where the rural Ontario custom of holding the fork in a tight left fist while cutting with the knife in the right hand came from.

Despite the lack of polish in country table manners, the tradition of hospitality established by the pioneers has continued. Its essence has always been abundance, and from early days visitors have remarked on the embarrassment of having to eat more than they wished in order to still the often-repeated, "Have some more—there's plenty!"

For many years dining rooms of the Victorian period were dark and sombre and the furnishings were as rich as could be afforded. Light over the tablecloth, whether from oil fixtures or gas, gathered the assembled diners into a circle of warmth and colour and left the rest of the room in shadows. Such rooms were still commonly seen in my childhood. I remember the dining room of my grandparents' old three-story house on Mutual Street in Toronto. It was a dark room. The only light came from a tall bay window doubly curtained with white lace and heavy green wool and crammed with plants. A drop-leaf tea table stood in its alcove with a brass red-shaded kerosene lamp on it and a shabby leather armchair beside it. Here my grandfather regularly sat to read *The Globe*, *The Christian Guardian* and *Blackwood's Magazine*.

The wallpaper was a deep red damask on which gilt-framed oil paintings were hung so high that they were never on eye-level for me as long as I went there. The gas light over the dining table was concealed by a square-shaped mottled red and black glass shade with a red bead fringe. Its glow seemed brilliant when it shone on the white cloth beneath. White linen damask (over a silence cloth and a soft old woollen blanket) was the constant covering of the table and hung to the carpet. Monogrammed silver rings held our accompanying linen napkins.

In the centre of the table was a glass vase of flowers, when they could be picked from the back garden, or a fern in a silver dish, when they had gone. Hemstitched and monogrammed traycloths and white crocheted mats were used under hot serving dishes. One whole drawer of the sideboard held various types of hand-made mats.

The chairs were balloon-backed, with buttoned leather seats, and my

English porcelain teapot and teacup from a set which includes tea plates and cake plate, all decorated in rose, green and yellow and having characteristic shapes of the '50s. / Author's coll.

Teapoy in maple and cherry. The box contains tea compartments and mixing bowls, c. 1835-40.

49

chair held both Volume One of the *Encyclopaedia Britannica* and a cushion. The mirrored walnut sideboard held half a dozen small rounded shelves looking like little compartments. On these were, as I remember, a pink biscuit jar (in which the change for the iceman was kept), a silver lemonade pitcher, a red, clear glass pickle jar with a fat stopper, and a pair of statuettes called "the French ornaments" which had been bought at the Chicago World's Fair. The silver tea and coffee service sat in the middle of the sideboard, flanked by a tray of tumblers turned upside down, together with a water carafe over which there was draped a small crocheted doily weighted at the corners with blue beads.

I remember particularly Friday night suppers in that room during the winter for I often spent week-ends with my grandparents. Most shopping was done on Saturday morning at the St. Lawrence Market and Friday's meals were "just what was in the house." Since it was one of my favourite menus this one was often repeated. It began with plates of oyster stew made with cream, and Bath Oliver biscuits to break into it. Then came a large platter of tender smoked bacon and two covered vegetable dishes of potatoes and turnips, both richly mashed with cream and butter. Of course there were the usual four or five dishes of pickles: chopped beet root, dilled cucumbers, chow chow and chili sauce. Dessert was ambrosial—my grandmother's sun-berries, so rich that only as much as would cover the bottom of a fruit nappie was served. Each berry was tasted separately and enhanced by the flavour of a beautiful sponge cake. Cheddar cheese from our own county of Prince Edward was always eaten at the end of dinner. It came to us regularly from the country by train, along with crates of fresh eggs.

The grace so earnestly said by my grandfather before we ate requested, "These creatures bless, and grant that we may feast in Paradise with Thee." It brought a chorus of "Amens," but imagination never succeeded in conjuring up any heavenly repast which could surpass our daily dinners.

Some of the requisites of an 1860 dining table are shown here: revolving cruet stand, soup tureen, celery glass, water pitcher, tumblers, and a large set of dishes. The china pattern, "Asiatic Pheasants," very popular between 1840 and 1860, was made by several English potteries in both blue and brown transfer printing. / U.C.V.

Kitchens

Looking out the door of the summer kitchen at "The White House,"

the old Fairfield home built in 1794 near Collins Bay, Ontario.

Stoves of the 1850s were thought to save labour but still demanded stooping and kneeling in the cooking and fire-tending. / Upper Canada Village

The settlers in the woods appear to be the most independent and contented people, in their way, I ever met with; perhaps with only a log house, unplastered, containing two rooms, one above and one below, with a large open fireplace and a log fire—a boarded floor, unplaned—one or two small glass sash windows and sometimes, at first, none; doors and gates with wooden hooks and hinges. A few articles of common household utensils—two spinning wheels, one for flax, one for wool, with reaves of spun yarn, hung around inside the house on wooden pegs driven into the logs; an upright churn—a gun or rifle—an oven out-of-doors at a little distance from the house, sometimes built of clay only, at others of brick or stone.

So wrote Joseph Pickering in *Inquiries of an Immigrant* in 1832. He was describing both a house and a kitchen, for they were synonymous in all of the one-room log cabins built in Upper Canada. Mr. Pickering was fortunate in seeing cabins nicely kept by contented families. Other reports describe inefficient and indifferent housekeeping, even squalor. This is not surprising for in many cabins there was no upper floor; the beds shared the room with all the equipment for living. And when there was no outdoor oven all cooking and baking was done on the open hearth in the room. It required conviction and endurance to keep the cabin clean and tidy.

Pioneers throughout the whole period of settlement brought with them their accustomed ways of living. Loyalists, Scottish crofters, destitute Irish, English gentlefolk, paupers, and Germans from Pennsylvania all had different customs and standards. For many newcomers life in a log cabin was no harder than the life they had left; they had always been poor and were used to making do. And in Upper Canada their hardships were lightened by a new independence and the promise of a future limited only by their capacity for work. The poor were not in the habit of recording their feelings and impressions, however, and the few firsthand accounts of housekeeping which have come down to us were written by literate people whose former circumstances were very much more comfortable than those they faced in Upper Canada.

In their first homes, most settlers had very little cooking equipment and a meagre choice of food. Nevertheless, they made the best of what was available, and prepared it according to the methods they remembered from their homeland. They adapted their familiar recipes to the cooking of native game, fish, wild fowl, vegetables and fruit. From the Indians they learned of other fare including that delicious dish corn-on-the-cob.

It was every settler's ambition to build a "second" house with a separate kitchen. But even when this became possible most people knew of few improvements to make in the planning or furnishing of the kitchen. Brick replaced stone in fireplaces, and more of them now contained ovens. Stone sinks were built into wide window sills, or wooden sinks were built along a

Town houses of the 1850s and '60s often boasted a massive "modern" stove set into the old fireplace chimney breast. / Mackenzie House, Toronto

A kitchen of the 1820s with its fireside equipment. A bar suspended from the ceiling dries or warms linen and blankets. Tansy tied in a bunch keeps away flies, and apples threaded on string are drying. The bellows used constantly to encourage the fire is by the oven. The long-handled peel used to take bread, cakes and pies from the oven stands beside the open oven door. Cupboards in the chimney provide warm, dry storage. A kettle and griddle hang from pot hooks and ring on the crane. / Upper Canada Village

wall. A lead pipe was added to take waste water to a pail, or even out through the wall to the yard where it made a puddle in which the geese waddled. Town houses sometimes had soapstone or tin-coated copper sinks.

There was no fixed rule regulating the location of kitchens in houses. They might be built as part of the ground floor, as rear or parallel wings, or in the cellar, and there are even records of kitchens in separate outbuildings. In York, in 1804, a two-story house, twenty-six by eighteen feet, had "an addition of 13 feet at one end, as a kitchen." A house was offered for sale in Niagara in 1795 with "four rooms on the lower floor, a commodious kitchen adjoining." In 1799 another advertisement specified "a dwelling house with out-kitchen" which could have been an extended wing or one of the first of those summer kitchens which were so ubiquitous in Upper Canada. In Kings-

ton in 1817 a house for sale was described as being "on the road to the Bay of Quinte, baker's oven in the lower part of it and an excellent kitchen." Another had "four elegant rooms and a complete cellar kitchen." And one offered "a large two-story house with a garret and a large cellar and kitchen."

Cellar kitchens were apparently not considered inconvenient for, except in very elegant houses, the food was eaten where it was cooked. A fine brick farmhouse of the 1820s, still standing in Prince Edward County, contains a cellar kitchen with an excellent cooking fireplace and oven. Since the house was built on a slope of land, the kitchen door opens into the surrounding dooryard. Basement kitchens were sometimes paved, as was the kitchen in a house advertised for sale in York in 1817.

The kitchen as a wing or lean-to, either beside or behind the house, dates back more than one hundred and fifty years. After heating stoves were generally available in the 1830s and it was no longer necessary for the family to circle the cooking fireplace for warmth, this was a practical move. It meant that in summer the heat from cooking could be confined to one room. In the one-room log cabins that were built as new settlements opened up, north and west of The Front, however, the kitchen continued to occupy the whole house.

In some cases the second houses were built around the original cabin kitchen. The house in which I live has such a history. Built about 1829 as a

log cabin with a loft bedroom above, it was enlarged in the customary way about 1840 by partitioning the downstairs area to provide two kitchen slip-rooms, one of which became a bedroom and the other a pantry. At one end of the house, a summer kitchen and a cool room were added, and across the end of these a long woodshed was erected. At the opposite end of the house, a parlour with a slip-room and another loft bedroom were built. Then the whole house was covered with clapboard. There was no cellar but the cool room, built entirely of stone, including shelves and floor, and lit only by a foot-square window, was a substitute. One could walk from the winter kitchen (the old cabin kitchen) through the summer kitchen to the woodshed without going outdoors. The pantry and cold storage were close at hand. It was an efficient arrangement.

Left: "Poplar Villa," built by J. Macdonnell at Point Fortune about 1820, had a basement kitchen with typical early fireplace wall. The openings, from the left, are: oven with ash-pit below, cooking hearth, alcove for cast-iron boiler with firebox beneath. / Public Archives

Right: The Schramm house north of Hayesville was rented in 1862 by the brothers C. and F. Brown, one of whom drew the kitchen. / Ont. Arch.

Earthenware. Above: salt-glazed stoneware beer bottle with "J.L." in cobalt blue; red-brown glazed jar; bottle in a pre-1850 shape. Below: kitchen jugs from Ontario potteries, a mottled-glaze and a brown-glaze once common on farms. / The Philip Shackletons of Ottawa

The great advantage of the built-on summer kitchen was, of course, that it left the principal family room cool in hot weather. Usually part of a lean-to built of unlined studs and boards, the best of the summer kitchens had a door at either end through which the hay-scented summer breezes cooled the air. In warm weather washing, cooking, milk-pan-scouring, churning, cheese-making, and preserving were done there. In winter knives and boots were cleaned in that room and overflow of all kinds was stored there.

Traditionally the well was just outside the summer kitchen door. There, lettuce, carrots and spring onions were washed and prepared for dinner while the housewife kept an eye on the stove only a few feet away. Some old summer kitchens with open fireplaces are still to be seen but from the middle of the century on an old stove or the winter-kitchen range, moved for summer's duration, was used for cooking. With these there was no need to keep the fire going all day. Paper and some chips would boil a kettle, fry some pork and potatoes for breakfast, then go quickly out. In fall and spring the summer kitchen was a nice cool place to keep food, though everything edible had to be covered, for mice were prime pests.

Summer kitchens were also catch-all rooms. Some had a half-ceiling on which were piled old trunks and boxes, broken furniture and utensils, and all the crocks and bottles for "doing down" meat, vegetables and fruit. The

buffalo robe for the sleigh hung in an old cotton tick over the rafters and from it the smell of camphor was wafted through the air. From pegs on the wall hung a broken bee "skip," skates, some squirrel skins, an empty birdcage and an old razor strop. (It was in this room, or the woodshed, that punishment was administered to recalcitrant children.)

In the cabin kitchens, the first stone cooking fireplace had lug-poles of wood or iron set in across the opening to the chimney, and from these hung pot chains or trammels. Cooking pots were suspended from the trammels by S-shaped iron pot hooks. A huge backlog smouldered on the hearth day and night. Even in summer some fire was always kept alive. Dog-irons held the smaller logs and sticks and supported the spit on which meat and fowl were impaled for roasting. A wheel and knob at one end of the long horizontal spit rod allowed the turnspit (often a small child) to rotate the meat till it was evenly and deliciously roasted, but not burnt. Another early way of cooking meat was by hooking it to a twisted hemp cord hung in front of the fireplace, which turned continuously as it untwisted and retwisted itself.

Equipment for the open hearth in the cabin kitchen was often limited to the spit, a boiler, a long-handled frying pan, a short-handled frying pan with three legs (called a spider—a name eventually applied to all iron frying pans), gridirons for broiling, trivets, ladles, skimmers, stirring-spoons, a teakettle and a bake-kettle. With bread dough in the bake-kettle which was set in the hot coals, meat on the spit, potatoes or corn meal in the boiler, and a kettle boiling for tea, the settler could look forward to satisfying his hunger.

To keep long-handled pans level when they sat on the fire unattended, the handle was rested on the spit, or on an iron stand called a jack. In the absence of either of these, an overturned chair served just as well. A long shovel, poker and tongs, and a homemade broom leaned against the chimney. Ladles and skimmers hung from the mantel shelf or lay on it beside the candlestick, sugar choppers, coffee grinder and pepper box.

The brick fireplace of the second house was usually equipped with cranes and ovens, which made cooking easier. Swinging the crane out towards her from the fire, the housewife could change the position of the hanging pots from the hot middle of the fire to the cooler end, and fill and empty pots without danger of burning her hands or gown. Fireplace ovens stood about three feet above the hearth and had recessed openings that were closed with iron doors on hinges, or thick wooden plugs with handles. Below the oven, just above floor level, was another space where ashes were stored.

In the second house, the utensils, though not improved, were more numerous. Most cooking vessels were still made of heavy iron which became coated with soot and were difficult to handle and clean. Joseph Pickering wrote in 1832, "Iron ore is plentiful and good . . . forges and furnaces are now so common that iron and cast ware is plentiful and moderately cheap." Still, most ironware was imported from Britain. Tinware, that is sheet-iron coated with tin, was in use at that time, but was reported to be expensive. It was less often advertised for sale in the country than in the town. There were cast-iron pots "lined with white metal" (probably tin) which were valued for cooking some foods (such as apples, which did not turn dark in tin as they did in iron). And there were standing toasters which turned on a pivot, copper and brass teakettles, all kinds of hand mills for grinding pepper and coffee, dripping pans, iron wire sieves, revolving gridirons, hanging griddles for pancakes, canisters, and a covered pan for roasting coffee.

Perhaps the most coveted cooking convenience was a reflector oven. This ingenious but quite simple contrivance was made of tin-plated sheet iron. It had four feet; the back feet were just an inch or so of iron rod; the front feet were formed by V-shaped pieces of tin which prevented the oven from tipping. The back of the oven was completely open and faced the fire; the front had

Top: Deep dish-platter, sugar basin and bowl decorated by stencilling or sponging under glaze in colours of blue, red, brown and green. This English earthenware was extremely popular in Canada after 1850. Middle: Blue feather-edged plate, the cheapest variety, and transfer-printed teacup with Spode's Stone China mark, both common items on the early dish dressers. Bottom: Sugar basin of early shape beautifully hand-decorated with flower sprigs but stained in spots from a hundred years of brown sugar. / All objects are from the author's collection.

Opposite page: A built-in kitchen dresser was the repository of china, pewter, cutlery and utensils. The china in this dresser is Staffordshire blue transfer printed in the 1820s. / U.C.V.

A crock and two churns in grey-buff stoneware, salt-glazed, with cobalt oxide (blue) decoration. Pieces of this kind were made in quantity after 1850. / Mr. and Mrs. Philip Shackleton, Ottawa

An unusual combination of dry sink and dish cupboard which was made in Prince Edward County.

a door which could be lifted to tend whatever was roasting on the long spit running through the middle from end to end of the oven. The spit, which was turned by a handle at the end, had small holes for the skewers that held the meat in place. The semi-circular bottom of the oven caught the drippings which could be poured from a spout at the end. Johnny cakes, puddings and pies could be baked on a rack when the spit was not in use. The ovens were made in lengths from one to four feet. (The little ones were for pigeons and other small wild fowl.)

The reflector oven has been given many names; tin kitchen, roasting kitchen and Dutch oven are common, though the last properly refers to a covered iron pot. It is said to have been invented in the eighteenth century, and recipe books published after the middle of the nineteenth still gave instructions for its use. There were also vertical tin ovens of this type, operated by a clock jack and having a vertical spit.

Some people simply had a tin-plated iron "hastener" which looked like a fire screen and reflected the heat of the fire on roasting meat.

Even in the first ten years of the century there were people of means in the province whose kitchens were as well equipped as those in Philadelphia, New York or Boston. Their tinware included "basins, tart-pans, dippers, cheese-toasters, tea-kettles, candle boxes, milk strainers, funnels, quart measures," all for sale before 1806. The distance between their kitchens and dining parlours made dish covers and hot-water-heated serving plates necessary.

For efficient cooking well-to-do people had smokejacks or expensive brass clock jacks at the open hearth. The smokejack was a horizontal vane placed in the chimney with a chain drive connecting it to the spit. It was turned by the up-draught of air and smoke. Clock jacks, hanging above the fireplace, were wound with a key and operated a system of wheels, weights, chains and cord which turned the spit. They would run for about two hours without attention from the cook.

Some fine houses had English-style ranges or hot plates built of bricks, usually beside the chimney, and topped by long cast-iron plates with holes for frying pans and pots. There was a firebox at one end with a flue connected to a space under the hot plate. The heat from the firebox filled this cavity and then passed up a flue to the fireplace chimney. The heat under the pots could be regulated by a damper. The iron range of the future was foreshadowed by this useful stove. The English hob-grate that was set into the fireplace and had iron shelves or ovens on either side was sometimes used in town houses, though more often in army garrisons.

During the 1830s advertisements for cooking stoves began to appear quite regularly all over the province. They were usually sold with "furnishings," which were all the boilers and pots to fit that particular stove's top openings. These included a large hot-water heater which looked like a later copper clothes boiler with a hinged half-lid on top. There were tin baking covers which could be fitted over half the stove top, and some stoves had a roaster at one end with a turn-back hinged door. Most had a back-closet under the right end where food or plates could be kept warm, or wet wood dried.

In 1829, Hooker and Church at Prescott were advertising:

> Cooking stoves, large and small, of the latest and most appropriate patterns, with apparatus [cooking utensils] complete. Manufactured from double tin and copper. . . . Their stoves are the wares of St. Maurice, Three Rivers, Lower Canada, and the Carthage Furnace, State of New York. Heretofore it has been necessary to resort to the United States to obtain these articles, particularly cooking stoves, but the subscribers having obtained them direct from the furnaces are enabled and determined to sell them as low as they can be purchased at any other place.

Though Upper Canada foundries soon began to make a variety of cooking

58

stoves, records show that many people believed American stoves, because of their constant improvements, to be the best.

In the next ten years, many stoves were bought, particularly in towns, and they changed the whole aspect of the kitchen. The continual cloud of smoke dust no longer settled on floors and furniture, and the usual sprinkling of ashes on food was gone. The family gathering around the hearth was transferred to the kitchen table where, by very inadequate light, the Bible reading, sewing and writing was done.

By 1850, the stove had supplanted the open cooking hearth in the winter kitchen in most new houses in town and country, and had been installed in front of boarded-up fireplaces in the old one.

Other changes and improvements also took place in the kitchen. "Yankee notions," as they were advertised (apple parers and sausage stuffers, for example) lightened work. The double boiler and other new utensils appeared, and some of these are in use in modernized form today. Matches became available and the fire could be allowed to die out between meals. In the towns coal came into use as cooking fuel, since wood was becoming expensive there. (On farms, however, the still-extensive wood lots continued to supply the fuel.) The greatest improvements of all proved to be the iron or zinc sink and the cistern pump which gushed water into it. Country women still sometimes refer to the sink as "the zinc," as it was called in early days.

Large farm families had little need for hired help in the house, but where necessary, girls from neighbouring farms often "hired out." There was no social disadvantage in doing this; it often provided a welcome change of scene, and better chances for marriage. But only in the larger towns was it possible to find domestic help willing to become servants rather than extra members of the family. In Toronto in 1837, John Macaulay was able to get a housemaid, cook and man of all work but his brother William, a well known Anglican clergyman who lived in Picton, wrote, "No good servants are to be found locally." His wife, Ann, in reply to a request that she find a local girl to go to Toronto as a nursemaid, wrote, "There is no one here whom I could recommend to you, and in fact it is too far away from this place for any but a totally disinterested person to go to Toronto. *My* principal objection would be that in general the people here in that station do not live *well enough* to make good nurses." My grandmother lived in the same town some thirty years later and told me of the succession of competent hired girls from farms who in her youth helped with all household chores including nursemaiding. They were so much part of the family that one who was greatly liked was married from the house, with all her relatives invited to stay for the celebrations. Her descendants today are progressive and prosperous farmers. "Helping," and "waiting on" were two different occupations, however. Those who did the "waiting on"—a cook who stayed in the kitchen and maids who answered bells—were only to be found in exceptional houses; most families did their own cooking and housekeeping.

These two pine dish dressers both have original brown paint. The upper one, c. 1830, has the customary moulding against which the old Ferrybridge ware plates lean forward. The lower one contains a dinner set of English Stone China made by Elsmore and Forster about 1850. / Above: Upper Canada Village. / Below: Dundurn Castle

The food available for the early cabin kitchens was extremely limited in contrast with the eventual agricultural abundance. Most settlers had some flour, wheat or rye, corn meal, potatoes, pumpkins, maple sugar and the molasses made from it, some hop yeast, some "boughten" goods like salt, pepper and coffee; as well as venison, bear, rabbits, coons, wild ducks, geese, partridge and pigeons. Wild grapes and nuts were gathered and eaten, and the small berries and plums were enjoyed in their seasons. Catherine Parr Traill said, "The wild red plum, skinned, makes good pies and puddings, and boiled down in sugar a capital preserve. The bush settlers' wives boil down these plums in maple molasses, or with a portion of maple sugar."

Pigs were cheaper to buy and easier at first to keep than cattle, and pork

Dough box in which bread dough was set to rise. The lid, turned upside down, made a kneading board—a very efficient arrangement. / U.C.V.

Painted dark brown-red and green, this pie cupboard with slatted upper sides and door was found in an old Scottish settlement. / U.C.V.

was the common meat. Fish provided a welcome change. Most families kept geese but saw that eggs were hatched rather than eaten. Milk, butter, cheese and hens' eggs were not at first the common staples of a pioneer kitchen.

Milky fluid in a bottle with a large cork was often kept on the window sill in an early kitchen. This was one of the most precious ingredients of pioneer cooking: yeast. It was available from the "emptyin's" of beer barrels or the mash tubs in the numerous breweries. Notices such as the one which appeared in a Cornwall newspaper in 1841, "Fresh yeast from Moulinette Brewery kept constantly on hand and for sale," were frequent. Yeast could also be obtained from a neighbour who had it from her mother, who had it from a friend. It kept for years. There were many ways of making leavening for bread dough but all recipes ended with, "Then add a cupful of good lively yeast," and this came from the bottle on the window sill.

Refined potash produced pearlash which was used in place of baking powder. It was called saleratus and could be produced at home, and eventually it could be bought. The hot biscuits so well remembered by many pioneers were lightened with it.

Brown bread was made from rye and corn meal (called "rye and Injun" in the States), and white bread from wheat flour which was precious enough to be frequently eked out with other grains. Kneading troughs or dough boxes where dough was punched and pommelled and left to rise were used throughout the nineteenth and early twentieth centuries and are one of the most commonly found farm antiques.

Bread was at first baked in a three-legged iron kettle with a high collar around the edge into which a lid fitted. (Pots were called kettles long before a spout and lid made one into a teakettle.) Coals were heaped on top and all around the kettle, which served very well when there was not a lot of baking to do. But the outside ovens and the brick chimney ovens took many loaves at once, and other baking too. A good fire of light wood was made in the oven and left till it died out. Then the ashes were raked out and the bread put in. An old lady in Dundas County told me, "First we put in the bread and pies, next cookies and cake, then shortcake and birds' nest pudding." The recipe for birds' nest pudding, a very old one, she described as follows: "Take some nice apples, pare and core them, put them in a pudding basin and pour a good rich custard over them." Brick oven bread had thick hard crust. Some of it was cut off and saved for bread-and-milk laced with molasses. This and corn meal mush, the other staple diet of the settler, made many cabin suppers.

Indians, neighbours, newspapers and cookbooks all contributed suggestions for food substitutes and ways to preserve food for winter. Meat, which was most important, was packed in barrels of salt and brine or, in the spring, smoked and hung in canvas bags. A side of beef might be preserved deep in the oat box in the icy temperature of the barn. Beans and peas, squash, blueberries and raspberries could all be dried and kept in paper bags. The chimney breast was festooned with dried and sliced pumpkin and apples. Baked beans were drained hot from the cooking pot into bowls lined with muslin. When they were cool and dry the muslin was tied around them and they were hung to freeze in the woodshed.

A cellar improved the chances for successful food preservation. Summer butter was packed in crocks. Eggs were put down in lime and salt where they could be kept for six months. Root vegetables and apples smelled up the cellar all winter. Fruit was made into preserves by the pound-of-fruit, pound-of-sugar method, with a little brandy added for insurance. Parchment or cloth dipped in brandy was tied over the glass or stoneware fruit containers. Pickling was done with everything from giant cucumbers to nasturtium seeds. When food became tiresome or slightly tainted, maple syrup, honey, molasses and spices made it more palatable. Root cellars, icehouses, refrigerators and Mason jars came to most people in the plentiful years following 1850.

Before the later years of the nineteenth century there were few Canadian cookbooks, and these contained for the most part recipes compiled from the United States and Great Britain. The earliest known is *The Cook Not Mad*, published by James Macfarlane in Kingston in 1831. A popular cookbook published in 1861 by William Gillespy in Hamilton, bore the title *The Canadian Housewife's Manual of Cookery—carefully compiled from the best English and American works, especially adapted to this country*. It is a small book and its recipes differ scarcely at all from American counterparts. It does suggest more uses for tomatoes than is usual. There are recipes for making tomato soup, scalloping, stewing, frying, preserving, pickling, baking, and making sauce and catsup, all with tomatoes. It also gives a recipe for an old-fashioned summer drink which I remember as being offered, with sugar cookies, to visitors. The recipe called for red currants and raspberries to be bruised together and added to water, sugar, cream of tartar and citric acid.

Between 1830 and 1850, a great many cookbooks and household manuals were published in Philadelphia and Boston. They were advertised in Upper Canada and were probably sold by book pedlars, as they were in the United States. It is these American books rather than the monumental work of Mrs. Beeton, with its English recipes and ingredients, that are still to be found in old farmhouses. *The Frugal Housewife* by Mrs. Child, and a cookbook by Mrs. Hale, usually in late editions of the '30s, turn up occasionally, but the works of Miss Eliza Leslie are found much more often. Her *House Book* and *Receipt Book*, both published in the '40s, probably give the closest approximation to housekeeping methods and cooking which were aspired to by women in Upper Canada. Catharine Beecher's *Domestic Economy*, 1842, was also popular and must have established many household practices. An 1859 volume, *The Family and Housekeeper's Guide* is so commonly found that it was probably given away as a premium. My own copy has the inside of both front and back covers pasted up with clippings of births, marriages and deaths of many families whose descendants are my neighbours in Prince Edward County.

When Catharine Beecher and her sister Harriet Beecher Stowe published *The American Woman's Home* in 1869 they instigated some of the most advanced and efficient methods of housekeeping ever proposed, and they gave dignity and a high sense of responsibility to the role of housewife. They proposed to people of modest cash incomes new ideas for organizing work and decorating the house.

All these books described for us the developing of increasing plentitude and better ways of making a happy home. Nevertheless, from the 1850s through the rest of the century the Ontario kitchen still required awkward and time-consuming work. Sinks were far too low, so were stoves; cupboard shelves were too high; things to be carried were far too heavy. But for many people they were good times. The abundance of food, the presence of both grandmother and the girls at home to help cook it, and the feeling that all comfort was the reward of that supreme rural virtue hard work, made farm kitchens the focal point of the happiest memories in Canadian lives. I remember the "pieces of meat" not recognizable as butcher's roasts which came out of the oven at noon, falling apart from tenderness, the great pots of mashed potatoes and squash or turnip. I also remember the horrid taste of preserved butter from the cellar crock which made even the lightest of tea biscuits inedible.

It was nice to be sent "down-cellar" to choose a preserve and see the rows of peaches, cherries, raspberries, strawberries, plums and Missouri currants. It didn't matter which was chosen; there were dozens and dozens of jars of each. The tea was weak, and the coffee too. But oh the pies, day after day, two to a meal—rhubarb in spring (the pastry shortened with bacon dripping) berries in summer, apples in fall, and pumpkin in winter. (British emigrants found the Canadian apple pies, with their generous additions of nutmeg and

Kitchen sideboard used in home of the present owner's great-grandmother. This was one of the most common pieces of kitchen furniture between 1850 and 1875. / Mr. & Mrs. W. E. Gronau, Hamilton.

Work table with storage compartments, factory-made about 1860. Some similar pieces still retain remnants of the original varnish finish.

Kitchen tables, from left: eighteenth-century turned-leg table with stretchers; turned-leg table prevalent from 1850 on; table with H-stretchers, the commonest early kitchen table.

Couch (opposite page), also called bench or settee, was a universal kitchen piece. Having a straw or wool-filled mattress, it often served for cat-naps between chores. Such couches were made of hardwoods in great variety from 1840 on and were usually stained dark red or black.

Kitchen chairs. Below: the slat-back, a common early style. Opposite, above: the Windsor, once found in every farmhouse; below: the arrow-back, a favourite for many years from the 1830s on.

allspice, rather sickly sweet, and made *theirs* with lemon peel and cloves.)

With particular pleasure I remember the threshing dinners. The whole household was up at 5:30. There were pies to bake. (Apple and lemon were standard.) When the pies were done and the oven was still good and hot a gargantuan piece of meat was put in to cook for hours. Potatoes and carrots were cleaned and put aside in big pots of water. A basket of tomatoes was peeled, cut up, and steeped in vinegar; dozens of cucumbers were sliced. Lettuce was chopped and sprinkled with vinegar and sugar, and pickled beets were put out. Great pride was taken in the variety of pickles that could be put on the table.

The womenfolk, which included all the local relatives and wives of some helping farmers, worked swiftly and competently. The tea and coffee were put on the back of the stove half an hour before dinner was ready. The table was set, plates with mountainous piles of bread were covered with linen napkins, and bowls of cabbage salad were covered with plates to protect them from flies. Basins were filled with water and laid out on milk benches outside the doors, and towels were pegged to the line for the men's washing up. Beginners like myself were warned, "Never let a cup get empty. Keep the coffee and tea pots full. Don't clear anything off the table."

The men filed in to the long kitchen, all waiting till the Thresher was seated at the head of the table before taking their chairs. The master of the house sat at the opposite end. The eating proceeded in silence—the women, who waited on table, speaking in whispers—until the Thresher had cleaned his plate, wiped his moustaches and tilted his chair back. Then there was loud talk and laughter among the men which ended when the Thresher glanced at the clock and pushed back his chair. In a minute they were all out, the table was cleared, the dishes stacked and the remains of food reheated if necessary. The women then sat down in a cluster at one end of the table and began to eat and gossip leisurely. Until the combine took over the work of the threshing machine, this was an unchanging autumn scene.

The washing-up was done in a tin dishpan which sat on the still-warm stove top in the summer kitchen. Dishes drained on an old japanned tray on a nearby table. The chairs, which were pushed back against the wall, were like those illustrating the pages of books on antiques except that they were covered with fresh yellow paint. The oilcloth-covered table had long H-shaped stretchers and might have been made in 1825. Only the cupboards were new, a concession to a bride of the 1880s. Till the arrival of the chrome suite,

Ontario farm kitchen furniture changed very little.

The very early furnishings of cabin kitchens have been described by a settler, Mrs. David Fleming, speaking of her father's house in the Cobourg area about 1835:

> The house was not very large, being 12 x 18 feet in size with no partitions. . . . We had very little furniture to decorate with. Two beds stood at the east end of the house and the window between. Under the window stood my father's chest; the table stood in the centre of the floor; three or four chairs with some stools of my father's make and the dear old clock on a shelf directly opposite the door. These along with my mother's chest, and a few dishes and pots, also the long-handled frying pan and bake-kettle were about all of our possessions at that time.

This is how many settlers' housekeeping began, though in the same year there were kitchens all over the province in both cabins and houses which had advanced considerably beyond this simplicity.

Very primitive homemade kitchen furniture is still to be found, but it is not easy to say when it was made. The same materials and tools produced it over a long period of years from the same necessity: no other to be bought, or no money to buy. There are, however, slat- and ladder-back chairs, Windsor chairs, fireside settles, tables with stretchers, dish dressers, and cupboards which can be dated pre-1840, all of them well made by chairmakers or by small woodworking shops. Inventories, wills, auction bills and advertisements list them for us.

The kitchen piece least often found today is the open dish dresser which was easy to build and was at one time in very general use in Upper Canada. Earthenware, china and pewter were kept on the open shelves, linen and cutlery in drawers, and cooking utensils and crocks in the lower shelves or closed cupboard. Dish dressers were as much part of the room as the mantel.

Dressers were essentially kitchen furniture wherever they were used—in Europe, the British Isles and North America. In France and in French Canada the equivalent dresser was called a *vaisselier*, and was often a decorative piece of furniture, with carving and fine hardware. In the United States most dressers date between 1730 and 1840; in Ontario they seem to have fallen into disuse at about the same time.

Dressers varied in height from five to eight feet; in length they varied according to the space on the wall where they were to stand. Scalloping of end-boards, cornices and shelves, and the cutting of spoon notches which were

Pine wall boxes were usually made at home. They served as salt holders or as catch-alls. / U.C.V.

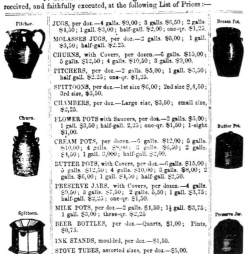

common in American dressers were unusual here. Cornices had a pleasing moulding, or just a beaded board, and a moulded base rather than feet was usual. Plates overlapped each other and frequently leaned forward on the gallery or guard moulding, which made them easy to remove. Cups, jugs and tankards hung from iron hooks inserted underneath or on the edge of shelves, and serving dishes stood on the counter. Knobs on drawers were always wood, and doors were closed by wooden or brass turn buttons. Most dressers were made of pine, but other woods were used—simply because they were available and not with the intention of making a fine piece of furniture. They were frequently painted the colour of the kitchen wood trim, and the colour changed as the room was repainted. The colours most commonly used at first were Indian red, raw or burnt sienna, yellow ochre, umber, Spanish brown and Prussian blue.

Another dish cupboard was sometimes built in a corner of the kitchen. This usually had two sets of doors, the upper ones often glazed. These corner cupboards gradually replaced dish dressers.

In early pioneer days the dish cupboard generally contained a scanty stock. William Canniff's description of the scarcity of tablewares is typical. In *The History of the Settlement of Upper Canada*, he remarks,

> Many had but one or two dishes, often of wood, rudely made out of basswood, and spoons of the same material. Knives and forks in many families were unknown. A few families had brought a very limited number of articles for eating, relics of other days, but these were exceedingly scarce. The wooden spoon was the most common article with which to carry food to the mouth. Bye and bye the peddlers brought pewter spoons, and once in a while the settler procured pewter and moulds and made spoons for himself.

Locally-made redware or stoneware dishes and bowls were sometimes available, but the additions to the dish dresser were usually bought from the nearest town store, at auction sales, or from pedlars, and were imported goods.

Using pine, beech, basswood, hickory, ash and maple, the farmer often made his own tableware, including the beautiful "knot bowls," which we call burl. A pioneer in the Bay of Quinte district, however, recalled that his family bought woodenware from the Indian encampment nearby. Although glass tumblers, goblets, wine glasses, hock glasses, cruets, decanters and cooling glasses were all mentioned in inventories in Upper Canada before 1812, advertisements offer only the general term "glassware" in shipments from England. Empty bottles were often for sale.

Pewter continued in use for many years because it was already on hand. Although pewter teapots, basins and porringers were advertised till about 1810, Britannia ware appeared alongside these listings. This was a hard pewter with a high, lasting polish, and was much in demand. By the 1830s all advertisements of pewter for sale had disappeared; instead, scrap dealers offered to buy "any quantity of old pewter." A typical advertisement was that of L. Bigelow in 1815 at York: "Cash paid for old pewter or tinware given in exchange."

Typical tableware advertising lists "Britannia metal table, dessert, and teaspoons; iron and double plated ditto"; "iron table spoons, mustard, and salt spoons," and "tinned iron spoons." The few forks were of iron, and knives

Opposite page: By 1860 most farm kitchens had a pump which drew soft water from a cistern in the cellar. A lead pipe carried the draining water to a small gravel pit outside. / U.C.V.

were buck-handled. The head of the house usually carried his own special knife in a sheath at his belt, and drew it to cut meat. Horn spoons and tumblers were common in Scottish settlements.

Thomas McCrea, a pioneer, described his walk from Merrickville to Brockville carrying one and a half bushels of wheat which he exchanged for "a dozen white bowls with a blue edge and one dozen iron spoons bright as silver, half a pound of cheap tea, the balance in fine combs and little things for the children."

Stone sinks such as this one were set in window sills and sometimes had a hole and pipe to drain off water to the outside. / Upper Canada Village

The "bowls with blue edge" (all of which broke on the return journey!) may have been the extraordinarily popular edged ware which, along with other tableware and the coarser bowls, pudding basins, and jugs used in cooking, was imported from England from about 1800 and sold everywhere. Edged ware varied in colour from white to cream and had a moulded edge which qualified it to be described as feather-edged. The "feathering" was painted blue or green, and occasionally reddish-brown. Platters, sauceboats, pudding dishes, tureens, all sizes of plates, soup plates, ladles, handleless cups and saucers called tea bowls, pickle dishes and jugs were made of edged ware. All these, or sherds of them, have been found in Ontario. Leeds, Wedgwood and other potteries in England produced great quantities of this ware in varying qualities. It was advertised for sale, listed in stock books and described on invoices from 1800 to 1836 throughout Upper Canada. A set of "neat blue-edged Queensware" was sold in Niagara in 1797; and a brown-edged service was auctioned at Kingston in 1815 consisting of "8 meat dishes, different sizes: 4 vegetable dishes with 3 covers; 4 dessert dishes; 19 dinner plates, 12 soup dishes; 9 small dishes; 4 sauce boats; 1 fish strainer; 1 salad bowl." Edged ware was bought according to quality and price, by rich and poor.

Also very appealing to the early housewife was the great choice of pattern in blue transfer-printed earthenware made by English potters. This blue ware, printed with Italian, English and Indian scenes, along with some designs of Chinese derivation, included the celebrated Willow pattern. Mocha ware and some sponge-decorated ware were cheap, colourful additions to the dish dressers. In old houses on the long-settled shoreline from Cornwall to Niagara even today one finds a few pieces of porcelain, a teapot, sugar basin or cracked cup and saucer which have always been there. They are all that remain of a once-prized tea set which was saved for and kept on the top shelf of the

KITCHEN GADGETS
1. *Coffee roaster*
2. *Hemp doormat, 1845*
3. *Grater*
4. *Sugar nippers*
5. *Pigeon roaster*
6. *Barrel*
7. *Bucket*
8. *Piggin for dipping water*
9. *Churn*
10. *Trivet holding pan*
11. *Spider*
12. *Gridiron*
13. *Fowl roaster*
14. *Roasting kitchen with clock jack*
Drawings are of objects in
Upper Canada Village
National Historic Sites
Dundas Historical Society Museum
Private collections

1

Paddle scrapes pan bottom

LID

2

3

4

5

6

7

8

9

10

11

12

13

14

Kitchen gadgets

Some homes, especially in Eastern Ontario, had a small room or shed off the kitchen, called the "sink room." Here dishes were washed and milk pans were scoured. / Upper Canada Village

In large homes the sink room was known as the scullery and until about 1850 it always had a fireplace or boiler for hot water as well as a wooden dish-drying rack. / Dundurn Castle

Clockwise: (1) Tea kettle on adjustable trammel shelf which hangs on crane. (2) Tea kettle suspended by pot hook from crane, with device for lifting hot lid. (3) Cast-iron tea kettle, one of many different shapes made. (4) Bake kettle which sat on the fire with coals heaped on lid.

dresser or cupboard. Most often these bear the gay Chinese patterns of New Hall, the soft glow of Staffordshire lustre or the black stipple-painted scenes of Caughley-Coalport.

As soon as settlements were large enough to make stores profitable, merchants in Upper Canada began buying stock from wholesalers in the lower province. From Montreal they brought up some of the great quantities of common tableware which arrived in each spring shipment from Scotland and England. The usefulness of these wares may be judged by reading the cargo lists. In 1823 a ship from Sunderland to Quebec brought "13,000 pieces of loose earthenware, principally brown dishes, trays, stew-pots, wash-pots, milk bowls, cream pots, and C.C. [cream-coloured] plates and dishes"; and a vessel from Newcastle landed at the wharf "4829 pieces consisting of brown dishes, milch bowls, beef pots, hand basins, broth pots, stew pots, jars, pipkins, jugs, porringers and butter pots, and 1800 pieces cream-coloured oval baking dishes."

Wholesalers in Montreal also carried astonishingly large stocks of edged ware, blue ware, dipt ware (which was Mocha and similarly decorated crockery), and all kinds of delph. "Delph" was spelled in various ways but it described what was also referred to as common china—the crockery suitable for everyday use. Among this common china, ironstone was plentiful. These were the kind of dishes advertised in early days as "suitable for the Upper Canada market," and they became the ordinary dishes of the dish dresser in all farm homes and in the kitchens of the richer houses. For the first fifty years of the nineteenth century the choice of crockery for the kitchen was so good that it remains among the best of our antiques today.

The early transportation of tableware to Upper Canada was difficult. Shipments were often taken from Montreal by cart to Lachine, above the most hazardous rapids, then loaded on batteaux and Durham boats for a journey full of dangers for such perishable cargoes. Half-way merchants like H. & S. Jones of Brockville were advertising in 1829: "[They] are now building batteaux which together with their Durham boats they intend to keep constantly plying between this and Montreal. On arrival at this place [goods] shall be shipped by the cheapest and most speedy conveyance to their destinations."

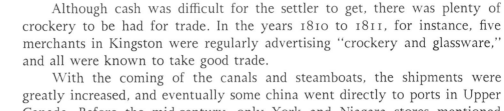

Although cash was difficult for the settler to get, there was plenty of crockery to be had for trade. In the years 1810 to 1811, for instance, five merchants in Kingston were regularly advertising "crockery and glassware," and all were known to take good trade.

With the coming of the canals and steamboats, the shipments were greatly increased, and eventually some china went directly to ports in Upper Canada. Before the mid-century, only York and Niagara stores mentioned American sources for the goods they advertised (which include tablewares), but travellers and pedlars no doubt distributed some Yankee crockery throughout the province. By 1850, Ogdensburg merchants advertised as far east as Cornwall, Detroit advertised in Chatham, and Buffalo advertised in Hamilton. Many of the advertisers sold common kitchen china.

After 1850, the cheaper late "ironstone, or granite ware" from England and Scotland was stocked by country merchants everywhere and often comprised the "best sets" for the farmhouse and the kitchenware in the homes of the affluent. Large sets ("enough for a threshing," which was a phrase used to describe anything enormous) were inexpensive, and cupboards soon became piled up with them.

The old tall, open, dish dresser eventually became a memory. Garnished with pewter and Britannia, blue feather-edged crockery, brown and yellow ware, and the dark glowing blue of transfer-printed dishes, it must have been a proud and lovely sight as the dishes reflected the great cooking fire. Canniff Haight, writing of the 1830s, said, "Who can ever forget the blue-edged plates, cups and saucers, and other dishes whereon indigo storks and mandarins, or something approaching a representation of them, glided airily over sky-blue hills in their pious way from one indigo pagoda to another. These things, I have no doubt, would be rare prizes to ceramic lovers of the present day." And so they are.

Opposite page: Feather tick, homespun blankets, patchwork quilt and goose-feather pillow await the sleeper in an 1850 country bedroom. / U.C.V.

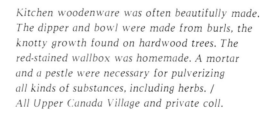

Kitchen woodenware was often beautifully made. The dipper and bowl were made from burls, the knotty growth found on hardwood trees. The red-stained wallbox was homemade. A mortar and a pestle were necessary for pulverizing all kinds of substances, including herbs. / All Upper Canada Village and private coll.

Bedrooms

A bed built in the corner of a log cabin has homespun curtains and a grey-and-white blanket bound in scarlet. The skin from an ox's head makes a cover for the seat of a rocker. / U.C.V.

This butternut chest once held family clothing, including ladies' gowns. The carpet is striped drugget, very colourful. / Upper Canada Village

Opposite page: Looking into two slip-rooms from a parlour. Such rooms always opened off a larger room and had no other entry or exit. There was space for only a bed, chest, candle-stand, sometimes a washstand or chair. / U.C.V.

The coming of night brought the settler a respite from weariness, hardship and anxiety. The family worked as long as it was light in summer, continued in winter to work on whatever tasks could be done by firelight, then went early and thankfully to bed, rising with the dawn. No one doubted the maxim, "Early to bed, early to rise, makes a man healthy, wealthy and wise." It is not surprising, then, that the bed was the most valued of all early furniture. The very symbol of warmth, peace and security, it was associated with family memories of birth and death. Its curtains afforded the only privacy available and shut out surroundings which were often discouragingly crude. In most inventories and wills the bedstead appeared first in the list of household belongings; it was often bequeathed to the wife or to the favourite child.

What we now call a bed, that is, a wooden or metal frame, with or without posts, was then called a bedstead. The mattress or tick was the bed; the pillows, bolster, sheets and blankets, the bedding; the top cover—a quilt, coverlet or bedspread—was the counterpane; and the curtains, valance, tester cloth, head cloth and dust ruffle were the bed furniture. Bedsteads of the early period were extremely large and heavy and probably were not "brought by the Loyalists" as often as family legends claim.

In many of the first homes of the farmer-settlers the beds were not bedsteads but makeshift platforms fastened to the wall in a corner of the room, with a single post at the outer corner. The mattress often consisted of evergreen boughs or straw. (Samuel Strickland, describing his house in Douro township in the 1830s, noted: "My bed was composed of hemlock brush picked fine and covered with a buffalo robe.")

As long as the first house contained only a single room the bedstead was its dominating piece of furniture. Small children frequently slept with their parents when they first left the cradle. Later they were packed into a trundle bed which was pushed underneath the bedstead in the daytime. Later still, when the roof was wholly or partially ceiled-in, a ladder led them to their own bedsteads in the loft.

The first partitioning of a house was usually to provide a bedchamber. This was done by walling off a narrow space across the end of the room, a space which might be divided again to make two very small rooms, known as slip-rooms. Sometimes one of the rooms became a pantry, but more often both became bedchambers. Any room set aside for sleeping was called a bedchamber —a name frequently shortened to chamber—and even the loft above a lean-to was referred to as the wood-house chamber.

The original bedstead was usually too large for slip-rooms; it had to remain in the main room and since it was the privilege of the mother and father to sleep near the fire, they retained possession of it. When a cabin was enlarged, or a new house built, the rear end of the parlour was often partitioned to make a fairly large parlour slip-room or parlour bedchamber, but bedsteads often occupied the parlour itself. In many old Ontario houses the head of the family continued to sleep downstairs in the kitchen or the parlour even after a bedroom floor was added. Here he would be quickly alerted by a flaring-up of the fire on the hearth, the call of alarmed cattle or the approach of a traveller looking for shelter. This continued to a certain extent throughout the nineteenth century, although the parlour bedchamber sometimes became the spare room for guests.

The downstairs sleeping rooms had an added advantage: they acquired some heat from the kitchen or parlour fireplace. Only the finest houses provided heat upstairs, and it was a splendid house indeed that had dressing rooms with fireplaces.

The earliest bedchambers, in most cases just slip-rooms, contained only a small bedstead, a candlestand, a pegboard on the wall for hanging clothes, and a chair, if there was space for it. For many years the bedchamber walls were painted with a white or coloured lime-wash for cleanliness. The settlers

were anxiously aware of the scourge of bedbugs and fought a continuous war against them, which began with the sanitizing of walls.

The later, upstairs, bedchambers generally had room for a washstand, commode, chest of drawers and a bedside table called a stand. At the foot of the bed there was always "the box"—which might be a trunk. Such a piece was listed in one inventory as a "small red morocco trunk"—and very pretty it must have been. The box was sometimes a blanket chest with a small fixed or sliding top tray, sometimes just a plain, large box with a hinged lid, painted (often decoratively), or varnished, or padded and covered with chintz. My granddaughter owns a box which has been used for four generations in our family. Each time it is recovered it reveals, in the tightly-tacked areas where fabric is difficult to remove, tag ends of the various chintz coverings it has worn over the years. In my childhood it first held toys, then clothing, and was known as my bedroom box.

In the country the furnishing of bedrooms altered very little over the years from 1820 to 1850. The greatest change was the growing use of three-quarter-post and low-post bedsteads which fitted easily under sloping roofs.

Clothes-closets were rare; instead there were movable wardrobes which, in ordinary homes, were simple, painted pine cupboards for corner or wall. Most frequently, however, clothes in regular use were kept under a chintz, dimity or calico curtain hung from a wall shelf supported by a pegboard. Bandboxes were kept on top of the shelf, clothing was hung by sewn-on tapes from the pegs, and a small tin tub for bathing was often hidden behind the curtain. Sometimes the clothes would be simply hung on a clothes-airer, or clothes-horse, which was a larger version of the rack used for towels. Clothes not in daily use were folded and stored in drawers and boxes.

It was not until about 1850 that washstands were in every bedchamber. In houses where niceties were observed there was sometimes a dressing table, though not necessarily of fine wood. Miss Leslie in her *House Book* of 1840 says, "Dressing tables of plain, unpainted wood with white covers and valances of muslin are not yet quite out of use." The upholstered and draped dressing table was adopted in the eighteenth century, became immensely popular for both men and women between 1800 and 1830, went out of favour, was revived in the 1860s, and went again completely out of fashion where it remained until its reappearance in the first quarter of the twentieth century.

Another piece of furniture described in 1840 as going out of fashion was the dressing-glass which sat on the dressing table. It was made of mahogany or walnut, with a small swivelling mirror hung between posts mounted on a base or series of small drawers. Since the height of dressing tables varied a great deal, at some it was possible to use the mirror while standing, by tilting it up; at others it was necessary to sit. The early-nineteenth-century dressing-glasses had straight lines and were fine and delicate, in the general style of Sheraton and Hepplewhite. Despite predictions, the dressing-glass survived well into the 1860s, becoming larger and heavier, with mahogany or rosewood posts and convoluted bases. Shaving stands (which had a pedestal base, small oval mirror, shelf and drawer) and long, swivelled cheval glasses were also frequently used in town houses in the 1840-60 period.

Sometimes the dressing-glass was used on top of a bureau. In Upper Canada and elsewhere during the nineteenth century any chest of drawers intended for a bedroom was usually referred to as a bureau, and this word, spelled variously "buro," "beauro," and "beaurow," appears in inventories to the confusion of modern students who connect it with a slope-front desk on a case of drawers. The top surface of the bureau was protected with a damask-linen or dimity cloth. Illustrations of the time show the cloth hanging over the top surface for at least four inches, which must have made it awkward to open and close the top drawer. On the bureau top were ranged pomade jars, pin-cushions, daguerreotypes, cologne bottles, trinket boxes and candlesticks. Pins

Opposite page: In many communities of German settlers the bedding included bolsters, large pillows, sheets, and a huge feather comforter. By 1840 bed-curtains were often shortened to half-length, as they appear here. / U.C.V.

75

It was usual to stand before high dressing tables like this one of the 1840s. / U.C.V.

Victorian dressing table with draped mirror. Directions for elaborate draping were contained in home magazines of the 1860s and '70s. / U.C.V.

of all sizes were essential to women and there were often two pincushions. There was apt to be one in which large-headed pins were stuck to spell out "Mother," "Love the Lord," or some other suitable sentiment. Such a prized gift was not to be desecrated by the puncture of useful pins. The other pincushion contained large shawl pins, straight ordinary pins with pewter heads (much coarser than the ordinary dressmaker's pins of today), and minikins which were very fine, small pins.

The bureau with attached looking-glass was first available only in fine furniture but by the mid-1840s it appeared in country-made maple and cherry pieces and gained popularity rapidly when factory-made sets of bedroom furniture came on the market in the 1850s.

It was not till bedroom sets were introduced that the chairs in the room matched the rest of the bedroom furniture. Most houses owned a dozen or half-dozen matching, all-purpose chairs which could be bought very cheaply. (John Turnbull of Belleville owned twenty painted chairs valued at 5s. 6d. each in 1827.) These chairs commonly had cane seats and were varnished or painted. They were used all over the house, particularly in bedrooms. (Being light in weight, they were suitable for a room where "redding-up" was done every day.) A rocking chair was always kept in a bedroom where babies were nursed or children rocked, and there was usually one in the bedrooms of elderly people.

Bedroom floors in ordinary houses were often covered with straw matting, particularly in summer when heavier carpets were in storage. Local weavers produced the rag carpeting and striped wool carpet popularly called drugget in Upper Canada, which often covered the floor of the best bedchamber. Venetian carpet from factory looms, which resembled drugget, sold very cheaply and was recommended for use in bedrooms. Sheepskins, plain or dyed, and home-braided rugs lay beside and in front of washstands.

The houses of the rich had amply furnished bedchambers. When Baron Grant rented the beautiful and famous *Alwington* in Kingston to the Government for the use of the Governor, Lord Sydenham, in 1841, he supplied an inventory of the furniture left in the house. One of the five bedchambers contained:

1 bedstead and bedding
1 dressing table and glass
1 carpet
3 chairs
1 chest of drawers
1 wash-hand-stand
1 clothes screen
1 press
1 long pier glass
3 boxes
1 set of bed-curtains
1 mosquito blind

All but one of the five bedchambers had bed-curtains, dressing tables, wash-hand-stands, and clothes presses. All had carpets, chairs and boxes. A servant's room had only bed and bedding, chest of drawers and a small table.

Andrew Hurd at Augusta (near Brockville) had in his bedrooms in 1839: toilet tables, stands, two high-, two low-post beds and two French beds, "buros," chests, window screens; and in the parlour chamber he had a carpet, six chairs, bedstead and furnishings, and washstand.

The 1845 American edition of Webster's *Encyclopedia of Domestic Economy*, a much-respected authority, was quite specific on the subject of furnishing. For instance:

The principal articles requisite for the dressing room and toilet table are, wardrobes, commodes, wash stands, dressing glasses, dressing case, with razors, shaving boxes, hat and clothes and bonnet brushes, hair, tooth and nail brushes, shoe lifts, boot and button hooks, tongue scrapers, cap and wig blocks, wardrobe powder for dry-cleaning silks, corn rubbers, toilet cushions, braid combs of various sizes, powder boxes and puffs, towel airers, toilet covers, work boxes and loaded pin cushions, candlestick stands, bonnet boxes, sponge and sponge bags, flesh brushes, soaps of various kinds.

The 1850 inventory of Mrs. Ann Macaulay's old-fashioned furnishings in the house in Kingston where she had lived for many years included chamber furniture such as cane-seat chairs, painted wardrobe and washstand, dressing tables, towel horse, looking-glass, black walnut bedstead, marble-topped washstand and a "beaudette" (bidet).

Spool turning on cherry dressing table of the 1840s. At that time attached mirrors began to supplant portable dressing glasses. / U.C.V.

The four squared' posts of early high-post bedsteads and the thick poles which held them together were usually plain, unpainted maple. Headboards, when they were used, were low, and footboards were rare. The support for tick or mattress was sometimes canvas laced or tacked to the poles, sometimes a loosely woven mat made of strips of elm or basswood bark or rope. Some beds were held together with mortise-and-tenon joints, but bed screws and the keys used for fastening them were for sale before 1816. Some beds were topped by a moulded cornice, others with ordinary testers. Not many of these enormous early beds remain.

The trundle, or truckle, bed (names dating from the sixteenth century in England) was so practical that almost every house had one. In these, wooden slats usually supported a straw mattress. Michael Scherck mentioned them in describing early bedrooms in the Niagara district:

> In the sleeping apartments of the family was to be seen the old family bedstead with high wooden framework on top enclosed by damask curtains, and with a white linen curtain or valance around the bottom of the bedstead, as well as the low trundle bed on wooden castors or rollers, in which the children of the family slept in the same room with their parents, often until they were twelve or fourteen years of age, and which in daytime was shoved underneath the large bed. When the farmer was short of bedroom space there was to be seen in the dining-room or kitchen the old-fashioned bunk, which served as a seat or bench in the daytime and a bed at night, the lower part being in the shape of a box, which when opened up, disclosed a quantity of bedclothing and made a comfortable place for sleeping.

Rosewood dressing table in Louis XIV style. Pieces of this kind were usually part of a matching set which included the bed, bureau, commode and dressing table. / Dundurn Castle

The bed last mentioned has many names; in western Upper Canada it was the bench, box, bunk bed, or settle; but east of Prescott the name used was *banc-lit*. Surviving examples of such beds range from the crudest ones made of planks to those with turned spindles in the back rails. All were of pine or assorted woods and all were painted. Their use spans the time between 1800 and the present.

By about 1825 high bedsteads with handsomely turned and carved lower posts of cherry or mahogany were being used in Upper Canada. (It was usual to ornament only the lower posts as the head posts were covered with headcloth and curtains.) The headboard, which was originally of inferior wood and finish as it was hidden by the headcloth, was mortised into the top posts. The footboard was shaped or scrolled. Countersunk screws ran through the tenons of the side-rails to make a firm joining, and the rails were equipped with small knobs or holes for the roping, or a shelf for slats. It took five people to put up or dismantle such bedsteads; the fifth person tightened the screws with the bed-key. Sometimes the job required the services of a carpenter or cabinet-maker.

The tester frame for these grand bedsteads was composed of four narrow strips of wood. The frames had holes in the ends which fitted over nail-heads or screws in the tops of the posts. On bedsteads which had moulded cornices the tester-cloth which formed the "roof" of the bedstead could be first tacked

77

Dressing bureau of bird's-eye maple with cherry mirror and knobs. It was made in Prince Edward County in the 1840s. / Mrs. L. Nethery, Picton

Country version, Sheraton-style dressing table, cherry with maple legs. Made in Kingston area in 1830s. / Mr. & Mrs. Philip Shackleton, Ottawa

Right below: Walnut marble-topped dressing bureau with fixed mirror and unusual arrangement of drawers. Made in 1856 for Rev. George A. Bull, of Barton Township. / Miss Mary Farmer, Hamilton

to a frame of slats and laid on the lowest ledge inside the cornice. Hidden iron or brass rods and rings held valance and curtains.

Tent or field beds were advertised and inventoried even before 1830 in Upper Canada. On these the canopy of tester-cloth and valance was hung over an arched frame which was hinged so it could be folded in half for moving or storage. Sometimes all parts of the bed furnishings, including curtains, were sewn together in one piece and supported on arched frames, but this was done after it was thought unnecessary to have curtains which could be drawn.

The early three-quarter-post bedstead, of which there are some beautiful examples in Ontario, discarded the tester altogether. On top of each post was a turned or carved finial instead of the flat top surface of most high bedposts. Bedsteads made of thin iron rods having a partial roof called a half-tester were made in England in the 1840s and are said to have been in use here, but the iron bedsteads commonly found are of a lacy cast-iron variety which was popular in the 1850s and '60s. These were advertised as being hygienic, as they could not harbour bed lice. (Although they still required the tester-cloth, valance and head curtains, they did not have the dust frill, which had often hidden dust rather than excluded it.)

By the 1840s the low-post bed had been developed in a great variety of styles. Those of painted maple with pine headboard and nicely turned foot-rail were most usual. This popular bed made the fortunes of many small factories of the 1850s where spool turning was perfected. They were finished in everything from red-filler to varnish, and imitations of wood-graining were common.

From 1830 to 1850 there was also a great vogue for "French bedsteads" (as they were advertised here), a reflection of the French Empire style. These had solid ends of equal height and were frequently of mahogany, though some were painted dark red with graining, or in light colours. They were placed with a side against the wall and bed-curtains hung either from a pole attached high on the wall or from a wooden form fixed to the wall side of the bed. On fine French beds curtains were suspended from a half-crown or coronet attached to the wall. The wide, draped curtains were held back by the head- and foot-boards and then hung to the floor.

The French beds were expensive and were used exclusively by the wealthy and fashionable, but their successors, the sleigh beds, which followed the same style lines but in heavier construction, were among the most popular of all nineteenth-century bedsteads. Usually made of mahogany, often veneered, the head- and footboards of the sleigh beds had an outward curve, and the side-rails, instead of having a straight top edge, curved up to join the head- and footboards with dowels. The bedclothing and spread were tucked behind these rails. Many sleigh beds that are found have fasteners of American patent—iron hooks that fit into slots to join rails and end boards.

Outward curves at head and foot appeared in amazing variety in iron beds cast by American foundries for a growing market from the late 1840s through the '60s. Although they were widely advertised and had the additional advantage of built-in metal springs, they are seldom found in Ontario today. Many, no doubt, were thrown on the scrap heap, for when their original white or green enamel paint wore off they rusted, and there was a long period after their first popularity when their truly elegant designs and fine castings were not appreciated.

Brass beds were manufactured in great quantities in the late 1840s in England and in the United States, but those surviving in Canada all seem to be in the style of 1880 to 1910.

A new style of bedstead, introduced in the late 1850s, was first made as part of a suite in good cabinet-shops but later became the standard bedstead of all factories, and remained in general popularity until the end of the century. Originally it was an ornate but richly handsome piece of furniture, usually walnut, with rounded footboards, low, moulded side-rails and disproportionately high, panelled, and crested headboards. The mass-produced stereotypes of this style found their way into almost every house. They were sold from $4 up and the greatest proportion of them, although simplified for economy, were badly made and finished. Their headboards were of ungainly height; sometimes they actually reached the ceiling. It was against these headboards that the stiffly starched pillow shams of our grandmothers were used to cover enormous feather pillows placed at a toboggan-slide angle. One sees them today at every country auction, in sad incongruity with simple farmhouse furniture, and the prices paid for them show that they have almost reached the category of antiques. They remain in use in old-fashioned houses throughout the province.

Because the legs of many early bedsteads were so high and so much bedding was used it was often necessary to use bed-steps. For at least the first fifty years of the nineteenth century, standard bedding consisted of a "bed," usually of feathers, laid on a "bottom" made of rope, lath, canvas or sail-cloth, a mattress laid on top of that, sheets, bolster, pillows, blankets, another thin feather bed on top for winter, and a light blanket or quilt in summer. There were innumerable variations in the use of feather beds; some people used them under, some over, a neater and thinner pad (the mattress) which was stuffed with hair, wool or sea-moss.

In many poor homes the only upholstery for the tired body was a tick full of barley straw, paper shavings, or a palliasse made of old blankets or quilts stitched together. When money was not a difficulty only health cranks completely abstained from the downy cosiness of a feather bed although many people used only the mattress in the summer months or placed a straw mat over the feather tick. How slippery this must have been! Yet all household manuals suggested it.

I was very young when I first slept in a feather bed. The bedstead was so high that I was lifted and dropped into the all-enveloping softness. It was a warm, breezy moonlit night; the blind cord banged on the screen; tendrils of Virginia creeper rustled round the window frame; the dimly seen pictures on the wall were all hung sloping forward in the old-fashioned way and seemed about to fall. The other end of the room stretched out forever and was full of frightening shapes. I slept, but was visited by a nightmare of strangulation and smothering that I still remember. Screams brought a kindly great-aunt who rocked me and made for me a much preferable blanket-bed on the floor.

For most people a good feather bed was a very desirable item. One listed in the Hon. James Baby sale at Queenston in 1833 was valued at £3.15s.10d., and in John Turnbull's inventory at Belleville in 1827 four feather beds were appraised at £20 the lot.

The making and care of a feather bed were onerous tasks. Feathers had to be plucked from the geese and were dried in baskets or laid out on papers on the attic floor. The filling of ticks and pillows was a slow and slippery business. Household manuals say that a boxed-tick with squared sides is best. This is certainly true but feather ticks are rarely seen that are not great flopping, lumpy, one-seamed bulks, almost impossible for one person to handle.

Filling ticks with straw or corn husks was easier, but still awkward. Straw was renewed every month by the perfect housewife; the common practice was to do this every fall.

The mattress—used in early days with the feather bed, later without—was made in the same boxed style we know today. The horsehair mattress was everywhere considered the best, but a good wool mattress, like those still made on farms today, was even better. Its resilience was perfect; it kept its shape but was comfortably soft. Wool flock mattresses (made from wool rejects) could be bought as well as made. Sea-moss, called also sea grass and

Country-style chest of drawers, of butternut with sumach inlay and pulls, c. 1840s. / U.C.V.

The warm tones of cherry and maple in this little chest look well against the bottle-green wall in a bedroom of the 1820s. A netted bed canopy was often used in the summer. / U.C.V.

ulva marina, was used as filling in many manufactured mattresses from the 1830s. As late as 1852, Stonnor and Jarvis in Hamilton were selling "sea-grass, hair, and straw mattresses." Wool mattresses could be remade for ten shillings. Although spring mattresses were made in Birmingham as early as 1845, they do not appear in advertisements or inventories in Canada until after 1870. The bed ticks which contained the feathers were often woven at home, but in 1806 they were advertised for sale in a shop at York. Good ticks were preferably made of linen, sometimes waxed on the inside to prevent the feathers from escaping; the opening, on the upper side, closed with buttons or tapes. Later ticks were made of heavy cotton ticking which was practically feather-proof, but not entirely so, for my grandmother described one of her childhood chores as feather-picking, which meant taking a paper bag and going through all the bedrooms to pick up loose feathers.

The feather bolster which lay at the head of the bed, and was at first an enlarged double pillow the width of the mattress, was still in use in the shape of a narrow roll at the end of the nineteenth century. It was customary to have two pillows for each bed and these were placed over the bolster to support the sleeper's head at an angle. The short length of the old bedsteads can be better understood if one realizes the inches that were saved by sleeping with inclined head and shoulders. In German communities the bolster or several pillows were often placed under the feather bed so that the occupant was sitting rather than lying. On such beds the top covering was often just another feather bed made like a comfortable, with tufting to hold the feathers in place.

The red, blue or black thread which marked corners of linen, cotton or linsey-woolsey sheets was the guide for making sure that the bottom of the sheet was never put at the top when the beds were made. Sheets were long, usually seamed in the middle, as sheeting was woven at home and in mills in narrow widths.

Linsey-woolsey sheets were particularly popular in winter. When I was young there were many old people who couldn't sleep in anything other than "winter sheets" in cold weather. When the weather was warm these linen-and-wool sheets, light in weight and fine in weave, became appropriate summer blankets. Russia sheeting, a linen twill, was sold everywhere in Upper Canada and was considered the best wearing of all bed linen, but families living far away from shops grew their own flax and wove many yards of linen for sheets, pillowcases, towels, shirts and underclothing. Cotton was scarce and considered uneconomical for sheets, both as to price and wearing quality.

The banc-lit settle, or bunk bed, was very commonly used in kitchens in Eastern Ontario. Usually made of pine, it opened out and down to provide extra sleeping space. / U.C.V.

Sheets were usually made of unbleached or home-bleached linen but pillowcases and feather quilt cases were often woven in indigo-and-white stripes or checks. The pillowcase openings were fastened with buttons or strings and this closure was sometimes hidden by a shirred frill, a style which continued in old-fashioned households to the 1890s.

Blankets, ranging from dingy-looking "Canadian grey" to indigo-checked, striped or plaid-on-white, were woven at home by itinerant weavers and by families of professional weavers who did all the work for a community. Most households did some home weaving, but people with access to imports could buy the much-advertised manufactured blankets of the period.

Many of the blankets brought in as trade goods by the fur traders were called Indian blankets, both in advertisements and in general speech. They were sold in ordinary shops as well as across the counters of the trading posts. Also advertised were the English blankets called Kersey, of a type of weaving which is mentioned by Shakespeare. (The name appears also spelled "Carsey" and "Kearsey" in Canada.) English blankets which are still made at Witney in Oxfordshire were sold here as early as 1810.

Among the most frequently advertised and inventoried blankets were those of fine quality described as rose, or rosed, blankets, in which a rose or a conventionalized rose design was worked in the corners. These embroideries, and other devices such as stripes or crowns, served to indicate the ends of blankets in uncut lengths. When George III and Queen Charlotte visited Witney in 1788 they were presented with "a pair of 14/4 blankets [meaning blankets three-and-a-half yards wide] beautifully rosed at each corner." Both professional and amateur weavers of American blankets frequently adopted the rose motif for corners and worked it in coloured yarns, calling the design Indian Rose or Cherokee Rose.

Thomas Empson of Witney filled an order for the Hudson's Bay Company in 1780 for 100 each of 1, 1½, 2, 2½ and 3-point blankets, the points referring to the respective weights. The point blankets were also advertised by general merchants throughout Upper Canada from the earliest times.

Old woollen clothing was cut into pieces for patchwork quilts which served as blankets, and it is in these preserved quilts that we find the bits of woven materials which are our chief evidence of the home industries of the past. Records show that eiderdown quilts were used but if they survive they have been so often remade that it is not possible to date them. Cotton comfortables were made with calico or chintz over batting and were quilted in large diamonds or squares. Beautifully designed unpadded quilts, sometimes stitched in magnificent patterns on fine white cotton, sometimes appliquéd in colour, sometimes pieced in colours, were used chiefly as counterpanes or spreads.

The mass of bedding ordinarily used got frequent airing and shaking and infrequent washing and remaking—all heavy, tedious work. Feather beds were taken out of doors, scrubbed with soapsuds and a stiff brush, put on stoop or shed roof to be rained on, then allowed to dry in the sun. While they were drying they had to be turned every day and they had to be covered with a thick cloth every night to protect them from the dew. When dry, they were heaved on to the bedstead with a great deal of shaking, pushing and smoothing with a bed pole.

A complete set of bed furnishings for the old high-post, flat-topped bedstead was:

1. Tester sheet or canopy which made a roof over the bed.
2. Valance—a short curtain on three sides of the bedstead, which hung from the tester below the tester-sheet.
3. Curtains—two or four pairs hung from underneath the valance at the four corners or at the two headposts, falling to the bottom of the counterpane or to the floor.
4. Headcloth, hanging straight or slightly gathered, from the tester to just

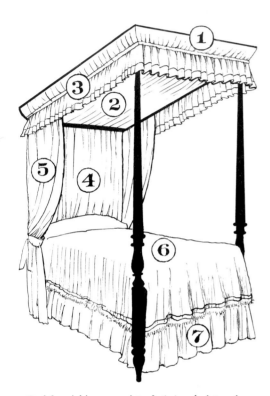

Bed furnishings consist of: (1) upholstered cornice, (2) tester cloth, (3) valance, (4) headcloth, (5) curtain, (6) counterpane, (7) dust ruffle or flounce. All wooden parts constitute "the bedstead." The mattress is "the bed." Sheets, blankets, bolster and pillows are "the bedding."

below the headboard.

5. Spread, counterpane, coverlet (or coverlid), made in one piece or with straight or shirred side pieces, which hung to the side-rails and under the footboard, if there was one.

6. Dust ruffle or flounce which hung from the side-rails to the floor on three sides.

The tester sheet, also called the tester cloth, was pleated and tacked to the four slats which formed the tester. There was at least one pleat to allow for shrinking but often the whole sheet was pleated or gathered. The material usually matched the rest of the furnishing fabric or the lining of the curtains, or else was a tea-coloured cotton.

Curtains on the earliest bedsteads (till about 1825) were meant to be drawn, and ran with rings over an iron rod held by pintles set into the posts just below the tester or by hooks set in the cornice frame. Later, when only head curtains were used, the curtains might be fastened by tape loops to small tacks in the tester frame and tied back to the headposts. The valance also hung by hooks and rings, or tapes, from the tester frame or cornice.

The dust ruffle was often made in three separate pieces, gathered and stitched to a band or tape, or made with a casing for a drawstring. In the first method it could be tacked; in the second it could be held fairly taut by drawing the strings and tacking the ruffle at the ends and middle of the side-rails.

The fabric of the counterpane might not match the rest of the bed furnishings and the dust ruffle was occasionally of another material, but surviving examples and the known custom of the period indicate that not only tester cloth, valance, curtains and headcloth were matching, but window curtains in the bed chamber as well.

Bed furnishing fabrics were advertised as such in Upper Canada from 1798. In the next thirty years the materials available included "calicoes, chintzes, moreens, prints, figured and embossed 'furniture,' damask, India calico, checked India calico, camlets and camleteens, twilled calicoes, and serge." Other fabrics are known to have been used, such as the very popular dimity and the expensive copper-plated English linen or cotton with lovely pastoral groups and scenes in indigo on white.

Early bed furnishings, which required heavy materials for warmth and privacy, relied on wool damasks and moreens, such as the set of crimson moreen bed-curtains listed in the inventory of John Turnbull's house in Belleville in 1827 and valued at £5. Moreen was a thick wool fabric, sometimes calendered to produce a watered effect as in moirés. It was advertised in Upper Canada from 1803 to 1852, though by the latter date it was considered quite old-fashioned. Cottons were perhaps as much used as wools for fashionable bed furniture. In William Firth's sale at *Holyrood House* in York in 1811 some of his bedchamber furnishings were listed as follows: "Superb mahogany four-post bedsteads on castors, with chintz and dimity furniture and large bordered, prime goose feather beds and pillows, best Whitney [sic] blankets, hair mattresses of very first quality." (Castors on bedsteads are not often mentioned in records but we know that they were in common use since they appear so frequently on the early bedsteads still in existence.

The name chintz, found in old records, does not necessarily mean the cloth of our contemporary dictionary's definition; instead it was commonly used to describe many types of coloured printed materials and may often have been used to designate calico. In the early period, dimity was a fairly coarse white cotton cloth woven in ribs or figures. At first it was often used to replace wool bed furnishings in summer; later it was used all year. Muslin was also in use for summer bed curtaining. As late as 1811 "china-blue furniture" was sold in Kingston. This fabric was printed by applying a paste of indigo directly on the cloth and then toning it with chemicals—an eighteenth-century technique. No old pieces of china-blue furniture are found today; one can only imagine the

The canopy for a field or tent bed like this one (c. 1830) was made in one piece and laid over a vaulted frame. There was usually a dust frill on all high-post beds / U.C.V

This simple cherry bed has tapering "pencil" posts, a style prevalent in 1820-25. Short bed curtains were called cascades. / U.C.V.

Left: A bedstead with "cannon ball" finials. The coverlet is handwoven quilted wool, with one side goldenrod, the other indigo. / U.C.V.

Opposite page, top: Posts, blanket rail and bed-screw covers of the 1840s Gothic-style bed are of exceptional quality. As on most beds of this period and earlier, the tick or mattress is supported on roping strung through holes or from pegs in the framework. / U.C.V.

fabric and wish that one could see a sample of it, as well as of such delightful-sounding material as "embossed brown Holland linen."

Records show that trimmings included curtain cords, tassels and fringes, broad white fringe, black and scarlet fringe for bed curtains and gimps (or furniture patch, as these braids were also known). The trimmings grew more sumptuous and available as the century progressed. They were used to edge valances, counterpanes, festoons (which were swags and drapes applied to the valances) and dust ruffles. Dimity trimmed with the broad white fringe was apparently common. Elaborate netting was made at home; sometimes it was used for trimming, sometimes it was wide enough to be used as a valance, or even an entire canopy.

The bedcover was, according to fashion, of fabric which matched the rest of the bed furnishings, but in actual use there was great variation. Inventories include many different names for bedcovers. Although we now use the word coverlet to describe a woven blanket-spread, it was synonymous with counterpane in the eighteenth century, and was later used to describe many different kinds of covering. Andrew Hurd's inventory at Augusta in Upper Canada in 1839 lists "two double coverlets at five shillings, two flowered coverlets at one pound, two old flowered coverlets at nine shillings, one birdseye coverlet at eighteen shillings."

Quilted bedspreads of great beauty were used from quite early times, and professionally woven bedspreads, called Marseilles spreads, were advertised from the early to the late nineteenth century. At first these resembled a kind of piqué, with small repeat patterns in diagonals, waves or diamonds, but after about 1840 they had elaborate floral patterns with large central motifs and deep borders. Around 1900 the name was given to cheap, loosely-woven, somewhat honeycombed spreads which were used mainly on children's beds or summer cottage beds. The mid-century Marseilles spreads were thick enough to cover the messy convolutions of feather beds, and when they lay snow-white and smooth on high- or low-post beds were as lovely a cover as could be desired. They were much valued and many were preserved for generations.

In modest homes a patchwork quilt often served as a spread, but there were probably few families that did not own at least one woven coverlet by the 1840s and '50s. Many housewives who did their own weaving produced

fine coverlets, usually in a variety of blue and white patterns. These, and the much more varied and intricate jacquard (reversible) coverlets were woven by professional weavers in magnificent colours. Two of the advantages of woven coverlets were that they washed beautifully and, though light in weight, served as warm blankets as well as spreads. Some coverlets were stored as heirlooms and bring ever-higher prices in the antique shops today; others served several generations and now scraps of them may be seen serving as pads on tractor seats or on the long-surviving kitchen couch in farmhouses.

Bedding and bed-furnishing was aired a great deal because the washing of it entailed a tremendous amount of work and was therefore done infrequently. Damasks and chintzes were never washed, only dusted, shaken and sponged; and since calico colours were not fast they too were rarely washed.

Despite all efforts at cleanliness, most houses harboured bedbugs and fleas. Vitriol applied to bedsteads was said to kill the bugs, and a bag of pennyroyal was kept in bedclothes to discourage the fleas. All travellers in Upper Canada complained about mosquitoes, for though window netting was available by 1840, or earlier, it does not appear to have been widely used.

Bedroom windows were not opened after nightfall, summer or winter. Still, some air leaked in. Storm windows were unusual; and window draughts in winter were only partially controlled by nailing padded laths around the window frames and stuffing cotton in the cracks. Few of the bedrooms were heated and on cold nights the bed-curtains were pulled close and the quilts piled on. Socks were worn in bed, heated stones or bricks were wrapped in flannel for the feet, glass hot-water bottles, and stone pigs with arched tops and flat bottoms took the chill off clammy linen sheets. Copper warming pans are listed in early auction sales and mentioned by writers such as Scherck but one gathers that they were not commonly used.

Low-post bed, necessary for story-and-a-half houses where the sloping ceilings would not accommodate beds with high posts. / U.C.V.

At bedtime candles or lamps were lit and carefully carried into the dark bedrooms to throw a dim light on whatever personal ablutions were thought necessary. Watches were tucked into the pockets designed for them in the bed curtains. Clothes were folded on chairs; nightgowns, nightshirts and night-caps were donned. Then it was time for prayers; only the most benighted Upper Canadian approached sleep without them.

Cooking & heating

The very first settlers often cooked outside their shanties in summer and suffered the fire hazards of a chimney made of sticks, clay and straw in winter. As soon as possible the first crude fireplace was replaced by one of stone, however, for the cooking fireplace was the heart of the house, the source of warmth and food, and the gathering place of the whole family.

The pioneer housewife, whether she came from the American colonies or the British Isles, was accustomed to cooking at an open hearth. She was familiar with the methods of making stew in a pot hung from a crane, baking bread in a bake-kettle in the hot ashes, and roasting meat and game on a turn-spit set before the fire.

There were certain drawbacks to cooking at an open hearth. Most fireplaces smoked excessively and it was often necessary to leave a door open in order to get a good draught. This made all but the hearth side of the room miserably cold in winter. To cut down on the smoke a shirred length of cloth was put across the front of the mantel. This held back some of the down-draught smoke and also caught some of the little clouds of smoke and ash which arose from the hearth as the bellows was used to encourage the flames. Now often called the frill and used only as a decoration, this cloth was originally called the fire-cloth or the chimney-cloth and its use dates back to the fifteenth century. It was usually made of thick old wool rather than cotton which scorched easily and often caught fire.

In many households, the first improvement in cooking facilities was a large stone or clay oven built outside the house. This was so cavernous that a very long-handled paddle, called a peel, was necessary to reach in to the back. The oven was heated with a hot fire of light wood. The ashes were then raked out and the bread and other food were put in.

When bricks became available, indoor ovens were built beside the cooking hearth. Most of these were heated like the outdoor oven, quite separately from the fire on the hearth. Some, however, were connected by a sloping flue from the hearth and could become intensely hot. These were less easy to control, but saved work.

When the cast-iron or sheet-iron cooking stove arrived, it did away to a large extent with the inconvenience of the open hearth. In the first half of the nineteenth century, though, cooking stoves were too dear for poor families, too low for comfort, and usually too small to cook the whole dinner at

Cookstove in the officers' quarters at Fort Wellington, Prescott. It has a boiling pot, the lower part of which fits in a pot hole. Stoves were sold complete with utensils. One, priced at $35 in 1839, had boilers, griddles, kettles, steamer, basin, dripping pan, reamer, and other equipment. / National Historic Sites

Opposite page: The stove shown here was made by Johnston and McGregor at the Northwestern Foundry, Smith's Falls, 1865-70. The low stove at left was used to heat flatirons. / U.C.V.

Stove and iron-ware advertisement. / Ont. Arch.

Late nineteenth-century nickel-trimmed stoves were advertised on bright-coloured lithographed pin trays like these. Well-known retailers of these stoves were the Adams Furniture Co. and the Dale Furniture Co., Toronto. / Author's coll.

once. Moreover, in summer they heated up the kitchen more than an open fire did. Consequently many people preferred to use the fireplace for cooking even though their houses were heated by stoves. The women of early Ontario did not easily relinquish their old methods of food preparation and the cheerful look of the cooking hearth. It was a long time before houses were built on the assumption that only a stove was to be used in the kitchen. Until then people who had a cooking stove sat it on the brick hearth and ran its pipe up the old chimney, or blocked up the opening by boards or bricks and put the pipe into the chimney breast above the mantel.

As late as 1854 cooking stoves were not considered essential, though in that year Mrs. Traill recommended in her *Female Emigrant's Guide* that the new settler's family invest in one. "It is more convenient and not so destructive to clothes as the great log fires," she observed. She named several makes of stoves—The Lion, Farmer's Friend, Burr, Canadian Hot Air, and Clinton Hot Air—and said, "A stove large enough to cook food for a family of ten or twelve persons will cost from twenty to thirty dollars. This will often include every necessary cooking utensil." But Mrs. Traill also advocated the outside oven: "Built of stones, brick or clay, [it] is put up at small cost and is a great comfort. The heating it once or twice a week will save you much work, and you will enjoy bread much better and sweeter than any baked in a stove oven or bake-kettle." The truth of her statement is borne out by the fact that the outdoor oven continued in use till the end of the century in many remote rural communities.

Though a few combination heating and baking stoves were advertised from about 1800, they are almost impossible to find today. These were not proper cooking stoves but they were efficient heaters and had a small oven space. There were American-made, ten-plate stoves of this kind, with legs that looked like the underpinnings of the old-fashioned sewing machine. A heating and baking stove more generally used was the very large double-stove which looked like one box stove on top of another. The upper half had a two-door oven which could be made very hot. Double-stoves were not set up in a kitchen, but in a hall or parlour, and were consequently not really convenient for baking. They were made in Lower Canada but were common throughout the settled areas and are still to be found in use.

No stoves intended only for cooking seem to have been advertised or inventoried in Upper Canada before the late 1820s, but in the 1830s there was scarcely a newspaper that did not list them for sale in all the principal towns. And they were included in almost all advertised auction sales. Many of them were Canadian made, but quite a few were imported from the United States by stove dealers and private people.

90

The British cooking stove of this period, which consisted of separate parts for building into the recess of the hearth, was rarely imported; its use here was almost entirely confined to garrisons. These cooking ranges had an open raised grate set in the bricks of the fireplace, with an oven on one side and a boiler for hot water on the other. They were economical of fuel and easy to work but usually burned coal which was not generally available in Canada in early times. It is quite possible that well-to-do English emigrants brought such fittings here and had them installed in existing fireplaces but there is no evidence of their general use. One of their features was a trivet hinged to the top bars of the grate, a trivet which could hold a kettle and be swung in toward the fire or away from it at will. Stoves such as these which survive in Ontario are usually in the old forts once occupied by British troops.

Experienced settlers knew the superiority of Canadian and American cooking stoves for use in this country. John Langton in the Peterborough area wrote to his father in England in 1837: "With regard to the cooking stove you mention, I would certainly oppose such a thing coming from England; there are plenty of cooking stoves of Yankee construction to be bought here with all the coppers, etc. for £10 or £12 and a great convenience they are, though they can never entirely supersede a fireplace in a kitchen. Some I have seen sent out from England are by no means so complete and being intended for coal are very difficult to heat with wood."

Some Ontario houses had another type of English cookstove. It consisted of counter-like stoves built of bricks which connected with the same flue as the fireplace. The top surface was either of bricks or an iron plate containing a series of "stew holes" into which stew pots could be fitted above the fire. Frying pans could also be used on these ranges.

Early cooking stoves usually had ovens at the side below the top surface. They were sold with kettles, steamers, pots, and boilers which fitted into the holes on the surface. Although they were at first expensive (John Turnbull of Belleville valued his at £20 in his inventory of 1827), they became progressively cheaper. The first Ontario stoves were made chiefly by the Normandale Foundry in Norfolk County (an example of 1831 is now in Upper Canada Village), the Marmora Iron Works, the Cornwall Foundry, the Bytown Foundry, Wood and Fulton of Osnabruck, and the Toronto firms of George H. Cheney Co., and J. R. Armstrong and Co. These companies all made stoves between 1829 and 1850.

A typical stove of the thirties is described by Anne Langton who, in 1838, wrote feelingly about the cookstove at Blythe Farm on Sturgeon Lake:

I sometimes wonder how we managed for those months when we had no fire in the house, and every culinary operation, from baking bread to heating water, was performed on a dilapidated cooking stove, whilst eight or nine meals were regularly served each day and ten or twelve mouths fed with bread. This stove stands about ten yards from the back door, under a little shed. It measures 2 feet 7 inches each way. The chimney pipe rises at the top, an oval kettle fits into one side, a deep pan with a steamer above it into the other side, and a large boiler on a bake-pan at the bottom, each hole having an iron lid, when the vessels are not in, on which you may then place smaller saucepans, or heat irons, etc. The front of the stove has an upper and lower door and a little hearth—formerly there was something of an oven within, but it was out of repair before I was acquainted with it, now there is only an iron plate, which enables you to have your fire on the upper or lower storey. Here was many a nice dinner cooked with all proper varieties for a party of five or six (sometimes more) besides the eternal almost daily breadbaking, and everlasting frying for breakfasts and suppers. We have now had an oven built. . . .

The small "hearth" she describes, a feature of most cooking stoves, was a kind of iron apron which extended in front of the stove and on which pots and plates could be kept warm.

Drawings for a stove patent made for Armstrong's Foundry of Toronto in 1858. / Public Archives

BACK

TOP

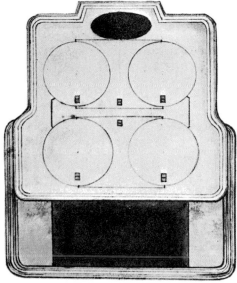

FRONT

SIDE VIEW.

91

STOVES ! STOVES !!

GEORGE H. CHENEY & Co.,

BEG to notify their friends and the public generally, that they have resumed business in the premises lately erected on the site of their old stand, No. 5, St. James' Buildings, King Street.

Having made a very great reduction in the prices of STOVES, and having at much expense effected several improvements in their patterns, their stock being *all new*, and manufactured under their immediate supervision from the very *best materials*, their long experience in the Stove business, and with their facilities for manufacturing, they believe it to be for the interest of parties wishing to purchase *Stoves, Coal Grates*, Copper, Sheet Iron, or Tin Ware, to call, examine, and compare prices.

In expressing their obligations for the very liberal patronage they have received during the past eight years, they beg most respectfully to solicit a continuance of the same, with the assurance that they will make every effort to give satisfaction.

Stoves and Pipes cleaned and put up in the best manner, by experienced and careful workmen.

Toronto, Sept. 28, 1849.   455-3m

BRITANNIA FOUNDRY,

Brantford, C.W.

B. G. TISDALE, Proprietor.

N.B.—Extra Furniture Given to Young Married People.

THE VICTOR.

NOS. 8, 9 & 10.   16 PIECES OF FURNITURE.

Price, $14, 16, 18.   (SEE OVER.)

CANADIAN FARMER.

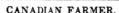
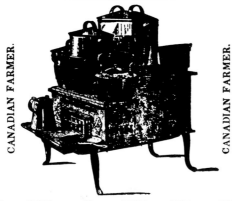

STOVES.

J. R. ARMSTRONG & Co.

City Foundry, 116 Yonge Street, and 2nd door east of St. James's Cathedral, King Street, Toronto, C. W.

MANUFACTURER OF

CANADIAN FARMER COOKING STOVES,

Nos. 6 & 7, (SEE THE CUT),

Burr Cooking Stoves.	*Box Stoves* 6 *sizes.*
Premium do. 5 *sizes.*	*Air Tight do.* 6 "
Bang-up do. 5 "	*Parlor do.* 7 "

Dairymaid Stove and Cauldron, 3 sizes.

The Canadian Farmer was patented by J. R. A. in June, 1850, and took the second Premium at the Provincial Fair this year, when the competition was very keen.   It is the best stove in use for the county, because,

1st. It takes larger and longer wood than any other—from 2½ to 3 ft.

2ndly. It has more holes on the top to boil—No. 7, seven holes, No. 6, six holes.

3rdly. The plates are thicker, being from ⅜ to ½ inch thick.

4thly. It bakes beautifully, and holds 9 large loaves of bread.

The celebrated BANG UP is better adapted for the town, where saving of fuel is an object—the oven being large and high.   And for roasting and broiling it cannot be surpassed.   The Dairymaid Stove and Cauldron, for steaming feed for cattle, boiling water, and for dairy purposes, should be used by every good farmer.   It took the first Premium at the late Fair at Niagara.

POT ASH KETTLES cast with the mouth up, two sizes weighing 800 and 1100 lbs.

POT ASH COOLERS.

SUGAR KETTLES, three sizes, and a variety of castings.

COAL GRATES of the latest and most chaste styles from New York.

N.B.—Old Iron taken in exchange.

STOVES.

MOSIMAN & BASS,

48 KING-STREET WEST.

Keep constantly on hand a variety of the most approved styles and patterns of

Hall, Parlour, Cooking and DUMB

STOVES,

STOVE PIPES,

SHOWER, HIP AND SPONG

BATHS,

TUBS AND WILLOW WARE,

With every description of

PLAIN & JAPANNED TIN-WARE,

Sheet Iron and Copper-ware,

To which they respectfully call the attention of their friends and the public of Toronto and neighbouring villages.

Advertisements for stoves: by George H. Cheney, Toronto, 1849; by J.R. Armstrong, Toronto, 1850; by Britannia Foundry, Brantford, 1867; by Mosiman and Bass, 1850. / All are from Ontario Archives

Many cookstoves had, as an addition, an oval oven of sheet iron with cast-iron end doors which fitted over the pipes of small cooking ranges and box stoves. The heat from the pipes passed through these ovens and out into the chimney. Iron trivets and wire shelves were also commonly fitted to stove pipes.

All sorts of gadgetry and improvements for stoves were brought out each year. Although Canadian foundries boomed with stove production by the 1840s and '50s, some people who could afford it went to Rochester and Albany to see the marvels of innovation in cooking stoves which were advertised there, and sent stoves back home by steamboat. John Macaulay, who in 1818 was agent in Kingston for the Three Rivers Iron Works of Lower Canada (and who therefore knew good stoves), wrote in 1837 that he was planning to go to Rochester to buy one of the new Rotary cooking stoves for his house in Toronto. This was an American invention with a holed top which rotated so that the cook could bring any of the apertures directly over the fire.

Most Upper Canada families burned the ever-plentiful wood in their cookstoves. Coal was generally sold in towns in the mid-1840s but was used in fireplace grates rather than in cookstoves. Mrs. John Beverley Robinson's account books for *Beverley House* in Toronto show £83.9s. spent for wood in 1848. In 1857 the Robinsons bought fourteen tons of coal from William Jarvis for £21—a fair indication of the relative uses of fuel. *Beverley House* was large and the Chief Justice's hospitality was ample, but coal in that year in Toronto was only £1.12s.6d. a ton, including cartage, so that fires must have burnt merrily and continuously.

By the 1850s town-house families sometimes installed cast-iron cooking stoves five and six feet high which were made for building into the fireplace. Many old mantels were torn out to install them. They had no feet but rested on a brick hearth and often had two tiers of ovens heated by a pipe at the back of the stove. They were usually of American manufacture. Few of them survive, unlike the countless varieties of free-standing cast-iron ranges which are still to be found.

To a woman in the mid-nineteenth century her cooking stove was of major importance. She confronted it every day of her life and the health and contentment of her household depended on her success in coping with it. Today most stoves are dependable but the coal and wood ranges which even in my childhood were still widely used both in city and farm kitchens were a gamble to buy. They demanded intimate understanding and knowledgeable handling, and could produce in the cook feelings ranging from satisfaction to despair.

Familiarity with a stove brought proficiency. A pushing and switching of pots and pans on the stove top controlled the degree of heat—stopping the boiling of vegetables, preserving the simmer of the soup and crisping the frying potatoes. A quick touch on the sliding draught door and a half-inch opening of the oven door stopped the meat from spluttering. A flip of the wrist drained the vegetables which were then covered and shoved to the back of the stove, along with the potato pan. A series of deft movements filled the firebox with light wood. A practised hand tested the oven and in went the johnny-cake and biscuits. Plates, serving dishes, the roast and yesterday's second pie were in the warming oven. The reservoir was steaming. The smells were heavenly. And the mistress of the house stood confident and happy, ready to dish out the noonday dinner to her family. An old man once said to me, "The grandest sight in the world is the woman you love taking an apple pie from the oven."

Women talked to their stoves: "You don't want to heat up," "You're slow this morning." And they reported: "That old stove has a habit of dropping a cake, but it sure knows how to do a pie," "A stove with a small firebox makes a good hot top, but the oven takes all day to bake potatoes." Bad

Above: Double stove, sometimes called Montreal stove, Canadian stove, or Three Rivers Stove. Designs used in casting were exceptionally fine. This stove kept a house in the Niagara Peninsula warm and cosy. About 1800-20. / Ontario Archives

York Foundry, operated by Sheldon and Dutcher, advertised in York in 1830. / Ontario Archives

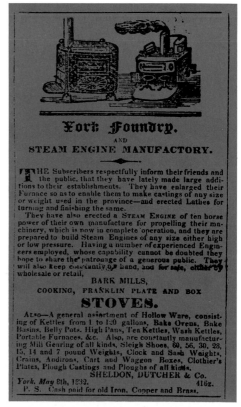

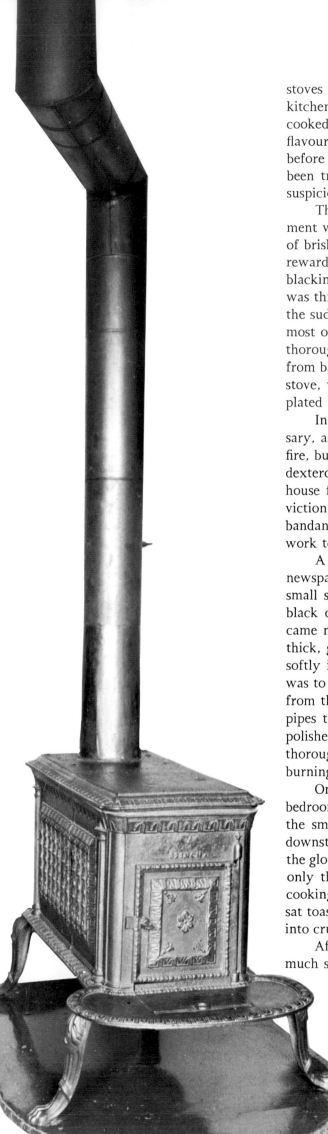

stoves produced cranky housewives and were apt to end up in the summer kitchen. There they served a second term and the tomatoes and pickles that cooked in great kettles right over their fireboxes made the air thick with flavour. Old and cracked stoves were relegated to the sugar shanty, but not before the old remedy for stopping cracks with wood ash, salt and water had been tried. New stoves were carefully chosen, but even then regarded with suspicion till they had proved themselves.

The stoves of my youth were gloriously nickel-trimmed, but this adornment was only beginning to be common in the 1870s and '80s. The half-hour of brisk work that it took to polish a nickel-trimmed stove was uncommonly rewarding. The stove had to be practically "let go out" before the inflammable blacking could be applied. I have often watched as the small blacking cloth was thrown in on top of a low fire, and have seen the quick flame, and heard the sudden "whoosh" as it was consumed. In winter, when the stove was hot most of the day, it was brushed with a turkey wing and, as a stop-gap for a thorough cleaning, was rubbed quickly with a rolled ball of waxed paper from baker's bread. Whiting, kept in a small jar on the window ledge near the stove, was rubbed on the nickel and polished quickly, and the huge nickel-plated kettle was not neglected. The shine of black and silver was beautiful!

In the spring and fall the stovepipes had to be cleaned. This was necessary, as otherwise the stove would not burn well and the pipes could catch fire, but it was a dreaded task. Some people (usually women) were neat and dexterous at it but I have known families who excluded the head of the house from the operation because he attacked it with such hatred and conviction that things would go wrong. Women tied up their hair in towels or bandannas, wore old sweaters and sacking aprons, and grimly accepted the work to be done.

A good housewife began by covering every exposed surface with old newspapers. Loosening the pipe elbows (called knees in early days) started a small sprinkling of soot and an acrid smell in the room. Scraping the thick black deposit from under the stove surface and the top of the oven lining came next. This was often a child's job and was considered a privilege. The thick, gummy soot was pulled out with a long-handled scraper and dropped softly into an old pan. When it came to cleaning the pipes the thing to do was to pop a paper bag over the open ends and carry them outside well away from the house. There an old mop was used to push newspapers through the pipes to clean them. The pipes were relacquered, or at least blackened and polished before the fire was lighted again, and the stove itself was given a thorough polishing. The sheen that resulted, and the smell of the now briskly-burning wood fire, obliterated all the misery.

One of the nicest things about a farm childhood was waking in a cold bedroom, where bright sun was shining through a frosted window, sniffing the smell of pine kindling and frying pork from the kitchen, and running downstairs in stocking feet to stand on the mat in front of the stove and feel the glow of kindly heat. There is a deep gratitude for warmth after cold which only those who have lived with stoves can know. Even when nothing was cooking there was a pleasant smell around the stove, for heaps of stale bread sat toasting in an old ironstone bowl in the warming oven, ready to be rolled into crumbs or fed, with jam, to a hungry child.

After 1900 the old nickel-plated monsters of rococo design changed to much smaller, chaste, square-looking stoves covered with as much enamel as

A single box stove of this type, c. 1840-50, was capable of heating more than one room if there was a "heat hole"—an opening with a removable door—between rooms. / U.C.V.

the surface allowed. The new stoves were easier to keep clean but many older women regretted the change. The warming ovens were too small. There was often only a narrow shelf on top not big enough for a platter. There was not enough variation of heat on the surface. But in the years between the 1860s and 1900 the wood or coal range was the chief joy of winter despite the chores of stoking and taking out ashes and polishing. It is a golden memory.

The first gas range was brought out in 1850 but for nearly thirty years it was regarded with prejudice. It was thought to be dangerous to health and likely to explode. Eventually, however, gas stoves replaced coal and wood cooking stoves in the larger towns.

Heating stoves, from the time they were first introduced, were readily accepted as a necessary part of life in Upper Canada. In 1861 Mrs. Edward Copleston, in *Canada: Why We Live in It and Why We Like It*, came to a conclusion long agreed upon by the inhabitants of Upper Canada: "Rooms heated by stoves were, to me, most suffocating and stifling, and, I imagined, must be injurious. I could not understand how people could exist in them—a doubt long since solved, for without them, I do not believe any human being could withstand the severity of this climate." We know that many people did survive the long numbing winters with only the fireplace for heat, but everyone aspired to a heating stove and a great many were sold.

Inventories and auction sale advertisements of the furnishings of large houses list heating stoves from 1800. In fact a few are mentioned in the 1780s, such as the "iron stove with its stove pipes" that belonged to Father Potier, a missionary at Windsor. When the early stoves were described at all they were called double-stoves or Franklins. (An interesting indication of popular speech of the time is the spelling of the word as "Frankling.") There must also have been a great number of small single-box stoves, as so many of these survive.

The Franklin was invented by Benjamin Franklin in the middle of the eighteenth century but was not patented. It was an open-hearth stove, a miniature iron hearth on short legs. For the next hundred years thousands of Franklins were made in America and many in England, where they were often called Pennsylvania or American stoves. Old Franklin stoves found in Ontario today are usually those cast in the Maritime provinces where they were more extensively used.

The Franklin was a great improvement over the large open fireplace since it held the heat and radiated it from all its surfaces. It used much less fuel and its narrow draught space helped to prevent smoking. It had no grates but burned wood on firedogs.

The Franklin could either be fitted into the fireplace or placed in the room. In the first case, its pipe could be let into the flue and the opening in the fireplace could be bricked up around it. If the stove was placed in front of the fireplace a fireboard could be used to close the opening, and the pipe taken into the chimney above the mantel.

Early Franklins were very finely cast and were quite beautiful in design. Those made after 1840, which was when grates were often added for burning coal, were coarser and less pleasing. Galleries, finials and bosses which appeared on those made from 1810 to 1830, were often of brass; later they were made of iron. A "dunce-cap," or an urn, which was placed on top of some early models, formed a heat chamber, giving even more heat in the room. Franklins were eventually made with double doors and could be used either open or closed.

The high double-stove of 1790 to 1830 which lent such welcoming warmth to homes and inns was a noble piece of furniture. It was distinctively Canadian and was rarely used elsewhere. It was too expensive to buy and cost too much to transport for any but well-to-do families. These stoves were made chiefly in Lower Canada, at St. Maurice close to Three Rivers where the forges had been established at an early date, but since they were mostly sold by deal-

Double stove, the upper part of which is an oven. Cast by Forges de Ste Maurice in Lower Canada, c. 1820. These stoves held long sticks of wood and gave intense heat. Detachable iron ash pan at front was called a hearth. / U.C.V.

Gothic parlour stove. These small heating stoves were brought out in constantly changing designs from 1840-60. / National Historic Sites

A Franklin stove manufactured around 1830-40. The Franklin stove was invented by Benjamin Franklin in the eighteenth century but was not patented. Early Franklins had a hearth and andirons; later grates were added, sometimes doors. Projecting into the room, Franklins radiated much more heat than an open hearth.

Typical late nineteenth-century base-burner stove, greatly beloved in farmhouses where it often took the place of a furnace, spreading heat throughout the house. With its self-feeding apparatus it could keep a fire going overnight. Mica windows shed a cheerful glow.

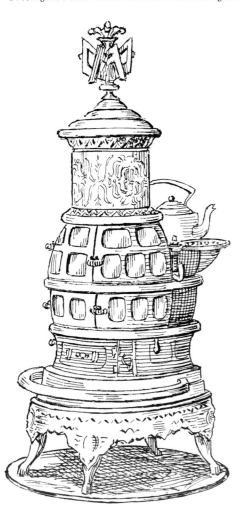

ers in Montreal they became popularly known as Montreal stoves. The trade name was double-stove, and both Americans and Canadians also called them Canadian stoves. Thomas Need, an author-settler, referred to one which was in a house on Lake St. Clair as "the large double Canadian stove which stood in the middle of the room."

The double-stove was simply an enlarged single-box stove with an oven, either the same size or slightly smaller, mounted on top. It burned long sticks of wood and when the fire was properly built up it produced a scorching heat. It was wise, therefore, to install the double-stove with plenty of space around it.

Both large and small single-box stoves were made by most Canadian foundries. They competed with stoves imported from Scotland, which were for sale everywhere and were commonly designated as Dundee stoves. (It is very likely that the patterns for Canadian single-box stoves were taken from Dundee stoves; the designs in both are very similar—fine and classical.) One advertisement in Kingston in 1818 pointed out that "the superior softness of the metal and durability of the Three Rivers stoves render them worthy of the attention of purchasers, as they are not liable to crack, like those imported from Scotland."

There are more single-box stoves in existence (some still in use) than double-stoves. They cost much less but they gave sufficient heat to really warm a fair-sized room and they were much easier to take down and store. One had simply to remove the nuts, bolts and rods, and all the plates could be stacked on the base. The legs were also removable. Single-box stoves were small enough to be used on the brick hearth in front of the fireplace but were sometimes placed on a small brick paving let into the floor in the middle of the room. They had no pot holes but a kettle could be brought to the boil on the top surface. Most of these lovely little stoves were made from 1800 to 1830. They gave a lot of heat for their size and were probably the most common heating stove for town houses. They must have been installed and handled rather casually, however, for in the *York Gazette* for October 22, 1818 Thomas Ridout, the Clerk of the Peace for the Home District, was forced to announce, "Whereas frequent fires have happened in the town of York owing to the pipes of stoves passing through roofs and sides of houses without being duly guarded, it is ordered by the Magistrates of the said district . . . that the pipes of stoves in the said town be made to pass into a chimney or a flue erected for that purpose."

A box stove in the parlour and a cooking hearth in the kitchen were the heating equipment for ordinary homes, but the houses of the wealthy often contained double-stoves for the hall and open-hearth Franklins for the principal living rooms. William Dickson at Niagara in 1802 had two Franklin stoves, and John Walden Myers at Belleville in 1827 had one double-stove valued at £10, and three other stoves ranging in value from £3 to £5 each. Stoves in bedrooms were rare until the late 1830s, but in good houses many bedrooms had fireplaces. Anne Langton had a "little stove" in her own room in 1839. Upstairs there were sometimes "dumb stoves," into which the pipes from the lower-floor stoves ran and from which another pipe entered the chimney. These took the chill off the sleeping quarters. Dumb stoves were simply heat chambers, cylindrical in shape, made of sheet iron. They gave off about as much heat as a warm hot-water radiator would today.

Box stoves were sometimes placed in a plenum chamber which was a closet or room in the basement. The stove door was flush with the opening to this space and when the stove was fed with wood the chamber was filled with hot air which was carried by ducts to the upper floors where it poured out of the cast-iron registers in floors or walls.

The early Franklins and the double- and single-box stoves all burned wood. In towns, well-dried firewood could be bought; in the country wood cost nothing but had to be cut one winter for use the next. The whole family took part

96

The modified Franklin stove with doors served as open fireplace or closed stove. This one was manufactured at Port Hope, Ontario, about 1850.

Small box stoves were often placed on a brick hearth or a sheet-iron floor protector in the middle of a room to increase heating efficiency. The stove pipe went through the ceiling to heat upper chambers. This stove c. 1820. / U.C.V.

Grecian-style stove, called Non Pareil, made by Morrison & Manning, Green Island Furnace, Troy, New York, 1840-50. It stands in the McFarland house, River Road, near Queenston. These once-fashionable stoves were imported into Canada in great numbers. / Niagara Parks

in this task and felt great satisfaction when they finally surveyed the full wood-shed and the beautifully arranged piles stacked outside. The children were usually required to make the cold, cold dashes to the woodshed to bring in fresh fuel for the stove.

The use of stoves was probably accelerated by a government tax on fire-places. For the first half of the nineteenth century, there was a special tax on any house with more than two fireplaces. At first this was levied regardless of the size or type of construction of the house and the assessment was a fixed sum which was added to the assessed value of the house. In 1811 an Act of Parliament established a method of grading houses according to the material of their construction. More than two fireplaces still called for an additional assessment, but now the amount was based on the type of house. For instance, if the householder owned a dressed log house under two stories in height he was assessed at £20 plus £4 for each fireplace more than two; for a brick or stone house under two stories he was assessed at £40 plus £10; and for frame, brick, or stone houses two stories or over he was assessed at £60 plus £10. If he put in a fireboard to close up one of his hearths and could persuade the assessor that he was not going to use it, he could save on taxes. He could also close up two fireplaces in the front of the house and put in one of the big double-stoves with which he could not only get as much heat and more, but which he could also use for baking. One stove, even though it heated the same space as two fireplaces, was only assessed as one hearth.

Dr. Nott's patent coal stove, forerunner of the base-burner, was sold in Upper Canada c. 1835.

Beginning in the 1840s, the shapes and designs of heating stoves became more complicated. By the 1840s, the most elaborate and fanciful castings were being made. The square and rectangular box stove was still made but was cast in bold designs and usually had pot holes. Many of the new heating stoves now had grates for burning either wood or coal and the most popular had doors which opened to show the cheerful flames within. Patents were taken out on mica windows for stove doors but they were not in general use until the 1880s and after. There were also two great improvements in stove design: a sunken space to hold the ashes, and a section of the hearth plate which could be lifted out so that the ashes could be easily removed. (When the hearth-plate section was pulled part-way out a fine draught was admitted.)

Some stoves were designed to look well in front of a closed-off fireplace. They had a pipe-hole at the back from which a pipe could be run into the old fireplace opening so that it did not spoil the appearance of the mantel and its ornaments. There were mound-shaped stoves of this type which were semi-circular in front and which looked very much like the new grates then being used. (The English called these little grates duck's nests.)

There were also oval sheet-iron stoves with decorative cast-iron placques applied to their sides; there were stoves both Gothic and Biblical in decoration; and, for the rich, there were stoves in the shapes of houses and churches. Canadian iron founders' advertisements depict conservative styles but "Yankee stoves" had exuberant shapes and designs, and they were sold everywhere on this continent.

Many stoves in the Greek Revival style were made at Troy in New York State and most stoves of this type which survive in Ontario show this as their place of manufacture. They were among the most decorative stoves of the 1840s and '50s, having two, and sometimes four, columns rising from the fire-box to a horizontal heat chamber from which the pipe went into the chimney. The columns were modelled on the various classical orders and an urn was often placed on the top. This was filled with water and acted as a humidifier. Another urn, purely decorative, was sometimes placed between the columns to cover a boiling-hole. It could be lifted off to accommodate a kettle or keep a pan hot. There was a register wheel in the hearth plate to provide a draught.

Mid-century America was full of inventive geniuses who tried their hands at anything, including stoves. (The word "new" was even more compelling then than it is now.) In this period hundreds of small improvements were made to both cooking and heating stoves and were heralded with vociferous advertising. Various means were devised for disguising a two-hole cooking stove so that it would appear to be a baroque or rococo parlour stove. The disguise usually involved a large removable top of lace-like iron work topped by some ornamental device or an urn. Such stoves, one supposes, would be useful, in the 1860s and '70s, to the numerous families in large towns who boarded but liked to boil a late-night kettle or fry an egg in the privacy of their parlours. They were frequently advertised as parlour cook stoves and sold for about $10.

Some stoves which were sold in Ontario were made of soapstone which was mined in the United States. Soapstone became increasingly popular as a novel stove material in the 1850s and '60s. It kept the heat exceedingly well, it was pretty—either soft grey or apple green—and it was "new." The soapstone stove was framed in iron, had iron doors and base, and was fed coal from the top by simply lifting off the lid.

England, the United States and Canada all imported some Russia iron for stove making. It made elegant stoves, with smooth, highly polished surfaces of a rather greyish colour. It was as satisfactory as ordinary cast iron for holding heat, and it was a novelty.

The universally-used heating stove of our grandparents, the base-burner, owes its inspiration to the ideas of a remarkable man, the Reverend Eliphalet Nott, head of Union College in Schenectady, New York. He was an inspired stove designer. In the 1820s he developed a new type of heating stove, first manufactured ten years later, which became celebrated both here and in Europe. It was illustrated in books and articles describing the great advances of science. Known as Dr. Nott's Patent Coal Stove, it was advertised in Ontario as early as 1835. It came in two sizes, one over six feet tall which looked a little like a cemetery monument, and the other three feet high which was used at fireplaces. The most important thing about these stoves was their method of producing heat. A hopper fed from above held enough coal to keep the fire burning for many hours, even overnight. The coal ignited and sank into the grate as it was blown upon by a draught above and below it. The grate could be turned over by a handle inserted in the side of the stove, to separate the clinkers and ash from the burning fire. The stoves were lined with firebrick and there was a commodious ash-pit. They were very efficient and could burn poor-quality coal impossible to use in ordinary stoves.

The principles employed in Dr. Nott's stove were developed into the base-burner, one of the most valued stoves in America. It was a tall, heavy stove, elaborately nickel-trimmed, and had an enormous firebox which could only be described as pot-bellied. Lively flames from the chestnut coal which was burned in it could be seen through sets of mica-windowed doors which extended around half the stove's circumference. Some base-burners had ovens at the rear, a surface on which to boil a kettle, and a swinging trivet.

The base-burner was constantly improved and by the 1880s almost all Ontario farm families relied on it for winter comfort, as did town families without furnaces. When well fed with coal it practically looked after itself, and was loved by all except the boys of the family who had to take turns getting out the clinkers which were inclined to stick fast in the grate.

Base-burners provided a focus of red-hot comfort in winter sitting rooms and spread warmth throughout the whole house. Smaller base-burners were often used in lower halls, and their heat ascended to the bedrooms above. These stoves demanded an enormous amount of cleaning and polishing, for the designs of their casting were intricate and covered the whole surface of the stove. They were so heavy that when the time came to remove them to the woodshed for the summer the whole family was called in to help. Nevertheless they were greatly appreciated and were kept shining brightly for they were the most efficient, economical and generally satisfactory heating stoves that had been invented.

British military cooking range with raised grate set in the fireplace bricks, oven on one side and boiler for hot water on the other. These stoves were used in garrison kitchens in the Colonial period and may have been imported by some English immigrants. This one is at Stanley Barracks, Toronto. / Toronto Hist. Bd.

Parlour stove with pipe hole at the back made by D. Moore, Hamilton, about 1850. / U.C.V.

Keeping clean

Simple necessities for cleanliness in a log cabin: rain water in a jug, basin which neatly swings into homemade washstand when not in use, chamber pot which belongs beneath the modest cotton skirt of a chair with a hole cut in the seat, braided rug on which to stand while washing, and miniscule looking-glass. / U.C.V.

Through most of the nineteenth century in Upper Canada women worked at hard, distasteful, physical chores in order to keep their houses decently clean. At best the results were not completely satisfying. At the end of an exhausting day's scrubbing in a kitchen of the 1840s the walls and ceiling would still remain permanently smoke-stained and there would be a lingering reek of wood ashes, sour milk, and snuffed candles. The rain-barrel water and homemade soap would have left their own particular smell. There would still be dust imbedded in the cracks and crevices in floors and woodwork where cockroaches and ants would only be in temporary retreat.

Standards of personal cleanliness were not demanding. Most people were thought clean enough if they washed their face, feet, hands and neck once a day, and if they cleaned their teeth once a week. Advice on care of the hair merely recommended brushing it to remove dust and occasionally washing it in cold water. Clothing that could not be washed was only inadequately cleaned at home.

Even among the privileged class, hot baths were taken only as medical treatment, and tepid baths were believed to be dangerous if taken less than three hours after meals. Until the 1860s, the bath was not regarded as pleasurable but only as a means of preserving health.

Dirt that showed was condemned, but the dirt that was unavoidably contained in curtains, carpets, upholstery, and in coats and gowns that were worn for twenty or thirty years with only brushing and airing, was accepted.

The opinion of most observers of the domestic scene in Upper Canada through the first quarter of the nineteenth century was that the majority of houses were clean. Old-Country immigrants, with the exception of some of the poor Irish families, were thought to be especially clean. The Yankees had the reputation of being "notional"; they cleaned as the spirit moved them. German settlers were considered to be exceptionally clean, a fact borne out by William Dunlop who, in describing a German house on the shores of the St. Lawrence during the war of 1812, said, "Floors, walls, and ceiling were

An iron pump succeeded buckets, well sweeps and wooden pumps, by mid-nineteenth-century, as the chief means of getting drinking and washing water. The pump of the old Servos house at Niagara appears here in a drawing made of a 1920 photograph. / Public Archives

Soft water was caught in barrels and tubs or was channelled from the eavestrough through a downpipe into a cellar cistern. The women in this 1830 frame house in Elgin County (which was photographed in the 1920s) no doubt got their wash water in this way. / Public Archives

sedulously washed once a week with hot water and soap vigorously applied with a scrubbing brush." Houses in the area between Montreal and Kingston were said by the very literate settler Mrs. Frances Stewart, in 1822, to be "invariably clean to a nicety . . . but these belonged to established immigrants who had been here for four or five years." John Howison, the traveller, also writing in 1822, said that the women in Upper Canada were "cleanly in everything that [related] to their houses, but negligent of their persons unless when dizened out for visiting." Mrs. Traill observed in 1836, that she was "delighted . . . with the neatness, cleanliness and comfort of the cottages and farms" in the upper St. Lawrence area.

The earliest settlers wanted grants of waterfront lands for easy summer transportation and for drinking, bathing, and washing. At the water's edge pots and pans from the nearby shanties and cabins were scrubbed; clothes, bedding and towels were cleaned by using shoreline rocks as scrubbing boards; and the river or lake served as a summer bathtub for the whole family.

The first well, when it was finally dug, was often no more than twelve feet deep. It was usually lined with stone and had a curbing or box of wood on top. Water was drawn up in pails by means of a chain, a windlass, or a sweep, which was a long pole pivoted on an upright post to act as a lever.

The settlers' first pumps, called sucker pumps, were made by inserting a rod in a hole bored lengthwise through the core of a log and affixing to the lower end of the rod a leather "sucker," or piston. Sucker pumps operated on the suction principle.

Rain water, that precious boon to cleanliness in which soap would actually lather, was caught in a barrel into which it drained from hollowed-out logs fixed to the eaves of the houses. And during a downpour every utensil that would hold water was rushed outside to catch more.

In winter, icicles and snow were melted but never came quite clean, and yielded so little water from so much frozen bulk that it was scarcely worth the effort involved. Everything and everyone became dirty. Warmth and food were the chief necessities and the thought of cleanliness was only part of the yearning for spring.

When houses were built with cellars, they frequently had large stone cisterns, the walls of which rose to within two feet of the ceiling. Despite the constant fishing-out of dead rats or mice and the laborious annual draining and cleaning, this supply of water, fed by drain pipes from the roof, was of inestimable value to the housewife. Eventually a noisy, squat iron pump was installed to raise the cistern water to the kitchen sink, and this pump still does duty in many Ontario farmhouses.

For many years the well sweep was a familiar sight in Upper Canada. It could be worked easily even by children. A long pole, called a sweep, was pivoted on an upright support and counterweighted so that a bucket on the end could be easily lowered or raised through the well opening which was usually surrounded by a stone or wooden wall. / Upper Canada Village

Soap, like candles, could be bought in very early times providing there was a store and the settler had cash or something to trade. Townspeople could exchange grease and ashes for ready-made soap. But the fact that soap and candles could be produced at home without cost, and by using materials which would otherwise be wasted, established these household industries in rural communities for at least a hundred years. The wife of the Reverend William Macaulay in Picton (who owned the first piano in the county) was not above making her own soap in 1838. Thrifty farm women in remote areas still save grease and make their own soap, though they buy their lye.

Lye was usually made in the woodshed or out of doors. The housewife set an ash or pine barrel with a small hole in the bottom on two rows of bricks or stout pieces of wood leaving enough room underneath for a wooden tub into which the lye could run. Inside the barrel she put four bricks around the area of the hole and laid some straw on them to serve as a filter. Then, for the best results, both ashes and unslaked lime were carefully dumped into the barrel in alternate layers, as well as three or four pailfuls of boiling water. After this a pailful of soft cold water was added every hour until the ashes were well soaked. Soon the lye began to drip and run into the tub. The next day, when the tub was more than half full, the lye was "tried" by putting an egg into it. If the egg floated enough to show a portion of the top "the size of a ten cent piece" the lye was just right. All directions, both verbal and written, mention the ten-cent-piece test. If more egg showed one ran quickly for additional water but if less showed the whole operation was a failure and there was nothing to do but empty the barrel, get fresh ashes, and start all over again.

Coal ashes were worthless for lye making. Hickory ashes were much the best, but oak and hickory together were considered good. Careful housewives strained the lye caught in the tub into the lye barrel which stood, along with the soap barrel, in the summer kitchen where it was handy for both indoor and outdoor clothes washing. The weak lye which came in the last drizzles from the ash barrel was kept as a general bleach and water softener.

It used to be said that a woman was "a great hand at the soap," or that she "always had luck with soap." But it was more than a matter of luck or skill. The weather, the quality of the fat, the ashes, and perhaps even the water undoubtedly had something to do with the success or failure of the project.

Everyone made soft soap, and some people used it for all purposes. All the fats and grease from butchering and cooking were rendered and saved in barrels or crocks and were prevented from becoming rancid by the addition of a weak solution of lye. On the great soap-making day in spring or fall the grease was melted again in a giant cauldron over a very hot fire, either indoors or out. A long paddle was used to stir the fat as it melted and the lye was slowly added. The mixture was always stirred in one direction. Then the intensely hot fire was let die out and a small, steady fire was established and kept going all day. The cauldron had to be watched constantly so that more fat could be added when the surface stopped looking greasy. More lye was trickled in from time to time while the practised eye watched for the soap consistency to "come." A dipperful of the mixture would be ladled out into a dish so that the housewife could see if it was the proper bright brown colour and clear, and if it was beginning to jelly when cold. When the soap was done it was ladled into tubs or pails and put down in the cellar or in the yard to cool, after which it was emptied into the soap barrel and given a stir every time anyone passed for the next three or four days.

Potash soap was much quicker to make than soft soap. It was produced by simply wetting potash in a cauldron, adding grease and stirring the mixture till it was all melted. The substance was then put in a barrel, water was added each day and the soap was stirred and stirred.

The potash used in this process was also homemade. If the men in the family had been cutting and burning a hardwood bush they often made potash to sell by gathering up the ashes, leaching them in wooden tubs, and boiling the lye they got till it left a residue in the bottom of the pot. It was quite profitable to make and for a great many years it was much in demand for the export market. Some potash was usually saved for home use and people who had none could buy it from their neighbours or from stores. Even ashes, provided they were from good hardwood, brought from 6d. to 9d. a bushel when sold to an ashery, and stores would trade goods for them.

Well-established families made fine, hard soap which required lard or suet, lye, water, salt, and—if one's taste and purse ran to it—perfume. If perfume were added, the soap had to be remelted and a tincture of musk, oil of bergamot, almond, or palm oil beaten in before it was put into moulds to harden.

The soap sold by merchants was advertised in newspapers from 1800 on, some of it simply as "soap." There was also common soap and yellow soap (which contained resin), and occasionally Castile soap, which was often called Castle soap or Spanish soap. But the most popular of all was Windsor soap. This was made chiefly from tallow, with a small amount of olive oil and soda. It was manufactured from 1820 on by the Roberts Windsor Soap Company at Windsor in England, as well as by other makers, and it is still made today. (The name indicates a special type of soap and not just a brand.) People also made Windsor soap at home. It was most commonly scented with carroway and it has been said that ordinary soap, perfumed with carroway, was often passed off as Windsor. Castile soap was made from olive oil and soda. It came in plain white, considered very pure and desirable, and in a "marbled" variety which had dark streaks of blue or red and was much harsher. Some Castile soap came from Spain but most was imported from Marseilles in France.

By 1850 countless varieties of toilet soap were available: rectangular and round, coloured and plain, scented (with almond, rose, orange-flower, cinnamon, gilliflowers, bergamot or cloves). Yardley, Knight, Pears and Gibb all made excellent soap, and shaving soap was also advertised. Windsor, Castile, and other manufactured soaps were used for the toilet. Hard soap, slivered to

dissolve readily, was used for washing clothes since soft soap was too slippery and wasteful in the tub. It was also generally used for washing dishes, and for this purpose it was dissolved by skewering a chunk on a fork and swishing it around in the dishpan. For scrubbing floors and woodwork the greasy-smelling soft soap was used.

In my youth, only pure Castile soap was thought suitable for washing children's hair, but in the early years of the nineteenth century it was considered too harsh unless accompanied by some spirits of wine, or rum, and then rinsed out in clear rain water. A dishpan on the back stoop during a rain storm was a familiar sight even in the city, where hair washing was postponed till some soft water could be caught. Between rains, women patted orris root or Fuller's Earth into their hair, and then vigorously brushed it out, leaving the hair sweet-smelling, dry and slippery. This practice continued from early days until about 1914.

Toothbrushes, shaped much as they are today, were advertised in Upper Canada by 1810. The bristles were fixed into thin wooden handles much broader than those we know. At least one manufactured dentifrice, Odonto, made in England by Rowlands, was available by 1800. Home manuals recommended the use of a piece of flannel to rub powdered charcoal, pumice or bath brick on the teeth. Honey mixed with charcoal was believed to whiten the teeth and the common mouth deodorant was limewater and a little Peruvian bark. Makers of dentifrices added pink colouring to the powder so that when it accumulated between the teeth it would be less noticeable. *Cooley's Cyclopedia* for 1850 states, "Very few persons, comparatively, wash their mouths in the morning, which ought always to be done. Indeed, this ought to be practised at the conclusion of every meal." It is impossible to say how many people took this, or any other such advice, but the fact that it was common for people to lose all their teeth by the age of thirty-five suggests that it was largely ignored.

One can still buy the short, pointed quills which some gentlefolk once used as toothpicks. Other people used wood slivers.

In simple homes the pattern of daily ablutions scarcely varied for a hundred years or more. It consisted of a great splashing of water in a rain water trough, at a spring, or under the outdoor pump in fine weather, and a perfunctory swilling of hands and face in a tin basin of water (often already used by other members of the family) in the kitchen, when outside water was frozen. Where more gentle living prevailed, washing was done at the washstand in the bedroom. Visitors and the elderly were usually provided with hot water brought up in a copper jug. In the homes of the rich, hot water

106

This boldly designed and neatly executed small country washstand was made around the year 1840. / Mr. and Mrs. Philip Shackleton

Right, top: Cherry washstand of simple country make, containing colourful ironstone basin and ewer of the 1840s. A copper hot water ewer is on the shelf below. / U.C.V.

Right, bottom: Small Prince Edward County walnut washstand of 1840-50 which exemplifies the type of stand made by cabinet shops before factories began turning them out in standardized shapes and sizes. / Author's coll.

jugs were filled from a boiler or cauldron in the kitchen or scullery and deposited in all bedrooms. It was a common practice to fill a bath with hot water or leave a jugful protected with a flannel cover in the bedroom at night on the assumption that the water temperature would be just right for morning ablutions.

By the mid-eighteenth century in England basin-stands were becoming part of the furnishings of fashionable dressing rooms. These were little more than pedestals with an open ring at the top to hold a basin. By 1800 these had evolved into wash-hand-stands, a completely descriptive term since the basins and jugs which accompanied them held only about a quart of water. Wash-hand-stands were small, delicately-made square or three-cornered tables with a hole in the top for a basin and sometimes a smaller hole for a soap dish, which was often made of pewter. A cross-stretcher below supported a shelf or a drawer which held a bottle or jug for water. The top surface was often surrounded by a shaped splashboard. On corner stands the splashboard was quite high and frequently had a small shelf near the top just big enough for a water carafe and inverted drinking glass or a candlestick. Beneath the top an apron concealed the lower half of the basin and below it was a single drawer or a series of small ones. The practice of keeping a filled jug in the basin and not on the lower shelf soon became general. These early washstands were made of solid or veneered mahogany, of japanned beach, or of common woods painted. Most of the fine ones were imported from England but the size and shape were copied here by cabinetmakers and handymen.

The Canadian adaptations of the early washstands did not always have an opening for the bowl, the apron was shortened, and a single drawer, the top of which became a shelf, was placed close to the floor. Maple, cherry or pine were used and the overall size of the stand was often increased. It is interesting that the shape and size of the early stands continued for a long time in Lower Canada, while those in Upper Canada evolved towards a much larger stand. Small wooden or brass knobs were used instead of the typical English hinged brass rings. The use of washstands was not confined to the bedroom; they were a familiar item in the library, office or even dining room.

From 1830 on bowls and jugs became progressively larger. In the 1840s they held about half a gallon of water. They were often beautifully decorated yet the sets were comparatively cheap. By the 1850s the bowls and jugs were sometimes accompanied by a soap dish, drinking- and tooth-water jug, sponge holder, toothbrush vase and matching chamber pot. All these pieces were placed on or in a washstand with towel racks at the sides, a low back-gallery, and a shelf beneath.

English furniture between 1820 and 1840, which was sometimes imported here, included some very handsome large dressing-washstands of mahogany, rosewood or walnut. Similar in shape and size to a dressing or toilet table, these were distinguished by having a hinged-lid top which opened back against the wall to serve as a splashboard. The revealed top surface, sometimes of marble, was cut to receive all the standard pieces of washing equipment. Some of these washstands were undoubtedly campaign furniture used by officers garrisoned here, and the numerous drawers and compartments in the base must have made excellent packing space when the piece was moved. When the settler John Turnbull died at Belleville in 1827 he left "a bedroom dressing and night stand machine" valued at £3, which may have been one of these.

Until it began to be made as part of a set in the 1840s the ordinary washstand looked like a table (with or without a cut-out space for the bowl). It had one drawer and a shelf. The best of the new sets included washstands with marble tops and back-galleries, the base of which contained one or two doors concealing a compartment divided by a shelf. Both table and cupboard washstands persisted as long as these pieces were made and were very familiar to me in my childhood.

Corner washstand of the 1830s, with hole for small basin. Towels were laid over the top of the jug or hung on a towel horse before racks were added to stands. / Dundurn Castle

108

From the 1870s and '80s every inch of washstand top, as well as the lower compartments, was needed to contain the toilet sets which now included tooth mugs, foot baths and slop jars. Some of the jars were made of painted tin, some of earthenware. The earthenware slop jars then being made were fitted with removable funnels, to be used in filling them, and had wicker-covered handles. The lid of the chamber pot was covered with a crocheted hood to silence the clang of china on china—a concession to modesty. The back of the washstand was no longer a simple wood gallery but a frame with a rod on which hung a stiffly starched embroidered linen curtain to protect the wall.

For the morning wash one lifted the heavy ewer which was filled to the top with the stagnant-smelling rain water and half filled the basin. Then, with nightgown still on, one washed face, hands and neck and dried them on a large linen towel which was then laid over the mat in front of the washstand. One next placed the basin on the floor and dipped in first one foot and then the other, braving the shock of cold water. The feet were dried on a turkish or terry towel.

Then came the job of tidying up. The slop jar, already half full from the previous night's washing, was taken out of the cupboard. The wash water was emptied first, after which the basin and tooth mug were emptied and rinsed with clear water, and emptied again. A small clean cloth on the towel rail was used for wiping out the basin and sopping up splashes. After breakfast the slop jar was lugged downstairs, out through the kitchen to the back of the dooryard, to be dumped under the lilac bushes. The chamber-pot was emptied in the privy. The house manuals suggested daily scalding of chamber pot and slop jar, but in practice this was more likely to be a weekly chore.

A more intensive wash, which took more time and involved undressing and scrubbing all over, was termed a sponge bath, even when no sponge was used.

The *Family Encyclopedia*, published in New York in 1860 and sold in Canada, states firmly, "One ought to bathe once a week the whole year through, in tepid water, and it will be of considerable service to add to it some soap." Apparently even at that late date many people regarded bathing as simply immersion in water.

Bathrooms were rare before the 1850s and were confined to the homes of the rich. Some of these had running water (cold, of course) which was piped in by gravity from a tank in the attic. A small stove in the bathroom was used to heat a kettle of water to take the chill off the bath.

Most families owned one or more portable tin bathtubs. These were usually painted on the outside in a plain brown or in imitation of wood-graining. Their interiors were either finished in a beautiful robin's-egg blue or marbleized. The most luxurious bathtub, which cost $5.50 in 1860, had a ring for hanging it up. It was called a plunge bath and was the same functional lie-back shape as had been used for a thousand years in civilizations where bathing was considered necessary or enjoyable. If the budget would not stretch to a plunge bath it was possible to be comfortable in a smaller version of the same thing, the hip bath, where, with knees up, one could be immersed in ten inches of water. There were little fins on the sides of this tub for resting the elbows. In the round bath, which looked like a hat upside down, one would sit on the broad brim while washing the feet, but the real bathing was done by standing up and squeezing a sponge all over the body.

It was recommended that baths be taken beside the fire. In many homes the only fire was in the kitchen, in either a wood-burning fireplace or a stove, and it was here that most baths were taken. The children bathed first, then the parents, often without change of water. In the houses of the well-to-do, fires were lit in bedrooms for bathing. Privacy was also necessary for the use of the bidet which was part of the furnishing in a well-appointed retiring

Gallon-size jugs and large basins were typical of the 1860s and later. So were colourfully patterned wash sets comprising basin, jug, chamber pot, soap dish, shaving mug, tooth-brush jar, small jug for hot water, and slop pail. / Dundas Historical Society Museum

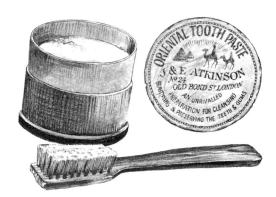

Toothbrushes, toothpaste and tooth powder were sold from 1800, but the brushing of teeth was not general for a long time after that date.

1. Round bath with seat
2. Copper-lined bathtub in wooden frame, with matching flush toilet, c. 1865
3. One of the forms of hip bath
4. Lidded box seat to hold chamber pot
5. Stand-up bath and water container, 1845
6. Commode chair, c. 1850 made by Brooks, Milles Roches / U.C.V.

room. The bidet, made of highly-glazed white earthenware, was a pan, often enclosed in a bench-like stool but sometimes encased in a deep pull-out compartment in English dressing stands. Army officers carried metal bidets with removable legs. They were also called sitz baths, although this term properly referred to a small tub in which one could sit after removing the clothing below the waist. The purpose was the same, however—to wash the lower parts of the body.

The fixed tub was not unknown even in the 1840s but only wealthy people ever even saw them before the 1870s when they were occasionally installed in good town houses. By that time fixed tubs were part of the house plumbing and no longer had to be filled and emptied by hand, as they had earlier. Made of zinc or copper, they were quite deep, had a sloping end, and were encased in wood. (The cast-iron tub was not made before 1880.) Their sides were so high that a wooden platform-step the length of the tub was often necessary. The wide wooden rims held soap and sponge dishes, a jug of drinking water and tumbler, and the toiletries of the time: cologne, Florida water, Butler and Crisp's Pomade Divine, and that other universally used soap ointment, Opedeldoc. Many people placed a blanket or heavy towel on the bottom of the tub, and ladies often bathed in their shifts.

Bathrooms were very often converted bedrooms, but even those planned specifically for the purpose were large, wallpapered, carpeted, and heavily curtained. Ordinary furnishings included stove, chairs, chests of drawers, towel and clothes racks, shaving stand and washstand. Oil paintings and engravings decorated the walls. I once saw such a bathroom in an old house on King Street in Toronto where the whole area above the bath was a badly-painted mural of Niagara Falls.

Water closets were rarely included in the bathroom fittings; they were in a separate small room. The chamber pot or commode was always present, however. "Going to the bathroom" was not a euphemistic phrase in the nineteenth century. The outside earth closet had various names. It was commonly called the privy, the outhouse or the backhouse, though sometimes people referred to it as the House of Parliament, a name derived from the English equivalent, the House of Commons. The origin of the name gongy or gong, sometimes used in Upper Canada, is tantalizing; it must have a relationship with gongfermors, the name given to those who emptied the cesspits of the Middle Ages. (The unenvied people who performed this task in Canada were called honey-divers.)

What were called inside conveniences included the patented earth closets of the 1840s which had reservoirs from which earth or sand poured into the pan at the pull of a lever. On their invention they were hailed as completely satisfactory and economical. Nevertheless they were beyond the reach of the average purse. Most people's inside conveniences consisted of the chamber pot genteelly hidden in a small lidded box in a low cupboard with a false front resembling drawers, or in a chair. All of these were called commodes, a name which originally belonged to a decorative chest of drawers. The original name chamber pot was shortened in more refined speech to chamber and by common folk to po. Another name, jerry pot, from Jeroboam, continues as jerry to this day. The commode appeared less frequently when washstand compartments and nightstands, or night tables, came into use. These stood beside the bed and provided a hiding place for the chamber pot. In the commodes the pot had been used *in situ* but the night-table pot was placed on the floor.

To change after bathing into clean clothes was not always possible, especially in winter when the family washing was only done about every five weeks. Advice to keep all soiled things together in baskets in the laundry was all very well when there was a laundry, but many people had no place for

The privy, the backhouse, the house of parliament, or whatever it was called, the outside earth closet was once a feature of every farm dooryard or small town garden—freezing in winter and buzzing with flies in summer.

Commode chair made by a country chairmaker is painted and has a stencilled back-rail in gay colours. / Mr. and Mrs. L. Donaldson, Galt

Commode chair with hinged seat (c. 1840) was designed, made and finished as a fine piece of furniture. / Dundurn Castle, Hamilton

The new rotary clothes dryer was advertised in the "Housekeepers' Guide and Catalogue" of Prowse Bros. of Montreal. / Author's coll.

dirty clothes except the floor of a closet or cupboard, and there they made a very attractive lair for mice and cockroaches.

Washing was done in the laundry, the kitchen, the summer kitchen, the woodshed, a wash-house in the dooryard, or out of doors, and it involved a hard day's work. The night before washday the washing was sorted and the white things were soaked in lye and water. On the day itself—traditionally a Monday, though washday was not necessarily a weekly event—great quantities of water were heated in pots or kettles. Most people had only a stove, a fireplace or an outdoor fire for this job but kitchens or laundries in large houses often contained a boiler for heating water and boiling clothes. This was a large brick stove with a copper cauldron fixed in its top and a small fireplace in the bottom.

When the water was heated the washtub was filled. Before 1850 there were few fixed washtubs, or taps to fill them. Most people used portable wooden tubs that had ears, or lugs, for lifting them. These sat on broad wooden forms called wash-benches. The clothes were scrubbed on wooden washboards with grooves or movable slats. The coarse cottons and linens were then boiled in a tin-lined copper pot or boiler, stirred all the while with a long hickory stick. Eventually they were lifted out with a pronged wooden fork. Dust cloths, rags and mops were then boiled in the dirty water. The fine things were not boiled; they were placed in a tub and scalding water was poured on them. All white articles were rinsed twice and blued in water which had a bag of indigo wafted through it. (Indigo was sold in the form of small round wafers packed in a wood box.) Coloured fabrics were treated with ox-gall which had an obnoxious smell. Ox-gall was universally used to set and brighten colours in silk, cotton or wool dresses and curtains, and for sponging silk and bombazine. A black bottle containing six cents' worth was kept in most households.

Ordinary shirts and coarse muslins were dipped into cold starch which was Poland starch mixed with cold water and a little salt. All fine things were "clear starched," with starch that was boiled till it was transparent. The articles were dipped in, squeezed out, and then clapped together with the hands till the starch was evenly distributed. A laundress was said to be good at "clearing and clapping."

Next came the drying and bleaching. Every household fabric had its own special wash techniques. There were even rules for using the best of all bleaches—the combination of sun and grass. The main wash was hung on horsehair clotheslines from morning till sunset, but all the smaller, fine things were laid on the grass. I remember table napkins being dampened and put out day after day to bleach out stains. In the dooryard of a house I once knew there was a small patch of grass where in summer the pocket handkerchiefs were laid out to dry. It was a child's task to take a little watering can which hung on the back porch and sprinkle the handkerchiefs (at the same time shooing off stray hens), so that they would bleach more thoroughly. In winter they were pinned to towels on the line.

Good ironing was a matter for justifiable pride. I remember the serious training in the art that was given to me. I was taught the exact flick of the fingers while sprinkling warm water on the clothes before rolling them up, the firmness required in the rolling, the snapping of the edges of table napkins and handkerchiefs to straighten them before pressing, the spit on the finger for trying the iron's heat, and the gliding of the wax "dolly" over its surface to prevent any sticking. Some things were not ironed but rubbed or shaken. Silks were often smoothed with the hands, laid between towels and weighted down. A Saturday morning task for me was the separate washing of yards and yards of ribbon from the lace insertion on my petticoats and nightdresses. These were never ironed, only wound tightly while wet around large wooden spools and fastened with a pin. When dry they had to be run through the lace with a bodkin.

In the early days the housewives used sadirons, with cast-iron handles,

1. Sadirons
2. Wax dolly
3. Tub with lugs
4. Wash bench
5. Scrubbing board
6. Wooden bucket
7. Birch broom
8. Charcoal iron
9. Fluting iron
10. Trivet

Laundry room. At rear copper clothes boiler is set in top surface of brick range on top of which stands an iron tray and wooden clothes pounder. Right of this is a small stove for water-heating, wringer, tubs and scrub board, clothes basket and an ironing table. At left is a folding drying rack, hamper and mangle. The racks on pulleys suspended from the ceiling were used to air clothes after ironing. / Dundurn Castle

which were heated by standing them upright on the hearth next to the hot coals. They were heavy and had to be wiped free of ashes before they could be used. In my youth irons were numbered by weight and had wooden clasp-on handles. Although they were heated on the range they were much lighter and easier to handle than the earlier irons. The wooden handles made a constant little click, click, click as one ironed. All flatirons retained their heat for only a few minutes; the cool one had to be heaved back on the stove and another snatched with a thick flannel pad. Large establishments had great long ironing tables on which two women could iron a sheet at the same time.

Many—perhaps most—townspeople had mangles by the mid-nineteenth century. These machines, some of which had rollers which could be heated, were fed, as a wringer would be, with folded bed and table linen. The articles they turned out were reasonably smooth but a final polishing-off was often done with flatirons. One could mangle linens from clothesbasket to receiving table, which spared the housewife the exasperating tangle of newspapers spread on the floor to protect the dangling ends of sheets and tablecloths.

Freshly ironed linen and clothing was often aired all over the house on ironing day—on clotheshorses, chairs, balustrades, beds, and even on the clothesline outside, and I remember that this gave us a sense of accomplishment and well-being. Our whole world smelled clean.

Articles that could not be washed in the ordinary way were cleaned. There were some fine commercial cleaners in the large centres as early as 1850. These establishments advertised that they cleaned "clothing, table and piano covers, rugs and carpets." Most people did their own cleaning, however, and every household fabric had its own special cleaning recipe. For example, household manuals suggested that a silk shawl be cleaned by sponging it with a clean cloth dipped into a jug containing soft soap, a teaspoon of brandy, and a pint of whisky or gin. It was then to be dried in the shade, brought in and squeezed through three cold waters, stretched and dried again, and then ironed.

It was believed that the smells of frying, roasting and baking clung to clothes during the washing and ironing, so boiled dinners were the rule for Mondays. From my own youth I can remember the fog of steam, the linoleum slippery with spilt water, the patient stirring-out of lumps in the starch (like other children I begged for the coloured pictures on the starch boxes), the smell of brown soap, and the soup plates full of lamb stew for lunch.

So many of the everyday smells of the nineteenth and early twentieth century have vanished! I can remember the taken-for-granted smell of horses in the drive-shed and its hayloft where we played; on the clothes of delivery men who brought milk, ice, tea and groceries; in the livery stables which we passed on the way to school. In winter we arrayed ourselves in clothing pungent with camphor. Our health was cared for with remedies that smelled; I remember the daily horror of fishy cod-liver oil, the colds which produced steaming Friar's Balsam, goose grease, mustard plasters, ginger tea, and horehound, the toothaches subdued by oil of peppermint or arnica. We found the dry smell of *poudre de riz* on our mother's powder puff exciting.

Wood-smoke and coal-oil smells in the house were usual, and the smell of apples in the barrel in the cold cellar and johnnycake coming from the oven were aromatic bliss. A good home was warm, in spots, always a little dusty; and the lingering smells of cleaning, washing, cooking and people were always present.

Keeping tidy

To throw away anything which could possibly be reused was deplorably irresponsible even fifty years ago, and in the early days of settlement it was wanton. Every girl growing up in a respectable home was taught that she must save much more than money if she was to become a good wife and housekeeper. The habit of thrifty saving was so inculcated in children that for the rest of their lives they believed that wilful waste makes woeful want. This made it necessary that there should be a place for everything, and everything in its place. All movable storage furniture such as cupboards, floor chests, chests of drawers and boxes of all sizes were crammed with stuff that might one day "come in handy."

From 1800 on, built-in cupboards with shelves for storage were as much a part of house construction as clothes-closets are today. These were usually thought of as dish cupboards but all sorts of odds and ends were stored along with dishes, particularly on the top and bottom shelves. Dishes were kept in the kitchen, dining room, or parlour, in cupboards which were often built across a corner or into the wall, their doors flush with the wall surface. Kitchen cupboards usually had solid doors in two sections but those in the parlour might have glazed doors on the top. Shelves were pine, sometimes almost an inch thick.

When their original usefulness had passed, all bedding and curtains and clothing were saved. The clothes that could not be cut down and made over were cut into strips of various lengths which were sewn to each other and rolled into great balls to be sent to the rag-rug weaver. Large worn blankets were sewn together, covered with chintz and quilted for bedcovers. Curtains were made into aprons, cushion covers, and into compartmentalized hanging pockets in which other little scraps were stored for patching. Old pocket handkerchiefs and linen pillow slips were bleached and torn in strips for bandages which were kept in little muslin bags sewn shut. I have helped with this household task myself.

Such an assortment of ribbons, braids, buttons, feathers and furs as a family collected in one generation! Anyone who has had to sort out and disperse the furnishings of an old house has been astounded at the contents of boxes and trunks, where such things as bits of silk, old thimbles, cooking recipes, the paw from an ermine tippet and a rusty tin nutmeg grater are found all neatly packed together.

Paper of all kinds was zealously stored. Newspapers were kept for years. Writing paper was precious, and little scraps of unused half-sheets from letters received were hoarded. Wrapping paper (called Nankeen paper when brown) and, of course, string were never thrown out. The blue paper that came wrapped around sugar loaves was always kept because it could be used to dye

Top: Splint storage boxes. Before 1850 boxes of this type were homemade. / U.C.V. Centre: Papier-mâché writing box in black lacquer lined with crimson velvet, c. 1835-1845. The owner's name, Georgina Rosalie, and the figure 28 are beautifully inscribed in gilt on the inside of the lid. / U.C.V. Bottom: Workbox covered with tooled leather, with brass handles, feet and lock. / Dundurn

115

Top: This black leather box, c. 1820, with iron lock, is lined with vivid hand-blocked wallpaper in blue, pink and brown. / U.C.V. Centre: Wallpaper-covered bandbox, c. 1820, typical of those once in every house. / U.C.V. Bottom: Pre-1850 boxes from Upper Canadian homes. Box covered with leather printed to imitate caning sits on wooden document box with brass bat-wing handles. Foreground box of brown leather has tooled lid. / All U.C.V.

things. (They turned out a rather unattractive mauvey-blue.) No one discarded the funeral cards of relatives and neighbours, and it is only of recent years that family letters have been tossed in the wastepaper basket instead of being tied up with ribbon or tape and put away.

Every small print, drawing, coloured label or clipping of interest that found its way into the house was saved and then, as a winter pastime, was pasted into old used ledgers. Children were offered such scrapbooks for their amusement when they visited the houses of older people. To find a little box of such pictures, saved for a scrapbook that was never made, is a special delight today.

Herbs and seeds, nails and screws, patches (of wool, silk and cotton), ravelled wool, hat trimmings and broken jewellery all found their way into boxes which were then put in drawers or on the shelves of cupboards. The housewife suffered no indecision; if it were saved it would one day be useful. To reuse anything was a prime virtue in homemaking—indeed almost an art. Every house needed (and had) boxes, large and small, plain and fancy. The gift of a box of any kind was greeted with pleasure and satisfaction.

Though wooden chests of drawers absorbed the bulky items of household hoarding, the decisive, hopeful putting-away of trivia was done with the aid of hundreds of small boxes. Many of them were boxes which had originally contained bonnets, gloves or dried fruit, but others—as country people still say—were "made a-purpose" for storage.

Thrifty families, from the 1830s to the 1880s made small pasteboard bandboxes covered with wallpaper, thereby unintentionally preserving for us samples of the papers which once adorned the walls of early homes. It is often possible to date the boxes by the newspapers which were used to line them and give them stiffness. The homemade bandboxes were used to store and carry housebonnets, collars, pelerines, fichus, lace and feathers.

Larger boxes, made of splint and also covered with wallpaper, were made professionally between 1810 and 1830. They were sold empty or containing a fashionable bonnet bought at a milliner's; sometimes they have the name of a bandbox maker or milliner on the inside of the lid. The custom of using these boxes for travelling went out about 1840, but for many years they continued to sit on the tops of wardrobes and in attics, crammed full of things to be saved. Travelling bandboxes often had tacks on the bottom to which a bonnet might be anchored with tape loops.

From the middle of the nineteenth century on, boxes were made which were designed to contain fine silk or beaver hats for men. These were often covered in white moiré paper with gilt binding, or in shiny black paper with red, and they bore the label of the hatter.

As early as the 1830s there were, in most Ontario towns, stores which specialized in fancy goods. They sold books, wallpapers, toys, needlework supplies, perfume, seeds, prints and engravings, china and ornaments, and "fancy boxes." The last-named items were particularly popular for storing trinkets, handkerchiefs or letters. These charming boxes, reminders of feminine hoarding, are sometimes found at auction sales but they rarely survive in good enough condition for re-sale in an antique store.

Inlaid and veneered wooden boxes, intended for no specific purpose but just for putting something away, were sold throughout the nineteenth century. They vary a great deal in quality. The workmanship of the inlay, the lining paper, and the small engravings that sometimes appear on the inside of the lid make them interesting to collectors today.

Boxes of papier-mâché and of wooden mosaic (called Tunbridge Ware) were very popular between 1840 and 1860. Both were imported from England, and were perhaps the most elegant and expensive of the boxes for diverse uses which were sold in that period. There was a wide range in excellence and price in papier-mâché boxes. The most expensive included painted scenes, flowers, birds, or animals, particularly dogs. There were also cheaper boxes with less painting and mother-of-pearl, which were, nevertheless, gay and charming. Fine jewel or trinket boxes, with removable trays, were often leather-covered.

The most generally used all-purpose storage boxes were the round, pine, splint ones which cost only pennies to buy and in which were kept everything from pills to huge cheeses. Those made before 1850 were handmade, with overlapped seams and hand-wrought nails. They were made in all sizes and they served to store spices, herbs, soda and other cooking ingredients. Their use was not confined to the kitchen, though; I once found one filled with desiccated rose leaves. The lovely faded colours of these boxes—red, yellow, green and blue—now make them popular with collectors. Their tops were sometimes ornamented with a punched design.

Painted and decorated tin storage boxes—tall and round or trunk-shaped with hinges—were more expensive than wooden boxes. They are found only occasionally today in pioneer German communities where there was once a tinsmith who knew the old European and early American tradition of insouciant, gay and colourful painting on tin. Tin was also employed for small boxes, with sliding or hinged lids, that were used to preserve candles from the mice which found them such a delicacy.

Every kitchen contained wall boxes which were usually made by the owner. They survive in a great variety of pleasing shapes and sizes, from the common knife-polish box, with its bath brick holder and scouring board, to large hold-alls on which the back-boards were cut in decorative shapes. Hanging spice or drug cupboards, which had small drawers, are not often seen in Ontario, however, except in very late examples.

There were other boxes, beautifully designed and made for special purposes, that have come down to us as part of our wealth of Canadian antiques. The tea caddy is one of these and the sewing workbox another. Although there were many types of tea caddies used in Ontario homes in the nineteenth century, the most usual was a wooden casket-shaped box lined with lead foil, containing two compartments for tea and one or two glass sugar bowls. Tea caddies were made of mahogany, rosewood veneer, maple, or occasionally of ebony. Brass stringing was often used on early caddies and mother-of-pearl on later ones. The workmanship was fine, the little brass locks and keys exquisite. Caddies made after 1830 were often of papier-mâché with gilt decoration in either a floral or Chinese design.

Most workboxes contained scissors, emery, bodkin, needles, punch and thimble, and there was a space for spools. The sewing tools were sometimes fitted into velvet or silk slots in a shallow tray that lifted out when "work" was to be taken from the space beneath. Wooden workboxes were often inlaid with contrasting wood or, if made of papier-mâché, with mother-of-pearl. A mirror or an engraving was sometimes set inside the lid. They were luxuriously lined with silks and velvets or with minutely patterned and delicately coloured papers. Every woman and girl in the family had a workbox and used it. It was an onerous chore for a child to be sent to tidy up her own box but it was a pleasure, as I well remember, to be allowed to take out all the equipment and materials of a grown-up's workbox and put them all back carefully in the right places.

Leather-covered travelling and storage trunk, c. 1820, with the owner's initials picked out in the original brass studs. / U.C.V.

Homemade blanket box decoratively painted with a design in brown and cream. / U.C.V.

Fine cabinet-made chest of drawers, c. 1825. It is made of butternut with veneered maple drawer fronts and carved walnut pilasters. The dressing-glass is of mahogany. / U.C.V.

A settler made this well-proportioned walnut cupboard for a log cabin in Prince Edward County around the year 1830. / Author's coll.

Writing boxes appeared in most houses from an early period. Ordinarily they held writing paper, penholders, pens, pen-cutters, pounce box or sander, and an inkwell.

There were several types of writing boxes but the most common was one in which the lid was lifted forward to become a sloping writing surface. Eventually it was made as part of a table or chest and became a writing desk at which one could sit or stand. Another early type of writing box was hinged in the middle; one half sat upright and contained slots for paper, drawers for money, and a long drawer for pens and ink. The other half rested on the table as a writing surface, and had letter compartments beneath it. When closed and locked, this writing box could be carried by a counter-sunk brass handle on the top.

The big boxes and chests which held a family's belongings on their arrival in Upper Canada became part of the furniture of their first home, serving as tables, seats and storage. Sometimes they were taken apart and the wood was used to build new furniture, but often, when replaced by something more suitable, they were moved to bedrooms and attics where they may still be found today. The boxes varied greatly in size and design. There were low, red-painted bedding boxes with blacksmith-made hinges and hasps, and large, often beautifully grained boxes, stencilled with owner's name and destination, in which clothing, china, silver and heirlooms were packed. They were so well made that even the most ordinary unpainted heavy boxes, which were advertised as "cart and wagon boxes" to be sold to settlers who were moving on, have survived.

When travellers mentioned that their boxes were tied on top of the stage-coach, they referred to the handsome, expertly made small trunks in which the best-equipped settlers brought their personal effects. These boxes had flat or domed tops, heavy locks and bale handles, and the leather or hide covering was often beautifully tooled and ornamented with brass-headed studs. The owner's initials were frequently set in studs on the lid or the front surface. Such boxes are sometimes sold very cheaply at country auctions today. The leather is usually dried, broken and curling, but it responds quickly to soaking with neat's foot oil, which the original owners also used to keep the leather in condition.

The common low chest, without legs or drawers but with a small fixed or sliding tray at one end of the interior, was not especially made for bedding but was often used for it. These chests were attached to a narrow moulded frame with rudimentary bracket feet, and had iron bale handles on the ends. They often stood at the foot of the bed and are still used in that way, either many times repainted or upholstered with quilt bats and chintz. The little tray often held cedar twigs or bags of rosemary or camphor but it was also a place for storing patches, braid, darning wool and curtain pins. The minty smell which sometimes still lingers along with that of camphor, came from dried costmary, called Sweet Mary in the country. (Lavender, so much used in England and the southern United States, was rarely available since it was not hardy enough to survive Canadian winters.) Small articles to be stored in these chests were wrapped in soft paper which came in light blue, buff, grey and rose. For a long time newspapers were never used to wrap white things, as the printing ink came off.

Mice, as well as moths, were a menace to storage in old houses, and the most satisfactory blanket chests were raised from the floor by legs. Some had legs formed by deeply notching the two long end boards. Others had bracket feet or legs and lids with close-fitting moulding that overhung on three sides. Many chests had, at the bottom, a single long drawer with mushroom wooden knobs or good brass pulls. And most of them had full-length trays. All such chests were painted red, brown, or green, and many had elaborate finger- or feather-painted designs. Early chests had wrought-iron strap hinges and mortise locks. They were mortise-and-tenoned in construction too, with broad dovetails. Late chests have rabbeted joints. Tall blanket chests with lift-top lids had as many as three simulated drawers, but only one that pulled out. All old blanket chests are today commonly called dower chests, but unless they are labelled with a woman's name and a date there is no reason to suppose that they were for anything but ordinary storage.

Blanket chests were made at home and in woodworking shops from the end of the eighteenth century until about 1880. Their styles did not change, and their dates are generally determined by examining saw and plane marks, the type of nails and locks, and the size of the dovetails. They were usually made of pine because pine chests were light to lift and carry.

Found in Merrickville, this pine storage cupboard (c. 1830) painted with red to imitate mahogany is one of the very best surviving examples of early country furniture. / U.C.V.

In early households closets were unusual and wardrobes were rarely used before 1840. Clothing was folded and laid away in a chest of drawers which was used for storing all underclothing, everyday dresses, the children's clothes and even the men's. The bottom drawer often contained the housewife's prized "good" silk dress which was only worn on very special occasions and might be the only one she had throughout her married life—a dress to be married and buried in.

Cherry and maple, pine, birch and ash were all used to make early chests. The boards of the drawers and on the back of the carcass were roughly planed pine or basswood. Before 1850 chests had hand-cut dovetails which were slightly uneven, quite large, and widely spread, unlike the narrow, neat dovetails of the factory product. Most drawers had iron or brass locks mortised into the centre top of the drawer front. Drawers were set flush into their openings without an overlapping bevel. On simple chests of drawers the tops were flush but on fine ones and on most chests of a late period the tops overhung. Even late chests show some evidence of hand finishing, since in furniture factories only planes and saws were power-driven.

Nineteenth-century chests of drawers were known as bureaus, though the original French word meant "desk." Cabinet shops seem to have used the term to describe a chest of drawers with a mirror attached, but at home, especially in the mid-century, the word was used for any chest of drawers.

The English and American highboy was an imposing piece of storage furniture of the eighteenth and very early nineteenth century. It consisted of a high chest which sat on a table-like form with legs. Or it might be a chest-on-chest which was made in two sections, one sitting upon the other. The highboy form is not reflected in Ontario chests except for a high chest of drawers with narrow bottom frame and bracket feet, which does occasionally appear.

The block-front chest, which required great skill on the part of the cabinetmaker, was not to be found in Upper Canada, though it did appear in Quebec and the Maritimes. It was made with a concave centre panel flanked by two convex panels topped with flat arches or carved shells.

Gentleman's mahogany clothes press with pullout shelves. It was brought to Canada from England by the Farmer family in 1834. Wardrobes of this sort were frequently used in good houses. / Mrs. Thomas Leith, Ancaster

Our best early chests are those which derive from the styles of Hepplewhite and Sheraton, particularly American interpretations of these designs. Some of the family chests which are treasured as Canadian may, in fact, have been brought across the border or made by American journeymen cabinetmakers. They were constructed of mahogany inlaid with other imported wood, or of cherry or maple, and had four graduated drawers with locks and oval brass plates with bale handles for pulls.

The Hepplewhite influence is seen in chests with inlay outlining oval or oblong panels in the drawer fronts, and in those with beautifully curved aprons and bracket feet. Sheraton designs show in chests which have three-quarter-round posts at the front corners, which are sometimes reeded. Both these

Built-in storage cupboards similar to those
found in nearly all early houses in Ontario.
Top left: Parlour corner cupboard, of pine
painted to imitate mahogany, about 1840, in
an abandoned house in Prince Edward County.
Lower left: Wall cupboard, c. 1810, in the
Lewis Bradley house near Clarkson, Ontario.
Right: Panels with Gothic arch of an 1850s
corner cupboard in Upper Canada Village.

styles were only produced by the few really fine cabinetmakers.

Other men, as appreciative of style but less skilful and lacking imported woods, turned out simplified versions of these chests. They combined figured maple with cherry to make some of our finest heirlooms. Our early cabinet-makers used cherry and maple as their mahogany and satinwood, and although their cabinetwork was neither as light nor as graceful as that of their superiors, the chests they made had a sturdy beauty.

Everyone needed chests of drawers but few could afford the best. Most families had to be content with pine, basswood, birch and ash chests of completely simple design, finished with red filler and stained or painted to resemble cherry, maple or walnut. These pieces had wooden knobs and either bracket, or short, rather ungainly-looking turned feet. Perhaps the most interesting of the simple chests were those painted and grained in imitation of veneer. The more refined examples of these had good brass pulls.

English chests of simple design, made of oak or walnut with excellent brass hardware, are sometimes seen, along with others of greater style made of mahogany. Most of these are family pieces brought out from the Old Country at various times.

It was not until the 1820s that chests were commonly made with a mirror attached, and even then the wall mirror and the swinging dressing-glass on its small stand continued in use. (English looking-glasses had been very frequently advertised in Ontario in the first ten years of the nineteenth century, however, even though popular tradition has it that mirror glass was practically unobtainable.)

The most marked change in the style of Canadian chests during the 1830-40 period was the introduction of free-standing columns or, alternatively, heavy scrolls resting on plinths and supporting an overhanging top drawer. Chests of this decade also had large, boldly carved paw feet at the front. These features originated in France and England, but the Canadian version took as its prototype the American Empire chest. A back-gallery was also introduced, at first either plain or cut in a scroll and later with "chimney pot" ends. As this style developed the top surface frequently had another section of small drawers (for handkerchiefs) attached to it. A mirror was sometimes suspended from socketed posts, on top of these small drawers or between them. A deep bonnet drawer also appeared as the centre top drawer of the chest. Mahogany crotch-grain veneer covered the finest of these chests and some had drawer fronts of figured maple.

Bracket-footed chest of drawers, c. 1830. It is made of butternut with maple knobs. / U.C.V.

While town cabinetmakers were producing such fashionable chests, they were being copied in solid cherry and maple and in pine and basswood in the country. The softwood chests were flatteringly painted in red and yellow to imitate their betters. About 1840, country cabinetmakers were also making chests of walnut, butternut, maple and pine, chests in which the free-standing column became a half- or three-quarter-round turned pilaster applied to the front corners. The top drawer did not always overhang, and the turned feet copied the pilaster turnings. The finish was often shellacked rather than painted or stained.

Varied and unusual details are sometimes seen on chests of this style and period. Though drawer handles were usually of wood, if the cabinetmaker had ample stock of old-fashioned hardware, like lion's head pulls, he sometimes used them. Bars of spool turning, matching the other trim on a chest of drawers, were also used as handles, and native sumach wood was occasionally used for inlay and for shaped drawer pulls. Pressed glass knobs, some of early Sandwich glass—clear or opalescent—were often bought by the owner to replace wooden ones. The earliest of these, particularly the opalescent ones, are now highly valued by collectors but originally they were quite cheap.

Chests made from 1840 to 1867 often had trinket or handkerchief boxes fixed to the rear of the top. Horizontal panels with half-round ends on drawer fronts were outlined with moulding, and keyholes frequently had wooden

Pine cupboard of unusual design, with deep scalloped frame enclosing the doors. It was made in Prince Edward County between 1840 and 1850. / Mr. & Mrs. Richard Hart, Picton

rosettes surrounding them. Wooden knobs were at first mushroom-shaped but increasingly, after 1850, carved wooden handles of leaf-and-fruit design took their place, until these became usual in the 1860s. The side ends of chests of this period showed a panel where the early chests of drawers had a solid board. Walnut and rosewood became much more popular than mahogany at this time, and marble was sometimes used for the top. Such chests were frequently sold as part of a set.

The 1850-60 chests, which conformed to a style then referred to as Louis XV Revival, or French Antique, were far removed from the styles of the first quarter of the century. Rosewood veneer or black walnut was used for these and there was no limit to the extraneous Victorian details that embellished them. Swing mirrors were set in frames of pierced and scroll-carved wood, some with neo-Gothic details and supporting posts like miniature spires. Keyholes had carved wood escutcheons. Aprons and corners were decorated with applied carved mouldings, and serpentine fronts were frequent.

Another new style of the fifties was the chest with walnut crotch-grain veneer drawer fronts and panels, two drawers at the top and three below, very large, round, grooved wooden pulls, and three-quarter-round corner posts ending in flat, round feet. These chests were as heavy as they looked, and the whole household took part in shifting them at housecleaning time. Factories and small cabinet shops adapted these details in cheaper chests, and as a result, we have the extremely numerous common Victorian chests of Ontario—one of the most interesting furniture categories for collectors.

The earliest clothespresses were made for men, or perhaps one should say for gentlemen, since very few men had enough shirts and waistcoats to fill the drawers of a press. There is a classic English style of press with three long drawers, or two long and two short drawers, topped by a cupboard with doors enclosing several sliding shelves. This seems to have been part of the furnishings of all well-to-do homes. Clothespresses in this style were made from the late eighteenth century until around 1820.

Another handsome press, which reflected the American Empire influence, was made in three sections, the two end parts slightly stepped back from the middle one. In this press the middle section has sliding shelves, while the other two have hanging space. A touch of Greek Revival style is seen on these, usually on the cornice, which places their style in the 1830s. They were the only types of clothespresses sold before 1840, when wardrobes began to be made.

Wardrobes were always included in a set of Louis XV Revival bedroom furniture but were also made and sold separately. Ponderous pieces, six feet or more in height, they had one or two doors, heavy cornices, and bulky feet. They often contained a central (or slightly off-centre) division that provided hanging space; the rest was fitted with drawers and shelves. There was usually one long drawer in the bottom. (This was too heavy for children to open and in my childhood that was where the Christmas presents were kept.) The two-door wardrobes sometimes had a mirror panel between the doors.

Inside the wardrobe there were pegs, occasionally a rod for hangers, and upper shelves for bonnets. We know from illustrations that there were turned wooden or cast-brass hangers for clothes, but it is impossible to find them today. Most women's good dresses had tape loops attached to them so that they could be hung on the pegs.

Few wardrobes were made after 1880 when the clothes-closet became a regular part of house planning. They are seldom used today; their size and their enormous weight make them difficult to move, and few bedrooms nowadays can afford the space they take up. Those that survive, however, almost always have a smell of camphor that overpowers the faint fragrance of the pomanders which once hung among the clothes.

Tall country-made linen cupboard finished with a stain in a dark brown colour. / U.C.V.

Opposite page: Painted and brush-grained door from the parlour of the old Keller house at Keller's Hill, North Marysburgh Township, Prince Edward County. All the woodwork in the parlour is finished in the same manner. The house was built between 1820 and 1830.

122

Painting & decorating

The old clap-boarded country houses of Upper Canada, painted yellow, red, green, grey or white, and sometimes unpainted, were set in rough stump-dotted clearings, dwarfed by the dark green forest. Their imperfect window glass reflected the light, their chimneys sent smoke curling through the trees every day of the year, and the long, low slope of their roof-lines was a welcome sight to every traveller.

No memory remains to anyone now living of the original appearance of these coloured houses in the primitive landscape. When seen today, even in isolated places, they are close to roads, surrounded by fenced fields, openly accessible, and part of the community. Their paint colour is almost invariably white if neglect has not left them derelict-grey. Only the ghosts of the forest remain—the gaunt skeletons of dying elms.

A knowledge of the early paint colours and their relationship to the landscape and the domestic interior is essential to a real understanding of the appearance of these houses and their furnishings. The tangible remains of our past—a blue-decorated jug, a bowl with a deep glossy brown glaze, a piece of brilliantly striped drugget, a sombre pewter plate, a rush-seated black chair with gilt stencils, all admired and collected now, can be appreciated much more if one can picture them in rooms with white or ochre walls, red-brown or grey-blue woodwork and yellow floors. These were commonplace backgrounds for simple furnishings.

Few of the early colours are at present fashionable; many of the combinations and uses of colour would never occur to us. Knowing and "seeing" the colours that provided the setting for domestic life affords a deeper understanding of the taste of the time, a taste which was circumscribed for many years by the limited availability of paints.

Perhaps the most important and interesting research that has been done on early colours in Ontario was in the restoration of first coats on houses, walls, wood-trim and floors in Upper Canada Village. The mixing and matching of paints was painstakingly done to reproduce what had once been there, even if the only remaining evidence was a patch no bigger than a hand. Those who worked on this project feared, at the outset, that the restoration might produce violent, or discordant, or repetitious colour, but were agreeably astonished at the final results. For instance, the intensity of the red walls and ceiling of the bedroom in Cook's Tavern (1835) was subdued by the mixture of Prussian blue and black in the wood-trim, and by the umber of the floor. The room was found to be cool in summer and warm in winter, despite uncurtained windows. The mixture of colour (Venetian red), whiting and glue size—the ingredients of an old recipe for "common distemper"—which made the wash used on three bedroom walls, produced a pink quite unlike any modern colour and provided a very flattering background to the furniture, curtains and bedspreads. The ochres used in the sitting room and dining room, the sage green of the hall and retiring room are typical wall colours of the period and combine as happily with the blue wood-trim as do the shades of red. The use of one wood-trim colour through most of the building is restful but never monotonous. To see furnishings in such settings is the best possible way to appreciate the colour palette of an epoch.

Both professional and amateur painters freely expressed their knowledge and sense of design. Much simple decorative painting was done by members of the household. The little extra curlicue, the freehand rose, the wave-like striping were often added with the certain knowledge that they would be admired. But it is to that forgotten band of men, the professional painters, that we owe a legacy of brilliant and beautiful decoration that adorned the sleighs, carriages, boats, walls, woodwork and furniture of our ancestors. Paints were advertised very early, and so were the services of painters, who could paint anything, who were proficient and full of traditional tricks and private fancies. These were the men who had more or less fixed locations and shops. There were undoubtedly others who, carrying palette and brushes, walked or rode across the counties, stopping to earn their keep, and a little more, by painting. We know they were here because their work has been discovered, identifiable as professional because of its highly developed decorative techniques. Some of these men were probably peripatetic Americans; others were Loyalist settlers or recent immigrants. They were skilled craftsmen, familiar with all types of painting, and were probably responsible for some of our now-treasured face painting, as early portraiture was often called. Their work and influence died away about 1850 but while they worked they added the pleasures of colour to the lives of the inhabitants of Upper Canada.

The use of colours during any period depends, of course, on the available range of pigments, but within that limit custom, fashion and individual taste always play some part. In early Upper Canada, judging by what is found, there were established customs for painting house exteriors and furniture, whereas colours for walls and woodwork were a matter of taste.

Advertisements of paints for sale began in the late eighteenth century. Benjamin Seymour, who kept a store at Fredericksburg near Bath in 1792, advertised only one colour of paint in that year—Spanish brown, which was priced at 17s.6d. a keg. Until 1820 those most commonly listed and defined in Upper Canada were:

> Spanish brown, a dark, dull red.
> Indian red, having a purple cast when from the East Indies; scarlet, when a substitute
> carmine, a brilliant red
> vermilion, a delicate red
> rose pink, white lead and pure lake
> Prussian blue, intense blue
> blue-black
> sky-blue
> yellow ochre, plain—light, spruce—dark
> chrome yellow, rich and brilliant yellow
> patent or Turner's yellow, light yellow
> Dutch pink, a straw yellow
> ivory black, called "the best black"
> Frankfort black
> lamp black
> umber, a brown ochre
> verdigris, a blue green
> red lead
> white lead
> turkey umber

The addition of white lead or lamp black gave some variety of tone to these pigments, most of which were crude and unstable. Raw linseed oil, which cost eight to ten shillings a gallon in 1802, was always advertised. The method of boiling it to increase its drying capacities was known to everyone. All kinds of brushes, including camel's hair "veining pencils" and gold and silver leaf appeared in advertisements as early as 1800. Turpentine, both spirits and oil, were for sale, although an early book warns against its use for outside paint as it "allows the paint to flake." Nut oil and oil of poppies were common mixing ingredients, and copal varnish and gum-shell shellack were listed.

Paints were sold by painters (most of whom were also glaziers) by carriage shops, cabinetmakers and by shops stocking glass or drugs. Drugstores in small towns continued for many years to carry paint and wallpapers. Dry pigments were sold in kegs, and semi-liquids such as the "lake" pigments like cochineal were put up in sheep or ox bladders. All brushes were rounded, not flat as they are today, and the smaller ones were called pencils.

A stencilled bedroom floor dating from about 1845. On a brown background there is a snow-flake design in creamy yellow alternating with a black outline figure. / Upper Canada Village

Floorcloth of painted canvas in a house in Salem, Mass. Such cloths were imported from England at high prices and were listed in inventories and auction sales of fine houses in early Upper Canada. / Essex Institute, Salem

Opposite page: The art of decorating walls with freehand and stencilled designs was practised in Upper Canada from 1800-1840. Top: section of stencilled wall in a parlour at South Bay, Prince Edward County, c. 1820. Centre: pale pink background with stylized carnations in rose and blue, on parlour wall of house just west of Brockville in Ontario. Bottom: section of stencilled wall in Player house, Lansdowne, Ontario, built in the 1820s.

Painters or their apprentices did much of the grinding of dry pigments on their own stone mills. Painting was a steady, respected trade, but held the dreadful hazard of painters' colic, the paroxysmal pains of which eventually attacked most men who worked in it.

By the 1830s Brunswick green appeared in almost all lists, and cream yellow, terre de Sienna, both raw and burnt, King's yellow and Venetian red were added to the commonly advertised colours. By 1860 it was scarcely necessary to specify the basic cólours in advertisements, but ready-mixed paints were being used and new names were given to mixtures. Thus in three colours recommended for shutters: bronze green was "five parts chrome green, 1 black, 1 umber"; and bottle green was produced by mixing Dutch pink and Prussian blue (for which a yellow lake glaze was recommended). Grass green was three parts yellow and one of Prussian blue. At this time barrels of paint were offered for sale, and in 1865 it was sold "in airtight tins ready for use."

All early paints appear to have been imported from England and were advertised by general merchants from Cornwall to Niagara. Quetton St. George of York listed "white and red paint," and "Spanish brown and yellow okre [sic]" in the Upper Canada Gazette in 1805. He concluded his advertisement with the information, "The same assortment will be found at Mr. Bolton's, Kingston, and Mr. Thomas Boucherville's at Amherstburg, who transact business for Mr. St. George."

Paints were cheapest in Montreal, where many Upper Canada merchants bought their stocks, but the prices rose proportionately as they were brought west. Some paints may have come in at the Niagara border, but the duty on these would bring the price in line with the English products. Very little documentary evidence on the cost of paints and painting has been found.

In Dundas County the St. John's Church records for 1845 show that $28 was paid for the work of painting the pastor's house (now in Upper Canada Village) "inside and out with two coats." The pastor himself bought the paints and paid $5.25 for the extra embellishment of the hall, parlour, dining room and study with "Mahoganizing." Elsewhere at about the same time, twenty cents a square yard, was given in an estimate of painting costs with no indication as to whether this included paint. All sorts of cheap substitutes for paint were described in journals and books in the first fifty years of the nineteenth century. Nicotine was used as a stain on raw wood; black paint was made from charred potatoes; beets stained whiting a rosy pink; barn paint was often melted pitch mixed with linseed oil and brick-dust.

There is a belief much held in Canada that most early painting on houses and furniture was done with a simple mixture of skim milk (some say sour milk) and pigment. Every published work on painting in the nineteenth century gives the basic recipe for skim-milk painting but it is not simple. The Amateur Painter, published in New York (undated but referring in the text to 1827 as "recent") says, "Take half a gallon of skimmed milk, six ounces of lime, newly slacked, four ounces of poppy, linseed or nut oil, and three pounds of Spanish white. Put the lime into an earthen vessel or clean bucket, and having poured on it a sufficient quantity of milk to make it about the thickness of cream, add the oil in small quantities at a time stirring the mixture with a wooden spatula. Then put in the rest of the milk, and afterwards the Spanish white. Milk skimmed in summer is often found to be curdled but this is of no consequence in the present preparation, as its combining with the lime soon restores it to its fluid state. But it must on no account be sour; because in that case it would, by uniting with the lime, form an earthy salt which could not resist any degree of dampness in the air." This recipe was for inside work; for outside painting two ounces more each of oil and slaked lime and two ounces of Burgundy pitch were added. This mixture was often coloured with the dry pigments used in oil painting.

Some dissatisfaction with the results of milk painting was voiced by both amateur and professional painters who tried it. They always referred to it as a substitute for "good painting." The complaint was that if the painting was done in warm weather the oil disappeared into the wood and left a flaky finish which soon wore off. Late autumn painting was recommended.

Cookery books, farm manuals and magazines all carried explicit and complicated instructions for painting and staining in the home. One feels that the slightest deviation from the directions would produce a horrible sticky mess, or a third-degree burn. (Muriatic acid was a common ingredient.) The professional painter must have been a welcome workman.

Between 1800 and 1850 advertisements included such services as "Ornamental painting, coach, gig and Fancy house painting; Ornamental painting and gilding on wood, metal or glass, in oil or burnished gilding; House building and painting; carriage and transparent painting; paper hanging and distemper colouring on walls and imitations of all kinds of wood and marble; ship, house, sign, carriage, chairs and ornamental painting; glazing, varnishing and paper-hanging; graining of various kinds of wood, gilding varnishing and polishing."

A typical early advertisement by travelling painters is the following from the *Kingston Gazette*, December 25th, 1810:

House Building and Painting

The subscribers hereby give notice to the inhabitants of Kingston, Ernestown, Adolphustown, and other adjoining places that they intend to employ the next season in this vicinity in painting houses outside and inside. Patent painting of rooms and etc. and the business of house carpenters and joiners. Their work will be executed with neatness and dispatch. Applications may be made at the dwelling house of Mr. Stoughton, innkeeper at Kingston, Mr. John Bell in Ernestown and Mrs. Douglas, innkeeper in Adolphustown.

Nathan Wheeler & Andrew Pickens

("Patent" painting is a term no longer used or understood.)

"Patent driers" were known but were not much used. Expert knowledge of their uses may have been worth special mention in an advertisement, for most paints dried very slowly. They also smelled strongly enough to warrant advice in all household manuals on how to alleviate the nuisance. The most common method of absorbing paint odours was to have a tub of water with a bundle of hay soaking in it. Vitriolic acid in a tub of water is also recommended "which in several days will absorb the smell."

Custom and the availability of paints dictated the colours chosen for the exteriors of early houses. Custom, among most Loyalist settlers, meant using the reds, yellows and greys of eighteenth-century America, and from all existing evidence, the earliest houses in the province were painted in these colours.

The log houses of the backwoods were usually unpainted inside or out until about thirty years after the beginning of settlement when records show that whitewash was used on inside walls and on outside door and window frames. Captain Charles Rubidge wrote, in 1820 in the Peterborough district, that he had painted the exterior log walls. There was little incentive to paint logs, for they lasted well without paint and, as a letter to the *Cobourg Star* in 1833 said, "A good log house is far more warm, comfortable and picturesque in the forest than a raw, gray, weather-boarded frame house, which unpainted (as such houses commonly are) looks very cold and uncomfortable."

Except for appearance there was no immediate necessity to paint, and some frame houses remained unpainted for the first generation. Air-dried lumber lasted a long time without paint. Travellers remarked on the "raw" look of new wood houses in growing villages. In *A Scotsman in Upper Canada* the old grandmother of the family who were ascending the upper St. Lawrence on their way to York compared the houses on the south side of the river with those on the north, and is reported to have remarked, "It's a

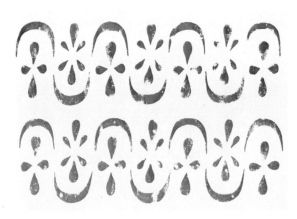

Wallpaper with gilt designs on a matte or satin-finish white ground was favoured for parlours from 1840 to 1890. This paper is in the style of the 1860s. / Author's coll.

Label that was on a shipment of wallpaper from M. Staunton who manufactured wallpaper in Toronto from 1855. / Mr. and Mrs. Douglas C. Brownell, Niagara-on-the-Lake, Ontario

Roller-printed wallpaper, c. 1840s, in which the design is the intense blue much used for popularly priced papers at that period. This paper was specially reproduced by silk screen from the original. / Dundurn Castle, Hamilton

wonder the Canadians don't paint their houses like the Americans do." In London in 1829 the forty or fifty houses of the village were described as "quite new, all of bright boards and shingles."

Still, it cannot be taken for granted that an overall packing-box colour prevailed throughout the province before 1820. Houses for sale were frequently described as painted. The owner of a house in Newark advertised it for sale in the *Upper Canada Gazette* for December 10th, 1795, as "that elegant new red house situated in Broad Street." Another in West Niagara is advertised as "the yellow house on Lot 1." And in York in 1799 a house is advertised to let, on the east side of New Street, as "that elegant Led [*sic*] coloured house, 2 stories high."

Canniff Haight, writing in 1885 in *Country Life in Canada Fifty Years Ago* said, "The house was a frame one, as nearly all the best houses were in those days, and was painted a dark yellow." And again, "The old homes as I remember them . . . were with very few exceptions wooden structures, clap-boarded, and painted either yellow or red. The majority, however, never received any touching up from the painter's brush, and as the years rolled on, became rusty and grey from the beating of winter's storms and summer's sun." Haight was writing about the Bay of Quinte district which, though on The Front, was isolated, and consequently conservative in its taste. Nevertheless by the 1830s the growing taste for white houses was following slowly behind the American, which had begun early in the nineteenth century. By 1847 the Reverend William Macaulay, writing of a journey from Picton to the Carrying Place in Prince Edward County, said, "It is surprising how rapidly the country is filling up with population. On my way to the Carrying Place where I had not been for some years I found all the desert and forest parts occupied and painted white farm houses where there were log huts."

Green, as a house colour, is not often mentioned, but Mrs. Traill, writing of a journey in 1832 along the St. Lawrence in Upper Canada, said, "I am delighted in travelling along the road, with the neatness, cleanliness and comfort of the cottages and farms. The log house and shanty rarely occur, having been supplanted by pretty frame houses, built in a superior style and often painted white lead colour or pale pea green." And Thomas Fowler, describing houses in Upper Canada in 1831, said, "The outside is done with finely dressed boards and painted white or yellow. The window shutters are generally grass green and varnished, and the roof slate colour. Now, these elegant mansions, with the verdant fields and the dark green woods have a light and graceful appearance, and one of these fine frame buildings will cost from ten to fifteen hundred dollars." A less enthusiastic traveller, Patrick Shirreff, described houses on the Bay of Quinte in 1835 as "whitewashed cots." Belleville in 1840 was described by Mrs. Moodie: "The dwellings of the wealthier portion of the community were distinguished by a coat of white or yellow paint, with green or brown doors and window blinds (shutters) while the houses of the poorer class retained the dull grey which the plain boards always assume after a short exposure to the weather."

Stucco houses seem to have been built wherever people who were already accustomed to them settled. Quite early ones were sprinkled throughout The Front. Mason's washes were used on these, and though usually they were white, recipes for both blue and yellow have been found.

By the 1850s, cream, buff, pearl grey and light lemon yellow were extremely popular as house colours, and most houses were trimmed with deeper or lighter tones, or with other colours. The white house with green trim was still a common choice despite the efforts of taste arbiters to change it. Fowler and Wells' *Illustrated Rural Manual* for 1851, listed "painting country houses white or red" under the heading of "Common Errors and Absurdities," with reference to house building.

The trim on brick houses was often dark green or brown. Red decorated a yellow frame house and very dark green or yellow a red one. Painting on window sashes varied with taste. On the old red houses it might be the same colour as the house; or it might be white, green or black. On yellow houses it was usually white. On white houses the frame of the window was sometimes painted green and the muntin bars white. The early-nineteenth-century custom, in the Northern United States, of painting muntin bars in dark colours (black, grey, red or Prussian blue) probably had an influence here. Roofs were also painted, following the American custom, usually red, but sometimes green, brown or grey.

Often only the main body of the house was painted, and the lean-to kitchen, sheds and other outbuildings were left without paint, or painted with a cheaper paint of another colour. A house might be white, while the attached summer kitchen, woodshed, drive-shed and outhouse might be painted red. Sometimes only the back wall of the house was painted another colour, and this is an interesting feature to watch for in old houses.

Old and unaltered wooden farmhouses are still to be seen in the country-side. Those most quickly recognized as old catch the eye of the passer-by because they are abandoned. Their windows and chimneys are broken, their roofs sagging, and lilacs crowd the front door. Always this kind of house appears never to have had a lick of paint, or very little. Perhaps only the window sash shows a flaking white.

A derelict look can develop rapidly. Thirty years without paint can reduce the exposed surfaces of a thinly-painted house to a soft, weather-stained grey. In many years of examining such ghost-like houses I have found very few which lacked some vestige of colour. (The places to look for it are under the eaves and at the corner-boards.) Reds and yellows are most usual.

The interior wood-trim of early houses was usually painted eventually, if not at first. There were exceptions, and when these are found today the naked pine boards in the partitions, door and window-trim, baseboards and chair-rails are truly lovely. I have seen a large abandoned log cabin in the Ottawa Valley where only the door and window frames were painted; partitions, stairs and stair rails were the soft toast-brown that only a hundred years of air and smoke can impart. Attics, back entries and summer kitchens were quite often left unpainted throughout the first years of the century and are still to be seen so today.

Scraping down to first coats of paint on woodwork in houses built before 1830 reveals the same colours repeated again and again. White, Prussian blue, Venetian red, Spanish brown, yellow ochre, umber, raw and burnt Sienna, and occasionally a green are found. The Prussian blue may have been much brighter than it appears when it is uncovered from beneath a later coat of dark grey. Some colours, too, have been affected by an original glaze.

The most common method of "improving" the look of paint on wood-work was to varnish or glaze it. Glazes were made from pigments such as Prussian blue, carmine, yellow lake or verdigris, which were used over similarly coloured ground coats. The dry pigment was ground in rubbing varnish, without oil, turpentine or japan, and was put on like varnish. This was not easy, as clouds or runs often appeared on the surface, but the effect of good glazing was as though a thin film of glass had been laid over the paint, greatly adding to its durability.

When an early house contains a room that was quite obviously a parlour, this room is usually found to have had a first coat of white. The fashion for white-painted parlours in Upper Canada seems to have been established by 1820 and to have lasted for at least thirty years. By the middle forties some houses had parlours finished with native pine, cherry, oak or black walnut—stained, oiled or varnished. A coat of gesso was sometimes given to pine wood-work. Over this a coat of light paint was laid, followed by a dark red, and

Wallpaper from an old Eastern Ontario house. There are alternate squares of grey and white with brown, tan and mulberry designs. It was a common colour combination of the 1830s. / Miss Hyacinthe Lambart, Grenville, Quebec

Wall painted in imitation of cream-coloured marble blocks, 1830-40. / Dundurn Castle

Wallpaper of 1846. The pattern, in shades of light grey, stands out against a white ground. / Courtesy Victoria and Albert Museum, London

English wallpapers, 1851. Top: Cream ground, grisaille floral stripes with brown chains on left, flowers on right in natural colours. Middle: Gothic grisaille tracery superimposed on a background of ultramarine blue. Bottom: Sprigs in two shades of green with very dark green shadows, on a cream ground. / Courtesy Victoria and Albert Museum, London

English wallpapers, 1841. Top: White embossed ground, ornament in shades of beige with pink scrollwork. Bottom: Columns and squares in shades of beige; scrollwork a pink colour. / Courtesy Victoria and Albert Museum, London

Opposite page: Gothic architecture was a frequent inspiration for hand-printed wallpapers, 1830-40, as shown in this paper which was reproduced from original. / Dundurn Castle

thereafter either an amateur or professional type of "mahoganizing" was effected by going over the surface with a brush while the top coat was still tacky.

By the mid-century and for twenty years after, both householders and decorators were much influenced by Andrew Jackson Downing, whose writings on architecture and household taste were accepted throughout the United States as the purest and finest expression of taste in the civilized world. His book, *Architecture of Country Houses*, published in New York in 1850, is often found in Canada; excerpts from it appeared in all periodicals and it was quoted everywhere. Recipes for paint mixtures and explicit directions for staining, graining and generally adorning a house were contained in his writings and he had great influence in this field, judging by the results still to be seen in old houses. Downing said:

> The interior wood-work of villas or country houses should be painted so as to harmonize with the prevailing tone of the room. It may be lighter or darker than the walls, and generally of a quiet neutral tint, but never the same colour, and never white, except in those drawing-rooms where white is relieved by gilding. In all libraries and other apartments the wood should be either oak or other dark wood, varnished, or it should be painted and grained to resemble it.

Downing's English counterpart was J. C. Loudon, who first published his monumental *Encyclopaedia of Cottage, Farm and Villa Architecture* in 1833. (Slightly revised editions continued to appear for many years.) Loudon was also an advocate of dark wood-trim. His ideas are very frequently seen, together with his original illustrations which were lifted from his book without credit, in such popular magazines as *Godey's*, which had a large circulation in Upper Canada. He felt that "all woodwork, avowed as such, should if possible, be grained in imitation of some natural wood; not with a view of having the imitation mistaken for the original, but rather to create allusion to it, and by a diversity of lines and shades, to produce a kind of variety and intricacy which affords more pleasure to the eye than a flat shade of colour."

Late methods of graining which grew less interesting as the gutta-percha tools succeeded the deft brush work of the decorator, are still much in evidence and are inevitably confused with the earlier techniques by the unpractised eye.

Graining was often used here for the "best" rooms, but the old custom of painting kitchen and bedroom in blue, red or grey was astonishingly persistent. About 1850 a rather disagreeable green seems to have been used, which has no name that I know, unless it is the "pea-green" often mentioned.

One trick with paint about which I have never read, but only seen, is the custom (still in use in parts of the country) of painting a line from two to five inches high on the baseboard of the wall where it meets the floor. The colour of the line was either the floor colour or black. Country people who still paint it today call it "the mop-line," which explains its purpose.

Marbleizing was a favourite method of finishing wood-trim in domestic hallways and vestibules. Sometimes it was used only for decorating the mantelpiece in a room, with the basic colour matching the other wood-trim. Some of these mantelpieces are beautifully done. I recall one which was oyster colour with very delicate veining in brown, pale yellow and deep orange. I remember another in terra cotta colour with yellow and black veining.

Marbleizing in a crude way was not beyond the skill of the average person and some fascinating variations have been revealed when old paint was removed from wood-trim. Some of this work resembles the effect achieved by spotting, candling, tortoise-shelling, sponging and the practice of painting over a ground coat with a series of wavy lines—techniques all quite common in New England. These simple, home-style methods were followed, no doubt, by those who came to this country with the memory of them.

English wallpapers of 1840. Top: Brown pin dots on cream ground with brown scrollwork enlacing pink, crimson and green motif, alternating with flower stripes of the same colours. Middle: Pale green ground with dark green dots, mauve and pink roses, green leaves. Bottom: Cream ground, buff pin dots, brown sprays and cobalt blue flowers. / All courtesy Victoria and Albert Museum, London

English wallpapers of 1835. Top: Pale cream, pattern dull yellow with brown dots, deep pink flowers, emerald green leaves. Middle:· Light grey ground with buff dots, spray and scrollwork, yellow and ochre with crimson outline, flowers mauve with crimson shading, emerald green leaves. Bottom: Graded pale grey ground, pin dots in buff, green sprays, blue flowers, yellow basket. / All courtesy Victoria and Albert Museum, London, England

No painting is ever done indifferently, but in Upper Canada few people have left us any record of their taste and pleasure in it. So we are happy to read of the concern felt by John and Helen Macaulay in their correspondence about their new house in Toronto in 1837. She asks, "Is the drawing room finished with black walnut? If not, I think the wood had better be painted white, and any little shade that might have to be added to make it correspond with the paper might easily be done." He replies that he will "make the dining room black walnut," but that they will paint the drawing room as she requests, as only the doors and mantel are "real walnut." He admires the drawing room of Mr. [Christopher] Hagerman where "the woodwork is white and the stiles are gilded," and suggests that they have this done in their house. It is difficult today to find any remains of the pastel colours and gilt which must have adorned such drawing rooms in town houses.

Most fireplaces in early houses had a board which could be fitted to the opening and fastened with wooden or brass turn buttons when the fireplace was not in use. Sometimes the fronts of the andirons were left out on the hearth and the lower edge of the fireboard slotted to fit over them. Fireboards were carefully fitted together and battened on the back. Their large smooth surface offered a perfect place for decoration and was often painted in two colours, marbleized, wallpapered, or filled with decorative painting. Occasionally a representation of the brick interior of the fireplace opening was painted in *trompe l'oeil* on the fireboard, with any addition in the way of flower vases, cats or dogs the painter fancied. Fireboards were decorated with landscapes, animals, flowers (in nosegays, vases or baskets), or with diagonal squares set with flowers and other motifs. How many of these designs are amateur and how many the work of travelling or shop-owning painters is not known.

Housekeeping guides always gave instructions for "painting the hearth." The actual bricks of the fireplace hearth were often plastered and painted red or black which made them easier to sweep.

When an old carpet was removed from a bedroom in a house brought into Upper Canada Village from Aultsville, an interesting stencilled floor was discovered. The date of the house was the early 1840s and the revealed floor suggests by its pattern and colours that it was of this date. The surface was badly worn and showed signs of having been renewed at least twice; the last painting had been protected with varnish. Successive coats of paint were removed and showed that the colour and design were the same right down to the original painting. The background was a bright tan; the pattern in alternate squares was done in black or creamy yellow. The lines of a simplified snowflake and of a conventionalized rose were blurred, and required very careful redrawing of edges to restore the clean-cut stencil pattern. The restored pattern and a square of the original are now to be seen in the Doctor's House at Upper Canada Village.

Another floor, much more elaborate in design, was removed from a house being demolished for the Seaway flood, but the boards were only discovered after they had been torn up and piled in a heap for burning. Workmen on the site believed that the boards had come from the kitchen. They were painted in a rich variety of colours—tan, red, green, orange, black and cream yellow —in a strapwork design. The existence of these two floors within a fifteen-mile radius suggests the possibility of many more still hidden by linoleum and carpets since the days when stencilling and freehand painting were probably used as much here as in the United States to beautify a house. This type of decoration took the place of carpets and rugs, and it was used in parlours, bedrooms and kitchens.

Floor decorating was in vogue in England in the early eighteenth century where painting was done on the wood and on oiled cloths that covered the floor. Both types of painting were popular in the States from the middle of the eighteenth century where stencilling, freehand painting, marbleizing and imitations of mosaic have all been found. That it was thought of here as an American custom may have been indicated in Mrs. Traill's account of her visit to an Ontario house in 1834: "We were introduced to the family sitting-room, the floor of which was painted after the Yankee fashion instead of being carpeted."

Floors in the "best" rooms of an old house usually had narrower boards than the others. These boards had fewer knot holes and were not inclined to shrink or warp, and so were valued. Painters advertised that they had methods of stopping the bleeding from knots and of disguising them completely. Parlour floors were often painted green, ochre yellow or grey, and were glazed. Kitchen floors were scoured with sand or wood ashes; other unpainted floors were oiled to keep down the dust. (Often only the parlour floor was painted.) Some general stores in the country still sell bulk floor oil put up in old quart whisky bottles. The "pumpkin yellow" which was such a beautiful and common colour on kitchen floors in the country when I was a child seems to have been a late taste.

From about 1840 there seems to have been a period when the over-painting of floors was done with a sponge or a cloth dipped in contrasting colour. Spattering colour from a brush tapped with a stick was also a late practice and is still done in some country places. I once watched a farm family of girls happily "spattering" the reverse side of a worn linoleum to which they had given a fresh coat of paint. Their mother remembered her own participation in the delightful art of spattering when she was young.

Town houses of well-to-do people had oilcloths in the entry hall and occasionally in the kitchen. They were often listed in early inventories. William Dickson's claim for his losses in the War of 1812 included "1 fine new oilcloth for hall" which was in his house at Niagara. This, he claimed, "cost in London £10." English oilcloth was imported to the United States and Canada. It was advertised by J. S. Buchanan & Co. at Niagara in 1838, "in the newest patterns." John Macaulay, in 1837, debated by letter with his wife regarding the use of oilcloth in the hall of their new home in Toronto, and felt that there would be innumerable patterns from which to choose. "English" oilcloth was advertised throughout the forties and fifties, and in 1864 the London, Ontario *Advertiser* carried an advertisement for English oil-cloth in all widths up to eight yards. In 1860 an American manufacturer patented a process for treating canvas with oxidized linseed oil and called it linoleum.

Although manufactured oilcloth was often recommended by housekeeping manuals of the late thirties and early forties, it was still too expensive for most people. Methods of making floor cloths at home were in circulation from the end of the eighteenth century, both in England and the United States. The existence of painted floors and floor cloths in America is known from written records, but is also clearly demonstrated by the extraordinary number of times a decorated floor forms part of the composition of American portraits and conversation-piece paintings.

Canvas, heavy brown paper and tow cloth were all used for floor cloths. Paper coverings were made by glueing together small pieces of brown paper to form a large square, oiling and sizing it, and finally painting it in patterns, usually geometric. Fancy borders were painted around hearths and built-in cupboards, as well as around the edges of the room.

Since directions for making floor cloths appeared in every manual and in most periodicals during the thirties and forties, it was probably a fairly common practice. The *American Woman's Home* by Catharine Beecher and Harriet Beecher Stowe (a book often found in Canada) included typical instructions:

Delicate maple table, c. 1810, decorated by hand with landscape and floral details in the manner taught to young ladies in the first quarter of the nineteenth century. / U.C.V.

Washstand, part of a painted and decorated bedroom set, 1845-60, factory made and sold under the trade name of "cottage furniture." / Mr. and Mrs. M. Philip, Markham, Ontario

133

This parlour chair, one of a set made about 1855, was beautifully grained in imitation of rosewood. / Dundurn Castle, Hamilton

Secretary-bookcase made in Prince Edward County, 1835-40. It was so well painted and grained in imitation of crotch-grain mahogany as to completely fool the eye. / Mr. and Mrs. Homer Talcott, Bloomfield

The floor of a kitchen should be painted, or what is better, covered with an oilcloth. To procure a kitchen oilcloth as cheaply as possible, buy cheap tow cloth and fit it to the size and shape of the kitchen. Then have it stretched and nailed to the south side of the barn, and with a brush, cover it with a coat of thin rye paste. When this is dry put on a coat of yellow paint, and let it dry for a fortnight. It is safest to first try the paint, and see if it dries well, as some paint will never dry. Then put on a second coat, and at the end of another fortnight, a third coat. Then let it hang two months, and it will last, uninjured, for several years. The longer the paint is left to dry, the better. If varnished it will last much longer.

Oilcloths were washed with milk and polished till dry, a practice still occasionally followed when I was a child.

Whitewashing, despite the inevitable drips, was a very satisfying way to clean a wall and was a common practice in Upper Canada before 1867. For cabins and farmhouses it was a stand-by. All that was needed was slaked lime and water and a large brush. Sometimes skimmed milk took the place of water. Susanna Moodie gives us a delightful picture of the results of whitewashing in her new home about 1836. "Bell had whitewashed all the black smoky walls and boarded ceilings." In this spotless room she had "snow-white fringed curtains and a bed with furniture to correspond, a carpeted floor, and a large pot of green boughs on the hearthstone." Even today woodsheds and summer kitchens get this antiseptic treatment.

Before and after the common use of wallpaper, which began about 1835, the kitchen and bedrooms and upper hallways of all types of houses were whitewashed, but many housewives added colour and glue size for permanency. Old recipes often list blue vitriol (still sold as a drench for sheep) as a "good" blue, along with chrome yellow, chrome green, Venetian red (to be used sparingly for pink), and lamp black for grey.

All these water colours, and others less common, have been found under layers of wallpaper in old houses. Pale blue seems to have been the favourite. Very dark shades of oil paint have been found on walls painted between 1830 and 1860. Red, green and a tan-brown—the red with the green and the tan with the green—are not uncommon. White for ceilings, perhaps with a little admixture of the wall colour, was most usual. Several dark green ceilings have been seen, and the use of this colour actually appears to add height to rooms. In one instance a green ceiling was used in an 1840 parlour where the walls had always been papered; in other instances the walls were green, either lighter or darker than the ceiling.

Plain painted walls and those with panels of one colour on a background of another were much in fashion for parlours in the forties and fifties. The colours are often those advocated by Miss Leslie in *The House Book*: pale grey, stone colour, or pale olive. Miss Leslie felt that these colours were most flattering to pictures, but she allowed the use of a "very pale pink or blossom colour, an extremely delicate light green or blue" when there were "only engravings." She advocated placing a bracket supporting a lamp on either side of all the principal pictures. It should be remembered that these wall colours were all seen at night by the light of candles, whale oil or burning fluid.

Despite Miss Leslie, some of the most interesting wall colours which have survived in Ontario are much more colourful and equally flattering to the pictures. The parlour of a house in Gananoque (1850) was painted a beautiful tangerine colour combined with smoky blue; and one at Ancaster had dark bottle green walls with mouldings and woodwork in deep dull red. Another house near Barrie followed the fashionable dicta of the 1850s with yellow-green panels defined with a broad brush line of purplish-red on an olive-green background, using bright yellow stencils as decoration. The wood-trim was mahoganized.

Sometimes the decorative painting on a wall became quite ambitious, and decorators of the mid-century occasionally gave a drawing room the air of a minor palace. Elaborately-shaped painted panels in frames outlined in gilt, cornices in imitation of plaster work, drawn and painted marbleized pillars, wainscotting done in the Renaissance, the Gothic, or the Etruscan style all enhanced the high-ceilinged rooms of town houses and villas.

Such paintings are in a tradition which goes a long way back in time. In England, churches and houses were painted with pictures from about the thirteenth century. Wall stencilling and painted canvas cloths covered with allegorical, Biblical and classical paintings have been found even in labourers' cottages from the seventeenth century, proving that they must have been as cheap then as they were in eighteenth- and nineteenth-century America. These were done by itinerant painters.

The art of stencilling was adopted and developed to a remarkable degree in the New England countryside of the United States where it has been carefully studied and well recorded. Enough evidence has been uncovered to determine regional styles and biographical data about its practitioners. The travelling artists equipped with brushes, stencils, measuring rod and tape, chalk and builders' cord made their way through farmland, villages and small towns, leaving varied and beautiful designs to which great attention is now paid. The same peregrinations must have occurred in Upper Canada where, one after another, houses with painted rooms are now discovered in the same localities. In the United States some eighteenth-century stencilling is known, but most can be dated, as it is here, in the years between 1800 and 1840.

Early accounts of wall painting refer to the material used as distemper. It was made up of glue, water and colouring mixed with Spanish whiting. Occasionally a coat of varnish was put on the wall before the work began, and advice to the stenciller included, "Mix a little varnish among your colours so that you may not be obliged to varnish them afterwards." The stencils were cut from heavy paper stiffened with oil and varnish. Long-handled round brushes were used. The painter mixed his own colours from a limited palette which consisted chiefly of yellow, green, black, pink and red. A warm red-brown was sometimes used, and a purple-red. In Ontario a blue wall has been described from memory but the room has long since been painted over. All colours appeared flat, with no shading.

The laying-out of the pattern of stencilling followed early wallpapering practice. There was usually a cornice border and another just above the baseboard. Borders were also painted around chair rails, windows and doors in the same way wallpaper borders were customarily applied. There is a great similarity between American and Canadian stencil designs. Certain motifs, such as stylized flowers, swags, tassels and urns, which appear on most stencilled walls are almost, or completely, identical.

The extent of the practice of decorative wall stencilling in early Upper Canada has only recently been realized. The first known research was done in 1959 during the restoration project of Upper Canada Village. None of the houses transplanted to the Village contained decorated walls, but a great many old houses from Cornwall to Adolphustown were examined for details of structure and finish. It was in one of these—the old MacLean house (circa 1820), just west of Brockville—that the first stencilled wall in that area was uncovered. In the course of renovations, when all wallpaper in the parlour and hallway had been stripped to the plaster a beautiful, early stencilled and free-hand painted design was revealed. The parlour walls were a soft clear pink. The frieze, about 12 inches deep, of a darker pink, had a figure like an elongated diamond with curved tails. This was painted vertically in sage green, striped and dotted with Prussian blue, the figures separated by small blue stars. Doorways were framed by a grapevine, blue grapes and sage green leaves climbing from an ochre urn with a small blue heart on its surface.

Painting on Wood in Water Colours.

LADIES in Toronto and the vicinity have now the opportunity, for a short time, of receiving instruction in this beautiful Art, at present so fashionable in England (for Tables, Cabinets, and all kinds of Fancy articles), from a Lady recently arrived from that country.

Specimens may be seen, and Terms ascertained, at the Store of Mr. H. Rowsell, Bookseller, King street, Toronto.

Oct. 19, 1847.   86

A kitchen chair of the 1850s bears a portrait of the family cat, charmingly painted. / U.C.V.

In one corner near the fireplace a garland of green sprigs and red berries rose from floor to ceiling. The wall spaces were filled by three figures: one a stylized wheel in ochre and blue, the other a group of nine blue carnations and two buds, and one of three rose carnations with a blue calyx. All had sage green leaves and were formally treated. The design over the mantel, partly obliterated, contained three large urns with flowers.

The original paint on the woodwork in this room was white, and the whole effect was one of extreme lightness and delicacy. The hall and stairway of the house were also decorated. Here a gold swag, boss and tassel were used to follow the line of the ascending stairs. Tantalizing details of other designs, including birds, were too disconnected to establish the complete pattern. The rooms have been replastered and papered, thereby removing forever the loveliness of an unforgettable early room in Upper Canada.

In 1960 a house in Prince Edward County, which appeared from the outside to have been built about 1875, was being vigorously housecleaned for new owners. The wallpaper in the parlour was removed to the plaster, revealing a painted surface of great charm, probably dating between 1800 and 1820 and having a distinct resemblance to those found in New England.

The background colour on the walls was a deep ochre, and a low chair rail divided the wall at less than a third of the height. Green and terra cotta were the dominant colours in the stencils, with a brilliant Prussian blue used for accent. The space immediately above the chair rail had a perfectly executed Greek motif in repeat. Urns, grapevines, formalized flowers, swags, tassels on rings and stars were also incorporated. There was one figure that suggested a candle flame and its radiance, or, if you like, a spread peacock's tail. (The same figure appears in the Brockville house and is seen on similar walls in New England.) The wood-trim was white. One whole wall of the room, including baseboard, chair rail and door, was acquired by the National Museum of Canada and, it is hoped, will one day be shown to the public.

This useful blanket chest with a lift-top storage compartment, c. 1820-40, is painted red with wavy and curly black lines. / U.C.V.

Another house where extensive stencilling was discovered in much the same way is in the little village of Jordan. The house was built by Lewis Haynes in 1829. The hall, when uncovered, showed a stencil of a shallow dish containing flowers on a background of deep rose. It is thought that most of the ground floor was decorated in the same manner with original wood-trim in black walnut.

The ceiling on the upstairs stairwell of an early nineteenth-century house in Sandwich shows a carefree design in celadon green on ivory. Every year one or two new examples of stencilled walls are discovered, and as people learn to recognize the historical value of such decoration more rooms will be recorded.

Wallpaper was known and admired in Upper Canada from 1800, but was more expensive than stencilling, and at first not generally available. The artists who decorated walls worked for very little money and were content with simple board and lodging. Hand-blocked "room-paper," on the other hand, was a luxury only available to the wealthy. The early papers were small sheets of various sizes; a typical sheet was eighteen by fifteen inches. The paper itself was often grey or brown and these colours consequently became the backgrounds for blocked designs. The paper was thick and easy to remove, though it often remained on a parlour wall for a lifetime. After a few years it was sometimes varnished in an attempt to make it washable.

Paperhangers advertised their services, but complete familiarity with the technique of paperhanging was as general in early rural Upper Canada as it is here today; most families were quite capable of papering their own walls. One of the benefits of wallpapering mentioned in early writings was that it kept out dampness, and those who could not afford wallpaper often resorted to papering with newspapers.

The first wallpapers were hand-printed with wooden blocks or with stencils. In many the design was block-printed and the colours "pencilled" on with a brush. Because only about fifty pieces could be printed in a day in the average factory, the cost was high. Both roller-printing and "long paper" were invented in the late 1830s, and the tax requiring every piece of paper to bear an excise stamp was repealed in 1836. These three factors allowed the manufacturers to produce more and cheaper papers for an ever-growing demand. Prices around 1840 for ordinary wallpaper ranged from a halfpenny to 1s.6d. a yard in England, with, of course, higher prices in Upper Canada.

Many advertisements in Upper Canada for room-papers considerably pre-date the low-price period. S. Bartlett in Kingston advertised in 1817, "a small assortment of paper hangings for sale if applied for soon"; and in 1818, in Kingston, Theodore Brocket offered "a very elegant assortment just received." A. Thompson and Company in Cornwall boasted in 1838 that they had a "choice assortment of paper hangings of the most modern and fashionable patterns." By 1846 Thomas J. Fuller of Toronto was advertising "4000 pieces of paper hangings of new patterns, also window shades, borders and fire board patterns."

Printed papers were pasted on fireboards and on linen window shades, the latter very effectively imitating the painted blinds which were popular from about 1820 to 1875. Brilliantly coloured border papers were also often used on painted walls.

It was quite common for people to buy a bundle of room-paper because it appealed to them and to use it many years later. According to family tradition, this was done with the fine early-1820s paper in the parlour of the French-Robertson house in Upper Canada Village. The pattern appeared in an English wallpaper record book for the last time in 1824, but the paper was not put on the wall for some years after that date. Store stocks of wallpapers were not quickly discarded and it was not unusual for a customer to choose a paper which had been made twenty years earlier.

Room-papers were sold in general stores, fancy-goods stores, bookstores and drugstores, or "medical halls" as they were often called. Paperhangers also carried some stocks, along with paints, for paperhanging was always a painter's, and sometimes a glazier's job.

Henry Orr, a paperhanger in Brockville in 1830, did "distemper colouring on walls and imitations of all kinds of wood and marble." In 1845 in Toronto, Alexander Hamilton kept wallpaper hangings constantly on hand, and as well as being a paperhanger was a painter, glazier and gilder. A Chatham paperhanger, J. Theodore Myers, listed his services in 1844 as "painting, glazing, sign lettering and ornamental painting, graining in imitation of oak, curled maple, mahogany, etc. Carriages, buggys, sleighs, cutters, lumber waggons, etc. done to order. Transparent window curtains painted in oil or distemper colours, wall painting, plain and ornamental." Such varied types of decorating were continuously advertised all over Ontario right up to the mid-1860s.

Most early wallpapers were English, imported through Montreal. The firm of Symes and Woolrich advertised in the *Quebec Mercury* the kind of paper used in fine town houses in 1821: "the best silvered paper-hanging with rich flock borders." Further west, less ornate papers were advertised by people like J. Wilson in his bookstore in Hallowell (Picton) in 1833, and were probably American. The cover on an 1823 account book which bears the stamp of A. H. Inskeep Paper Hanging Manufactory, New York has been seen

Handmade and decorated wooden workbox with roof as lid, c. 1800-20. It was inspired by some eighteenth-century ivory boxes. / U.C.V.

here. Where there was easy water transportation from the United States, a good deal of American paper probably was imported.

John and Helen Macaulay at Toronto in 1837 debated American versus English papers, sending to Rochester for samples which came quickly by boat. But they did not consider the price of 5s.6d. per piece "of the English size" justifiable. John wrote, "I have therefore determined to take the kind which Burnham has at 2/3 which is, on the whole, neat enough. I shall return all the others, for although neat in their way I am not sure we should like them as well as the English patterns we selected at Rowsell's [the bookseller's], the green flower you will recollect which corresponds with the green in our carpet, and is a genteel paper. I have taken the green leaf at Regnier's for Annie's room and her dressing room, and the two neat papers from Rowsell's for the other rooms." Ordering from American dealers was probably quite common, for the 1851 *Canada Directory* includes an advertisement of a Rochester shop offering "paper hangings, borders, fireboard views and window curtains [blinds]."

It is possible that some early French papers were used in Ontario, since they were certainly used in Quebec and the Maritimes, but mention of French papers does not appear in Ontario records till the 1850s.

Among the first Ontario manufacturers of wallpaper were the Barbers of Georgetown, who were making wallpaper in the late 1850s. *The Grand Trunk Directory* for 1862 stated that they had the largest wallpaper factory in America. In 1864 the Barber mill was leased to Race, White and Company who made wallpapers, window shades and fireboard patterns, while the Barbers continued to produce the paper for them. They took back their lease on the wallpaper factory in 1866. M. Staunton who had sold wallpapers in Toronto for some years commenced its manufacture in 1855.

As many as sixteen layers of wallpaper have been found in old houses, but the average number is eight. It is usual to find not more than two really old papers, the top layers consisting of the cheap (ten cents a roll) papers of the 1870s and 1890s, when "housecleaning" included repapering every two or three years.

The early designs so far found on wallpaper salvaged from walls in Ontario are rarely comparable to any on the fine papers of the Regency period now preserved in museums. This is because most stripping of papers for research has been done in small rural houses. The backgrounds are usually found to be straw or tea coloured, very much the same colour as the unbleached paper on which they were printed. On this background some have good blue or dull rose designs in block printing; a few are roller-printed in stripes or conventionalized figures; others show an all-over pattern of a small rural scene. Only two colours are usual in a paper, the second being a yellowish cream or white.

Papers that can be dated from the 1840s, however, show a much greater range of colour and design. The first paper on the parlour of my own house (an addition of 1840) had a white ground, with widely-spaced gilt fleurs-de-lis as a pattern. Many papers of this period show a "pin-work" background of small dots which housewives approved as it concealed blemishes and fly specks. Some marbleized papers and some with Gothic and other architectural patterns have been found.

Most common of all 1840s papers are those with small geometric designs or trellisage on unbleached paper on which the predominating colour is an intense blue often compared to the tablets of indigo and blueing sold at the time. Browns, reds, light blue, green and white were also used in similar patterns.

Wallpaper by the 1850s was priced low enough and appeared in such an enormous variety of appealing patterns that it was commonly used to decorate almost every room in the house. Many patterns were floral, in stripes or cascades of flowers, larger than life-size, with "fillers" of flower bunches in

138

between the stripes. Others were composed of rococo architectural motifs. The *Anglo-American Magazine* in Volume I, published in Toronto in July 1852, carried an article on "Selection of Paper-Hangings" which said:

> A diamond trellis pattern, with a small plant creeping over it, looks well in a small summer parlour. For a common sitting-room a small geometrical pattern is very suitable; being well covered, it does not show accidental stains or bruises, and in the constant repetition of the design there is no one object to attract the eye more than another. These are sometimes called Elizabethan patterns; they are much used for staircases, halls and passages, but they are not to be chosen at random. A large pattern on a narrow staircase, and in a passage not more than eight feet in height has a very heavy and disagreeable effect. A light grey, or yellow marble. divided into blocks by thin lines and varnished, will be found suitable for most passages. . . . A safe rule with regard to paper-hangings is to choose nothing that looks extravagant or unnatural.

Judging by the papers uncovered in old houses, this advice and all the rest contained in the article was cheerfully ignored.

Wallpapers were described as "handsome," "neat" or "pretty" in contemporary accounts. "Handsome" included the bold patterns depicting wood, marble, stone, cathedral architecture, flock and embossed papers, as well as those sold in panels showing allegorical or historical figures. "Neat" meant well designed and carefully printed; and "pretty" described all floral and fanciful designs, some of them done in twelve or fourteen colours.

There was no feminine prerogative regarding the use of "pretty" papers in the nineteenth century, and many a gentleman's study was enhanced with paper bowers or realistically portrayed roses and lilies. People were cautioned by doctors against the use of green wallpaper which was thought to exude arsenic to a harmful degree, but other than that wallpaper was accepted by everyone as a requisite of home furnishing.

The linings of old trunks and boxes and the covering of band boxes of early years are one of the best sources of old wallpaper patterns. They are usually well preserved and exhibit some of the best paper-staining (as the colour printing was called) that one can find. In such boxes examples can still be found of block printing over newspapers, a method of avoiding the paper tax which had already been paid on newsprint.

Eighteenth-century chest brought from Pennsylvania by Mrs. Edward Lyons and her family when they settled in the Dundas area on what is now the Ancaster highway about a mile from Binkley's Hollow. It is painted and decorated in the German style. / Dundas Historical Museum

Small painted washstand with boldly contrasting decoration. / Mr. and Mrs. J. E. Flanigan

The door of a zommo, part of a cottage set, was decorated with blue scrollwork and with a hand-painted scene framed in gold leaf. / U.C.V.

Modern documentary reproduction of early papers has gone a long way to interest people in wallpapers of the Victorian era and to show that the dark reds, bottle greens and purples usually associated with the period were a late development and not at all representative of the charming, freshly-coloured early designs. As yet no exhaustive study has been made of the fascinating papers which lined the rooms of Upper Canada.

Amateur painting of furniture falls into two categories: either elaborate, carefully executed scenes or decorative designs, or simple embellishments made with stripes, circles or scrolls in contrasting shades or colours.

The earliest art of amateur painting on furniture was regarded as proof of "accomplishment" of young ladies in the same way as was the more common embroidering of pictures. As a pastime, furniture painting dates from the eighteenth century. That it was still an admired craft in the nineteenth century is shown by an advertisement in the *Toronto Patriot* on March 3, 1848:

> Painting on wood, in water-colours. Ladies in Toronto and the vicinity have now the opportunity, for a short time, of receiving instructions in this beautiful art at present so fashionable in England (for tables; cabinets; and all kinds of fancy articles) from a lady recently arrived from that country. Specimens may be seen and terms ascertained at the store of H. Rowsell, Bookseller, King St.

The fancy articles mentioned probably included the workboxes and tea caddies one sometimes finds, on which the painting, though in effect unstudied, is done according to a style formula.

The use of finger, brush, feather, sponge or cloth to make a pattern by wiping a sticky second coat of paint to show a lighter coat beneath, was a technique widely practised in home decoration on all sorts of furniture. Occasional pieces show a more ambitious attempt to decorate by the use of feather or brush painting in flat black on reddish brown or ochre. Examples of the use of a plate to make outlines for a series of overlapping circles on a chest have been seen. Star forms and wheels within wheels are other favourite motifs.

Storage chests were the most commonly decorated pieces. The removal of a hundred years of paint may uncover as many as three different designs. Surprisingly good pieces of amateur decoration may turn up anywhere. A rather crudely-made, chamfered-leg desk-on-table was bought for Upper Canada Village with a heavy layer of brown paint on it. Careful removal of the top coat revealed an ochre colour and a delightful freehand painting in black. It was lightly and easily painted, but with a sure sense of spatial design, and is now one of the treasures of the museum.

The use of contrasting colour on mouldings and panels is far more common in the Dutch or German settled parts of the province than elsewhere. Here also the stylized painting of flowers and fruit (somewhat in the manner of tinware decoration) has a definite kinship to European peasant design.

It is a pity that the awakening interest in early Canadian furniture was so firmly associated with the taste for raw wood. By the stripping off of paint, countless designs of great variety and excellence have been permanently lost to us. Painting was a requisite of furniture finishing in early days, and its decoration was an expression of art and style. Both the colours and the designs are extremely valuable to our appreciation of the domestic life of the time.

The early practice of both chairmakers and cabinetmakers was to paint all cheap furniture. The several kinds of wood used to make an inexpensive piece were concealed under one or two coats of paint. Chairs were given a red filler coat so penetrating that it is still the despair of the finisher who tries to uncover the raw wood. For added attraction brush strokes of brilliant yellow were often used to fill the scribing marks on the posts, legs and arms of chairs. Red, grey and blue were customary colours for common chairs; Windsor chairs were traditionally painted green, but some are found with first coats of black or sand. Cheap chests of drawers, cupboards, storage chests, desks and tables were painted according to the prevalent custom of time and place, usually red, yellow or blue. Dish dressers, wardrobes, storage cupboards, table legs, chests of drawers and desks were sometimes given an extremely durable, thick coat of a very dark brown glossy paint which, seen today, shows that the cleaning and handling of more than a hundred years has only worn off the knobs and edges of the flat surfaces.

During the 1840-60 period some furniture was made on which apparently a penetrating water stain was used, in a light red with deep yellow for contrast. The intention was to imitate the more expensively finished cherry and maple pieces of this period.

An "ebonizing" technique was sometimes practised on better maple furniture. In this process a dye, probably logwood, was used to stain one feature of construction such as the legs, apron or corner blocks of a table. The deep black, well varnished, afforded dramatic contrast with highly polished figured maple.

Some furniture was stained with red ochre mixed with hot glue and water, then varnished, producing a passable imitation of mahogany. Madder and fustic were used for a light brown mahogany colour. A coat of logwood "liquor," followed by a brushing with common ink, made a good black. Brazil wood and pearl ashes were the chief ingredients for "rosewood pink," and turmeric was used as a yellow stain.

Ordinary beds were painted or stained a dark or light brownish-red, but some interesting examples of about 1850 have fine imitations of maple and walnut painted over a combination of cheap woods. Complete sets of bedroom furniture and chests, commodes, dressers, beds, washstands and nightstands were treated in this way.

By the mid-century some sets of painted and decorated bedroom furniture were turned out by small woodworking factories, under the names of cottage furniture and enamelled furniture, both here and in the United States. These had great popular appeal and are of special interest now. Such pieces are not often found with original decoration today, but their mass production supposes a widespread ownership on this continent. No mention is made in Canadian advertisements of the decoration, but this undoubtedly followed the type so widely advertised across the border. Such enamelled bedroom sets, in pale blue, green, grey or ivory, decorated with fine scrolls and flowers, were part of the stock-in-trade of many American furniture makers.

The cottage sets, finished in dark background colours, are even more interesting. An outstanding set, which now includes only a bed (sleigh style), dresser with glass attached and zommo, or nightstand, with one drawer and cupboard below, is in the spare room at the Farm House in Upper Canada Village. The three pieces match but were bought separately in Toronto and in the Eastern Townships of Quebec. Various woods are used in the set, but the finish is an extremely skilful imitation of mahogany. In the centres of all panels are pictures framed in flattened ovals embellished with formalized leaves done in shaded gold leaf. These frames contain scenes, painted freehand in many colours, of parks, forests, houses, hunters and even polar bears. Each one is quite different from the others; the largest, on the bed head and foot, is 10 x 13 inches; the smallest, on the handkerchief drawers of the dresser, are 2¼ x 3¾ inches. Missing from the set are, probably, a chair, washstand and table. This kind of set was originally sold in the United States for under fifty dollars. Quite commonly found are odd pieces from sets which are painted as mahogany with only the faintest attempt at graining, and with yellow stripes around the turnings. They occasionally have a broad band of yellow, pale blue or white on the edges of the flat surfaces and a few leafy brush strokes of yellow on a drawer front. Most furniture finished in this decorative style is comparatively late. Its vogue ended about 1870.

Decorated washstand, c. 1845-60, in one of many patterns offered in cottage furniture sets. / Dr. and Mrs. Charles Danby, Kingston

Chest of drawers in Empire style (Prince Edward County, c. 1840), painted and grained as mahogany, with black and gilt pilasters. / Mr. and Mrs. Homer Talcott, Bloomfield

Pictures on the wall

From about 1880, for many succeeding years, the sober faces of deceased relatives gazed down from the parlour or dining room walls of every Ontario farmhouse. Enlarged from ordinary photographs to chalky indistinctness, they were framed in standard gilded plaster frames measuring at least 18" x 25". Photographers and mail-order companies got the names for their assiduous soliciting of orders for framed enlargements from local obituaries. These portraits were so popular that some people had the whole living family done.

In one of the houses I knew best there hung on the wall not only the likenesses of the departed but their coffin-plates, engraved with birth and death dates and mounted on red velvet. The metal plates had been removed at the time of burial, a not-unusual custom. Many thousands of these photographs and most coffin-plates have been consigned to attics or auctions by descendants who never saw the people they represent and who find such morbidity distasteful. These large and almost always unattractive photographs were the last expressions of the old tradition of a life-size family face as an ornamentation for a wall.

Portraits of various kinds were part of the furnishing of Upper Canada houses from the earliest times, for settlers brought with them some miniatures, a good many silhouettes, and a few oil or watercolour portraits. These are now scattered, not many remaining with the descendants of those who brought them.

While there are practically no records of door-to-door travelling portrait painters in early Upper Canada, they were such familiar figures just south of the border that it is likely they sometimes crossed it in search of patrons. The itinerant painters and silhouette-makers who are known to have been here established temporary headquarters in towns where they advertised their services to the surrounding countryside.

Such an itinerant was Mr. Bouker who, at Barret's Tavern in York, in 1808, advertised that he "took" profile likenesses, two of one person, and one framed, for one dollar. Another was Mr. Seager, "artist from England," who in 1832 took rooms at Mr. Campbell's National Hotel in Brockville and stated in the *Brockville Gazette* that he intended taking profile likenesses in the best style, in fifteen-minute sittings, for one dollar each. He went on to advise "those gentlemen who may wish to procure a just resemblance in his forcible and elegant style to make an early application."

Both of these men made silhouettes, an art which originated in France in the mid-eighteenth century and spread to England and America where it was constantly practised till the daguerreotype was introduced in the 1840s. Two principal methods were used to produce these inexpensive but quite identifiable portraits. The most common silhouettes of profile busts and full-length subjects were either cut out of black paper and pasted on light-coloured board or they were cut out of white paper and the sheet of paper, minus the cut-out profile, laid over a dark background. This last method was called hollow cutting. All bust-length silhouettes, however they were done, were known as profiles. Some profile artists were extraordinarily competent in cutting likenesses directly from paper while observing their sitters, but others used the simple method of tracing a shadow thrown on a screen in a dark room by placing a light behind the sitter's head. Consequently, silhouettes were often called shades. There were patented machines for foolproof shadow tracing. Since these tracings were life-size, they were reduced by the use of a pantograph, still used in art studios and as a fascinating toy. The user drew a pointer over the large outline of the shadow to produce a much smaller replica traced out by a pen at the other end of the pointer. On a small finished profile, touches of bronze paint or even watercolours were used to highlight a cravat, a riding-whip, a curl, a ribbon or a nosegay.

The second method of producing this poor-man's portraiture was by painting an India ink silhouette and adding a little background in watercolour

Opposite page: The subjects and the artist of this picture found in the Barrie area are now unknown. (Another portrait of the same mother and child was painted on the reverse.) Furniture painters, sign painters and amateurs all portrayed Upper Canadian faces. / U.C.V.

This engraving of a Winterhalter portrait of Albert Edward, Prince of Wales (later Edward VII) was sold by the thousands during his visit to Canada in 1860 at the reasonable price of $1.50. / Miss Gillian Toles, Toronto

An engraved portrait of Governor Sir Charles Metcalfe was issued in 1845 for 12/6 and was a popular picture for families where there was political interest and ambition. / U.C.V.

Silhouette, 1836, by one of the greatest practitioners of the art, August Edouart. The subject is the family of Mr. Stewart Derbishire who became Queen's Printer for the United Canadas. He was the great-grandfather of the present owner of the picture. / Mr. Anthony Adamson, Port Credit

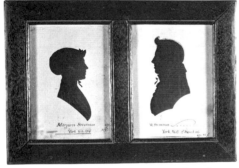

Profiles of Mr. and Mrs. Stevenson, done in York in 1816. / Mr. M. F. Feheley, Toronto

Advertisement in the York Gazette, April 30th, 1808. For one dollar Mr. Bowker, a well-known itinerant profile cutter, would produce two cuttings, one framed. / Author's collection

PROFILE LIKENESSES.

MR. BOUKER returns his thanks to the Ladies and Gentlemen of York for the great encouragement he has received from them, in the profession in which he has practiced in New England, through New Brunswick, Quebec, Montreal, &c. having in the tour taken some thousands of likenesses.—Two likenesses will be taken of one person, and one framed, for one dollar.

His stay at his room in Mr. Barret's Tavern will be very short, as he now intends going by the way of Niagara to Detroit.

York. 29th April, 1808.

or ink. These are seen less often than the cut silhouettes.

Not all silhouettes were done by professionals. Young girls, especially, were encouraged to memorialize their families in this way and learned the technique as part of their education at academies. Fortunately many silhouettes survive in their original frames which are charming and greatly enhance the appearance of these small portraits. The styles of the frames used for silhouettes became conventionalized, ranging from ebony with gilt bosses and ring for hanging, to gilded gesso, to polished mahogany with gilt liners. They were advertised as "profile frames" in Kingston in 1818. Especially beautiful were those where the glass under the frame was reverse-painted in black and gold to form a mat for the profile. Some shades were mounted on pink card, once bright but faded to the most delicate of backgrounds in the surviving examples. English shops sold profiles of the Royal Family and other celebrities. J. Cawthra who kept a prosperous general store in York in 1806 advertised that he sold profiles along with his hardware and groceries. It may even have been possible to acquire for a humble parlour a silhouette of George III.

In those days, before there was any photographic process, the silhouette and the drawn or painted portrait (executed in oils, tempera, watercolours and pastels) were widely used to express family love and pride. Established artists

144

Watercolour portrait of a Prince Edward County family, Robert and Jane Grimmon and their son Robert. / Mrs. Bruce Hart, Picton

Sara Editha is the name of this young woman, painted in watercolour in Dundas County in the 1840s. Wallpaper, chair, hair-dressing and gown reflect the period taste. / U.C.V.

such as Hoppner Meyer and George Theodore Berthon were commissioned by families of wealth and distinction in Upper Canada and have left a rich collection of portraits. Less well known artists, such as Morton Manners who advertised as a portrait painter at the Neptune Hotel at Niagara in 1838, and Peter March of Toronto, added to their income by instructing others. They were often employed as drawing masters at private schools. In the portrait paintings of their pupils, which still come to light in Ontario, we find stylized composition combined with naïveté. The cult of the primitive has unearthed from trunks and attics some of their valuable delineations of faces, clothes and backgrounds which now tell us in childlike terms what our ancestors looked like.

The public face as decoration for the home included a portrait of Lord Sydenham engraved by Hoppner Meyer in 1842, and his later engraving of the Honourable Robert Baldwin. An engraving of Governor Sir Charles Metcalfe sold for 12s.6d. for ordinary prints and 20s. for proof impressions in 1845; the Sartain engraving of Soanes' "Lord Elgin" in mezzotint, 20" x 16", sold for 10s. in 1859. Perhaps the most widely circulated portrait of public interest, after that of the Queen, was the engraved Winterhalter portrait of Edward VII as Prince of Wales. It still hangs in Ontario farmhouses, and those who frequent country auction sales are very familiar with that charm-

THE DAGUERREOTYPIST.

PALMER'S
DOME-LIGHT PREMIUM DAGUERREAN
GALLERY,
CORNER OF KING AND CHURCH STREETS.

WM. JOHNSTON,
ARTIST AND PHOTOGRAPHER
Takes Pictures in Oil and Water Colors, and all styles of Photography, in the best styles of the Art.
River Street,
PARIS, C. W.

ing boyish face. The account books of Abram Southard, cabinetmaker in Picton, list ten sales of "Prince of Wales" in 1859, for nine of which he made frames ranging in price from $2 to $4.75. The engraving itself cost $1.50.

In 1848, the British-American Photographic Gallery on King Street East in Toronto, advertised, "The price of a portrait is now so low that no one need be without a faithful likeness of an honoured parent or a beloved child." The first photographs, which were daguerreotypes, sold for one dollar all through the 1840s and '50s. Almost every town boasted a "Daguerrean Parlour" and every family patronized it. The silver-coated copper plates were covered closely with glass and stamped metal mats, then enclosed in an embossed velvet-lined case with a hinged lid. Daguerreotypes became part of the picture-furnishing of a house and were propped on mantels and bureaus everywhere. With the short-lived ambrotypes of the 1850s, they succeeded in capturing the visual essence of their period. The high hats and stocks of the men, the enveloping bonnets and crinolines of the women, as seen in the shimmering darkness of the daguerreotype plates, give a far more vivid sense of the past than most later photographs.

From the mid-fifties, a thin paper photograph pasted on a small card,

Sentimental subjects and brilliant colours characterized Berlin wool pictures of the mid-nineteenth century. This one is at the McFarland house. / Niagara Parks Com.

One method of making feather pictures was to buy a lithographed background, a collection of coloured feathers and instructions which produced pictures like this, c. 1850. / U.C.V.

Opposite: At top, a charming Berlin woolwork picture now in the Old Stone House Museum, Sault Ste. Marie. At bottom left, a silk embroidery picture of the finding of Moses, by Christiana Campbell, Niagara, 1823. The faces and the baby are done in watercolour. In the McFarland house maintained by the Niagara Parks Commission. At bottom right, a typical example of the art of embroidery on silk, combined with watercolour, as taught to young ladies till about 1830. The picture adorns the walls of Dundurn Castle, Hamilton

called a *carte de visite*, replaced the daguerreotype in popularity. These were rarely framed for the wall, but as the photograph grew larger through the sixties revered family faces, in walnut or gilt oval frames, formed part of the Victorian décor of Ontario homes. It is interesting to note, however, that Macdonald and Company at 41 Yonge Street in Toronto were advertising in 1858 "Photos, plain, $1.00; Ambrotypes coloured and put up in a neat Morocco case, 50¢." But the painted portrait was still a desirable object and the advertisement continued to say that the company also offered "portraits in oil or water-colours for $5.00 to $20.00." Before 1870 most photographers, in their advertisements and labels, styled themselves "artists."

Along with painted portraits, professional or amateur, framed needlework decorated early walls. Samplers and embroidered pictures were particularly popular. Many needlework pieces found today can be identified as of Canadian origin. They were chiefly the work of families with some daytime leisure, because fine stitchery by candlelight was very difficult. The sampler stitches were taught by mothers to girls as an exercise, preparing them for the long years ahead when their sewing skills would be essential. The embroidery was an accomplishment thrust upon young ladies who attended academies and convents. In 1829 the Brockville Seminary for Young Ladies taught "Plain and ornamental needle work and embroidery in cotton, silk, worsted and chinelle [*sic*]."

The early samplers were done on canvas or handwoven linen in cross-stitch, with linen thread or twisted silk of few colours. The alphabet and numerals formed the most common design made by young children, accompanied of course by their names, the date, and sometimes a quotation from the Scripture. Older girls showed their capability with drawn work and stitchery of buildings, scenes, flowers and fruit, or by cross-stitching a long poem. Few samplers show dates later than the 1840s and by 1850 this genteel art was beginning to disappear.

Embroidered pictures made between 1800 and 1840 are found in Canada but they are rare and highly valued. They were worked with silk thread in an over-and-over stitch then called satin stitch. Most of the pictures were under 18″ x 20″, which was the size of the beautiful pale-coloured satin especially recommended for them and often sold with designs already stamped. The subjects of the pictures were rarely original; if not done from stampings they were designs borrowed from Bible illustrations or from coloured engravings of pictures, by Morland, Wheatley, or Angelica Kauffmann, of idyllic peasant life and classical allegories. The colours in embroidered pictures were originally light and time has faded them; but in their old gilt frames and coloured mats they still suggest how lovely they must have looked on a delicately-tinted wall in the glow of candlelight.

Wool-work pictures found in Canada usually date after 1840 and are vivid examples of the Berlin wool craze which started early in the century but reached its height at the time of the Great Exhibition in London in 1851. The pictures were done in tent stitch, which we call needlepoint today. Berlin, Germany, supplied the brilliantly dyed wool for wool-work pictures, and a great variety of patterns. Dogs, cats, flowers, fruit, children, castles and Biblical scenes were stamped on canvas for those who mistrusted their sense of design.

Towards the middle of the nineteenth century, families whose land was cleared and who were prospering built new and larger houses. The populations of villages and towns greatly increased, and new houses were built there also. Most houses contained more rooms than formerly, so there were additional walls to be adorned. For many women the dawn-to-dark bondage of hard work was beginning to relax. But moral strictures of the time insisted that there be no idle hours. Magazines for women, such as *Godey's*, *Graham's*, *Peterson's*, and the *National*, all American but sold everywhere in Canada,

presented with every issue methods of occupying leisure time. Drawings and detailed directions for ladies' handwork of all kinds were given. Among these were hundreds of ways of making pictures for the home.

Many of the resulting productions are skilful copies and we are amazed at the general excellence of the work. Others show individual choice in colour and design and a breaking-away from the printed instructions. It was the women who lacked recommended materials and colours who often produced the most interesting pictures that remain to us. Such pictures are among the last of Victorian trivia to be appreciated for their decorative value.

Among the most varied and lovely of the handwork pictures were arrangements of flowers made from wool. The strands were painstakingly wound on shaped wire to make leaves and petals and the flowers were assembled in the shape of a wreath or bouquet. This was tacked on to a coloured velvet background. Another method of making wool flower pictures was to embroider and pad the flowers directly on velvet. Both of these types of pictures needed a deep box frame.

For the making of marine pictures (a hobby greatly favoured by Queen Victoria in her youth) shells and moss were gathered on the lakeshore and seaweed begged from friends who lived by the ocean. Shells were polished; fronds of mosses and weeds in grey-green, dull red and dark brown were washed, dried and pressed for the composition of charming pictures. The shells were glued on boards in shapes of animals or people, or simply in colourful arrangements. Moss and seaweed were most often used in a traditional arrangement. A small basket with a handle might be cut in half lengthwise and glued to a background, then filled to overflowing with moss and weeds. Sometimes a landscape was painted behind the basket and an appropriate popular poem of the period copied out beneath it. A verse in common use began, "Call us not weeds; we are flowers of the sea, And lovely and bright and gay-tinted are we."

The collections of seeds, burrs, teasels and other weeds which made up the farmers' wreaths so much loved by Ontario women, offered extraordinary variety for colour and design. They were mounted in a case as small as 8" x 10" or as large as 20" x 24". Infinite time, patience and glue were required for their making. They are found now with hundreds of seeds fallen to the bottom of the case, soiled backgrounds and cracked glass. And, alas, no one has the patience to restore them.

There was one type of art creation which could only be successfully produced with store-bought supplies: wax flowers. Boxed sheets of tinted wax and the various instruments for slicing, heating and curling them into petals and leaves, together with terrifyingly detailed instructions, were sold in fancy goods stores. The wax flowers which were arranged under bell-glasses were usually nicely coloured; those in wall cases tended to be white and funereal, often surrounding crosses, anchors or photographs of dead relatives.

Other wall ornaments, equally morbid to modern eyes, are the hair wreaths and hair trees that were made in great numbers. It is a mistake to think that all hair pictures were memorials to the dead. Hair trees were traditionally made of hair from the heads of the whole family, living or dead. It is true, though, that when people died locks of hair were often clipped and saved. The trunk of the hair tree contained the wiry grey and white hair of the elderly; the leaves were corn-coloured baby locks. It was easy to work with hair, which was strong, resilient and seemingly indestructible. If the worker's sense of design or ability to copy from instructions was good, the finished pictures, in their elegant maple or black and gold box frames, were among the more decorative of sentimental handiworks.

When feather pictures and cases of feather flowers became popular about 1850, there were plenty of feathers to be had from the farmyard, from old bonnet trimmings, and if money could be spent, from the milliners' shops.

Dyed tips of ostrich feathers, in authentic colourings, were glued to birds copied from a book, to produce a gay picture. / U.C.V.

A popular farmhouse wall decoration was a "farmer's wreath." This one is 30" high and contains corn, pumpkin seeds, walnuts and filberts. All sorts of farm produce such as gourds and grains were employed. / U.C.V.

Opposite page: A favourite wall decoration was a tree or wreath formed of hair cuttings from every member of the family, from babies to grandparents. / Dundurn Castle, Hamilton

Poultry feathers were ideal for cutting and curling into petals. Special dyes were sold for colouring them, and stems and artificial leaves could also be bought. Flowers, both real and artificial, were dissected so that the size and shape of the petals could be duplicated with a suitable feather. Rectangular, stencilled, black and gold box frames were favoured for feather flowers.

There was another kind of feather picture, one for which small, brightly coloured feathers were clipped, flattened and glued on a drawn or printed design. The composition, usually a flower garland, was often embellished with painting. Birds were also drawn and their outlines filled in with their own colour of feathers pasted flat. These were gay pictures, often used in bedrooms.

There has always been a great satisfaction in putting a lot of little things together to compose something larger, and the making of collage pictures was as happily practised in the mid-nineteenth century as it is now. Huge pictures were formed from a completely heterogeneous collection of cutouts, a process which must have occupied whole winters' evenings and ruined many valuable engravings. Much more creative were the pictures of actual places and buildings, usually farmhouses, which were built up with pasteboard, paper, moss and twigs, and enlivened with painted backgrounds and details. Not many of these topographical collage pictures exist today but they are found in widely separated counties, indicating perhaps that the art was known and practised throughout the province. Elaborate versions of such collage work which have been brought from the British Isles are also found here.

Tinsel pictures in America were very different from those produced in nineteenth-century England. In the 1830s and '40s cheap English prints of moderate size pictured street vendors, actors and actresses in various roles. They were titivated with colouring and bits of lace, silk, glass beads and coloured tin foil on the surface. Few of these were brought to Canada. The indigenous tinsel pictures of the late 1850s, through to the '80s, were equally fascinating, though a different sort of creation. Picture glass was laid over a drawn or printed design, the outline of which was sketched on the glass in the same colour of paint as the background. Small details of branches and leaf-veining were then sketched with opaque green paint on the glass. Then the background colour, either black or white, was mixed with varnish until it became semi-transparent, and was then applied to all but the spaces within the outlines of the design. The composition—which frequently involved roses, leaves, birds and butterflies—was then painted in transparent colours mixed with varnish. When all was completely dry, tinfoil pieces in various colours, crumpled to add glitter, were stuck on the underside of the glass, behind the design. This produced what has been described as "a gorgeous array of brilliant colours with sparkling aids." Putty or a coat of varnish held the foil and was reinforced by a piece of cloth and a thin board backing. The result of this rather tedious handiwork was often strikingly effective, but many failures are still to be seen in Ontario farmhouses—pictures in which white backgrounds are dirty grey, rose-reds are muddy, and blue-greens are sour and dull. However, the best of the tinsel pictures, which were then called Oriental or crystal paintings, are very good indeed.

For $1.50 anyone in Canada could get from Boston, post-paid, a copy of an extremely popular book called *Art Recreations*, published in 1859 by J. E. Tilton and Company. It was a fat, badly printed omnibus volume which was found even in farmhouses where the only books consisted of the Bible, the Almanac and the old school texts. In fact, it was worn to tatters in almost every type of house. *Art Recreations* gave explicit directions for making "paper flowers, moss work, cone work, feather flowers, hair work, leather work, Oriental painting, Grecian painting, wax flowers, shell work and sealing wax painting." Some of these "recreations" had already been known and practised for many years; others were new. Among other subjects, the book

Theorem painting done at Port Hope about 1830. It measures 12" x 16" and portrays red and pink roses, pansies, morning glory and a sprig of wheat. The vase is sprinkled with ground-up mother-of-pearl. A separate stencil was made for each flower and through this the paint was delicately rubbed or brushed. Details were added freehand. / Mrs. G. L. Macdonald, Toronto.

Calligraphic drawing was responsible for a great many stylized pictures like this one done by William Z. Dulmage in the mid-1800s at the village of Milford in Prince Edward County. / Miss Ann Farwell, Cherry Valley

dealt with "pencil drawing, oil painting, crayon drawing and painting, theorem painting, gilding and bronzing, Grecian and Antique painting." Both clever and fumbling fingers tackled these pursuits, and some of their work survives today, either treasured in the homes of people old enough to remember the grandmothers who made them, or reposing in antique shops ready to be discovered and newly appreciated in modern homes.

From this kind of involved mechanical instruction, and from the innumerable English and American drawing books with their models for amateur copyists, Upper Canadians with artistic strivings produced "art." No encouragement for spontaneous, original expression was offered by either manuals or instructors. The place to be painted might be a scene on Lake Ontario but the technique of rendering would be that already demonstrated as satisfactory in dealing with the wilder parts of Italy or of rural England. The local scene was treated in the same way as were mountain peaks, Tuscan villas and donkey carts, or thatched barns and cottages—all were softly shaded and romanticized in the drawing books. Actually it was easier and just as commendable not to bother to look outside at all. Copying was the only method of instruction and the only certain way to produce an acceptable picture. The style of the authorized models constantly influenced amateur painting in Upper Canada. The only significant exceptions were in the work of those engineer-artists, usually officers of the British garrison, who preserved

Early drawing books supplied the subjects but copyists often made alterations. The watercolour, done in the Galt area, shows a child with a kitten but a Brockville girl drew her with a puppy in 1842. / Author's coll.

Upper right: Amateur artists added objects copied from drawing books to their Canadian scenes. Windsor Castle appears in this one, c. 1850. / Miss Ann Farwell, Cherry Valley

Kate Douglass took home from Maple Lodge Academy, Simcoe, examples of her watercolour art. / Mr. & Mrs. Philip Shackleton, Ottawa

for us accurate, beautifully drawn pictures of the country as it really was.

This is not to say that the copyists and method painters did not produce work of value. It was rewarding to them and time has lent it interest for us. The amateurs were prolific and the province still has a wealth of little-known art work in forgotten portfolios and albums, on the walls of sitting rooms and bedrooms in the country, and now, fortunately, in the collections of small regional museums.

There are still to be found a limited number of glass pictures, a craft-like type of painting done in colour and in reverse on a sheet of glass. Some of these are heirlooms from England, done by a method introduced in the eighteenth century. Mezzotints were water-soaked, laid on a turpentine-coated piece of glass and rubbed with a damp sponge till the outline of the picture was transferred to the glass. (Many people will remember doing this with "transfer pictures" in their youth.) The glass pictures were finally painted in colours mixed with turpentine; details and highlights were filled in first and then the background. These pictures were made by both amateurs and professionals. The subjects were chiefly religious and *genre*, the latter often depicting the décor of the period with great charm.

By 1820, and for about twenty-five years thereafter, a much freer kind of glass painting was practised by professionals for mirror friezes, glass clock doors and decorative glass pictures. Outlines were drawn freehand and painted with oil colours thinned with shellac, varnish or linseed oil. Portraits, allegories, public buildings, still-life groups, children at play, and all sorts of fancy floral designs were the common subjects.

The glass used for reverse paintings was usually extra thick, but even so the mortality of these pictures has been high. There are more clock-door paintings than pictures left, and the door paintings are now sometimes removed and framed. The naïve designs and brilliant colours and the old reflecting surface make them charming wall decorations.

The technique of painting on glass, and painting and drawing generally, were often taught to amateurs. Many of the men who taught painting and drawing were professionals whose living was assured either as shop workers or itinerants. Their designs and skill were in demand for signboards, carriage doors, fancy chairs, tinware and clock faces, as well as portraits. As instructors they taught a stylized method.

Although the drawing books supplied the subjects and inspiration for most amateur art work before 1850, there were other sources—the Bible in particular. Famous pictures were sedulously reproduced; even the classical landscape scenes on transfer-printed earthenware plates were reproduced with pencil and paper. For the lady artist all floral subjects were considered suitable; they were sometimes drawn from nature but more often were concocted from details of published drawings and paintings. Artists' supplies were always available. Reeves colours were sold in York in 1802, and "veining pencils" (brushes) in 1800.

The art of painting on velvet was at its best between 1810 and 1840. Mrs. Cockburn's school in York advertised in 1822 that classes in drawing and painting on velvet would be provided at a charge of £1.10s. per quarter. Flowers, done either freehand or with the use of a stencil, were the principal subjects. Freehand painting on white cotton velvet produced a recognizably different effect than stencilling or theorem painting. In the latter no colours overlap; each is confined to the outline provided by the stencil, called a theorem. Theorems could be bought already cut or they could be made by cutting out a design in horn paper. When watercolour was applied through theorems to paper it was called oriental tinting; when it was applied to silk it was Poonah work. Theorem painting succeeded and supplanted the embroidered picture as a fashion. Many examples of it are brilliant and elegant, and usually more attractively composed than the freehand velvet painting.

In the 1860s, pictures were sold for Grecian or Antique painting, accompanied by "tints" and full directions for their use—a trend which showed the waning of any individual expression in amateur painting. In Antique painting colours were applied to the back of prints or engravings which had been made more or less transparent with coatings of varnish and turpentine. The final effect was one of antiquity though the finished product rarely justified an advertiser's claim that no other pictures could be made to "so fully resemble a canvas oil painting." Prints to be antiqued were copies of famous paintings, and reproductions of "modern" art such as "The Barefoot Boy," "Age and Infancy," "Hiawatha's Wooing" and the well-known "On the Prairie" (measuring 16″ x 22″ to 19″ x 27″). They cost from one to two dollars. There are now very few examples of this once-admired art.

Penmanship was much admired as an accomplishment for men and women alike. An American, P. R. Spencer (1800-1864), established a system of very clearly formed rounded writing, slanting towards the right, which lent itself to artistic exploitation. Manuals were published showing how written words and sentences could be used to form the composition of pictures, and how the same flowing lines could be used to draw "penmanship pictures." In nearly every community there were one or two people who excelled in this skill, and their pictures, which have a folk-art quality, are now much prized. Calligraphy in German, with Gothic letters and hand-coloured motifs associated with peasant art, made delightful wall decorations in those parts of the province settled by German people from Pennsylvania. This decorative technique, known as fractur, was employed mainly for birth, baptism and marriage certificates.

While many pictures were made at home, prints, engravings, lithographs and eventually chromo-lithographs were in regular supply in most stores and in the stock of pedlars. As early as 1803 Schofield and Mosley advertised in York that they sold "prints, glazed and framed," and maps and prints were again advertised in 1806. The subjects of early prints were not specified in advertisements but inventories and detailed claims for losses in the War of 1812 listed "Views of Niagara" most often. Portraits of generals, admirals, political figures, battles and English scenes, particularly those featuring abbeys and cathedrals, seem to be next in popularity. Maps were esteemed as wall decoration and could be "stained" (coloured) and framed to order. Bartlett's engravings of *American Scenery* were issued in parts with twelve plates in each, and were advertised in 1828 for $1 for each part. In 1833, six views of Montreal were listed in the inventory of the Honourable James Baby. E. Whitefield of Hamilton, in 1852, sold "large views of Canadian cities" and a "View of Hamilton from original drawing made by himself [in the] best style of

Tinsel pictures were made by reverse-painting the background and filling in the design with crinkled coloured foil. Oriental painting, as it was called, was a very popular female pastime of the 1850-70 period. / Dundurn Castle

This watercolour drawing which resembles and equals the exquisite floral painting on early porcelain was done by an amateur but talented artist in Toronto around 1830. / Author's coll.

155

Engravings were popular, though expensive, and those of David Wilkie, R.A. were sold in some quantity in Canada. This one. "Blind Man's Buff," is dedicated to George IV. / Dundurn

Floral watercolour paintings in eighteenth-century style were treasures. / Author's coll.

tinted lithography. Painted in tints, $5.00, fully coloured by hand, $8.00; also Toronto, Montreal, and Quebec, 30" x 36"."

The celebrated paintings of Sir David Wilkie, engraved in England, were very popular in Canada, a fact demonstrated by the number seen today in old homes and in auction rooms. In Mrs. John Beverley Robinson's household account books a folio of his engravings priced at £1.16s.6d. is noted in 1852.

American lithographic prints were very popular; those of Currier in the 1830s and '40s, and Currier and Ives after 1857, were for many years printed in black and white and were hand-coloured. D. W. Kellog, who lithographed the same sort of "prints for the people," operated from 1833 on, while Sarony was popular in the 1840s and '50s, and Louis Prang from 1865 to 1892. The Currier and Ives and Kellog prints were sold in all types of stores and from door-to-door for six cents to a dollar, while Prang prints sold at fifty cents for a folio of twelve pictures. Prints were often used as awards of merit in schools and Sunday schools, and everyone had them. Moreover, everyone liked them. They set a standard of artistic taste in rural districts which has been satisfied ever since by calendar art. This was in spite of criticism such as that expressed by the Reverend H. Christmas who, in *Canada in 1849: Pictures of Canadian Life or the Emigrant Churchman*, recommended that emigrants should bring "religious and loyal prints—coloured scriptural subjects with texts attached,

156

Currier and Ives brought five- and ten-cent art to the farmhouse. Colourful lithographs depicting farm life, sporting events, history, fruits and flowers could be bought from the village store or from pedlars. This one is "Golden Fruits of California." / Author's coll.

home scenery of school and village churches. Portraits of Her Majesty, Prince Albert, and the Royal children, Wellington and Nelson, views of Windsor Castle, the House of Parliament, our cathedrals, and such like . . . [are] greatly wanted to be largely disseminated in Canada to supplant, as far as possible, the influx of tawdry sheets portraying The Signing of the Declaration of Independence, portraits of Washington and General Taylor, the Capitol, the Mexican battles." There *were* English, French and German prints to be had but not in as great variety nor as cheap as the American ones.

The making of frames and framing of pictures was done by cabinet-makers in small towns and by "framers and gilders" in larger centres. Old frames often bear the labels of their framers on the board backing of the picture. One such frame, made by Abram Southard in Picton in the 1840s, informs his customers that he has "Picture frames, oval or square, carved, veneered or plain, of walnut and mahogany, curled maple, gilt and gilt and velvet (something new) on hand or made to order—particular attention paid to framing—all kinds of fancy work, Grecian oil painting, crayon drawings, etc. A large and splendid assortment of lithographs for Grecian oil paintings, Oriental and Italian or Diaphanic painting on glass." This last was transparent paper printed in colours to imitate stained glass. It has had a long life for use in the windows of old-fashioned vestibules, halls and even bathrooms.

Small woodcuts, line engravings and lithographs were coloured by hand and sold for a penny apiece. Once prevalent on farmhouse kitchen and bedroom walls, they were discarded long ago and are rarely found today. / Dundurn

157

If we judge the manner of hanging pictures from paintings of interiors and illustrations in books from 1800 to 1875, it is evident that most people pleased themselves most of the time. It was common, at the beginning and also at the end of the nineteenth century, to hang pictures above eye level. Rectangular pictures were commonly, but not always, hung in the narrow space between the top of a doorway and the ceiling, in the 1830s, and were often tilted forward—a practice popular again in the 1890s. Small pictures were often grouped together as they are today. Great care was taken that gilt should not tarnish or become fly-specked; in fine houses gilt-framed oil paintings were shrouded in muslin during the summer months, and the gilt coated with copal varnish annually (which explains the messy encrustations sometimes seen on old gilt frames). The staining, graining or painting in colours of simple, common, wood picture frames was not entirely an amateur art but was practised by the professional sign and fireboard painters. Few such frames are found in Ontario but all are charming and to be treasured.

By 1850, the sampler, the embroidered picture, silhouettes and even some engravings had been banished upstairs or put away, but only in fashionable houses. For most people, pictures were furniture. During that part of their lifetime when I knew my maternal grandparents, they lived in three different houses. After each move their pictures, many of them dating from the sixties, were hung in the same rooms as before, at the same height, and in the same relationship to each other. In the parlour, narrow gilt-framed watercolours of the Hudson River hung in a group of four. Chenille-embroidered roses on white satin in a heavy gilt frame were always over the sofa. On another wall was a mahogany-framed engraving of the marriage of Edward VII and Alexandra. Two oval-framed photographs of my great-grandparents were always there. The only latecomers were some flower paintings by the "girls" of the family, and an enormous sepia-toned Marcus Stone called "Two's Company." And so it was throughout the house, where engravings of "Sir Walter Scott," "Wellington," "A View in the Trossachs," a map of British North America, an "Oriental" painting of birds, some silhouettes, and a chromo-lithograph of "Little Miss Muffet" were all part of what seemed then to be a never-changing scene.

Someone sketched a delightful-looking child in Brockville in 1829. Unfortunately the name of the subject is obscured. / U.C.V.

The lights of home

Homemade candle lantern with wood sides, pierced
tin top, and metal socket. Lanterns were among
the most beautiful of all handmade objects. / U.C.V.

Pair of brass candlesticks with thumb pieces for raising the candle as it burned down. This type of candlestick was in common use in Upper Canada before the mid-century. / U.C.V.

Henry Lingwood,
TALLOW CHANDLER,

LATELY from England, has commenced the bufinefs in this town, which he intends to profecute with unceafing affiduity. It will conftitute his ambition to render his candles equally as profitable and pleafent to the confumer, as thofe which are imported. He hereby humbly folicits the public to favor his patriotic plan by their encouraging cuftom. The candles will be fold at Mr. DUN's STORE at 2s per lb. in retail, and 1s. 8d, wholefale.
Sept. 20.

Candles like those sold by Henry Lingwood, who advertised in the Upper Canada Gazette in 1797, were carefully conserved. Many homes had a save-all, a small pan with an upright pin which would hold a used candle so that it could be burned to extinction. (The pans were used independently or were set in a candle socket.) There was also a tin box of "ends," but they were strictly for family use; it was not thought genteel to commence a "company" evening with half-burnt candles. / Ont. Arch.

For the penniless pioneer the best light after dark was that from the fire on the hearth. Some settlers gathered pine knots in the forest, burned them on flat stones in the fireplace, and worked by their oily light. They provided at least as much light as the little iron grease lamps common to most households—lamps no better than those used by the ancient Egyptians, Greeks and Romans. Candles, which brightened the nights of the rich, were used sparingly in log cabins; the tallow candles made at home guttered and smoked, had to be trimmed constantly, smelled abominably, and gave a very feeble light. The light from whale-oil lamps was not much brighter. Small wonder, then, that most settlers regarded night as a time for sleep.

Rush lights, although used extensively in early houses in England and Europe, were apparently not much used in Canada. Wrought-iron holders for rushes, some with a candle socket attached, have been found in Ontario but it is likely that these were brought in by settlers accustomed to their use. The settlers would have been accustomed also to the method of preparing rush lights, peeling them almost to the pith, drying them, soaking them in tallow and grease, and leaving them to harden. But the rush used for lights (*Juncus Effusus*) does not grow as tall or as thick in Canada as it does in England, and it does not give as satisfactory a light. It is probable, then, that candlewood (splints from the heart of pitch pine or fir, and occasionally from birch) was used by preference, in the rush holders. There was no necessity to snuff the splints periodically, as they burned steadily, and they are said to have been much brighter than candles.

Far less bright were the dirty little lamps called grease lamps, pan lamps, fat lamps, slut lamps, or crusies. (The name crusie was very generally used in Scotland and in North America, though not elsewhere.) These were small round or pear-shaped dishes made of iron, with a handle or hook for hanging them up. They contained animal or fish fats and a cotton wick. (Sometimes a rag in a saucer served just as well. Michael Scherck, writing of early days at Niagara, called such a makeshift lamp a "witch.") Grease lamps gave a very feeble light, dripped oil continuously, and unless the wick was poked forward, went out. The best of the grease lamps, called double crusies or Phoebe lamps, had two pans, one above the other, the lower one for catching drips.

An improved version of the primitive grease lamp was the Betty, which also burned fats (tallow, grease or whale oil). It had a lid, a small trough for the wick, and a pick which was used to brush off the charred wick and pull it up into the spout. (This last piece of equipment was appropriately called a pick-wick.) The cotton wick was inserted so that the ends hung out of the wick channel. Bettys with holders for two wicks are sometimes seen. They were generally made of iron, occasionally of tin, and once in a while of pewter. Two or three inches in diameter and about an inch deep, they were leaf-shaped, oval, round or triangular, and their projecting channels were an inch or more long. Attached hooks, chains or spikes allowed the user to hang them on a nail or peg or the back of a chair, or to stick them into the chinks of a log wall. They also made it possible to lower the lamps into a pot so that cooking food could be inspected. Many Bettys were raised on small footed stands or mounted on shaped wooden blocks.

In some parts of Ontario both the grease lamps and the Bettys were colloquially called Dutch lamps, as many of them were brought by German settlers. Michael Scherck refers to them by this name. It is difficult to determine the age of any of these lamps. They are known to have been used in the sixteenth century in Europe, and were certainly in use in Upper Canada in the eighteenth and nineteenth centuries, but the old and the less-old all look very much alike.

Tallow candles, both moulded and dipped, were for sale in Upper Canada by about 1800. Moulded candles cost from 16*d.* to 2*s.* a pound; dipped candles cost 12*d.*—prices much too high for most settlers. Saving and rendering every bit of fat for the making of candles was one of the first principles of established housekeeping. Beef and mutton fat were the best, but pork was also used.

Autumn was the time for candlemaking. Large iron kettles, each half-filled with boiling water, were hung over a good fire in the kitchen fireplace. Into these went the tallow, to melt. Two long rods were laid parallel between two chairs or tables and placed across them were half a dozen short candle rods (often made of elder), each suspending, at two- or three-inch intervals, wicks of hemp, tow or loosely spun cotton, firmly twisted. The short rods were lifted one at a time and the wicks dipped into the melted tallow. After repeated dippings the wick cores became candles or, as they were often called, tallow dips. It was necessarily slow work, as hasty dipping made brittle candles which cracked. About forty dozen were made during an annual dipping.

Running tallow into moulds was less work but still slow. There were large candle moulds, set in wooden frames, which made up to twenty-four candles, but six- and three-candle moulds were most common. The wick was tied to a wire or nail laid across the top opening of each mould, and hung to the bottom of the cylinder where it was held by a knot. Melted tallow was carefully poured in around the wick. All wicks were twisted until the early nineteenth century when they began to be plaited and could be bought in stores.

Practically all homemade candles were of tallow. (Beeswax candles were frequently made at home in the United States, but this practice is rarely mentioned in Upper Canada records.) Rendered tallow could be bought for 1*s.* a pound, and unrendered for 9*d.*

Wax candles were imported from England. Perhaps the "London moulded candles" advertised in Upper Canada in the 1830s were some of these. The best candles that could be bought were made from spermaceti wax which was found in the head of the toothed whale. This highly prized substance made a pearly white, translucent candle which burned with a pure, bright flame and was enormously superior to the tallow candle. Spermaceti candles were constantly advertised for sale well before 1820 in the towns of Upper Canada. They were made by chandlers who accepted all kinds of goods in exchange.

About 1845 candle manufacturers began adding stearic acid to their wax. The new formula produced a candle with a good clear flame which did not flicker or sputter and was practically smokeless. An improved wax, paraffin, was used by chandlers from about 1850 on.

Since makers of candlesticks have continued to produce old shapes and styles for use today, it is often quite difficult for owners and collectors to distinguish the old from the new. Early candlesticks were made of tin, pewter, brass, glass, china, pottery, silver and Sheffield plate, and many candlesticks are made of these same materials today. However, all old candlesticks show distinct signs of wear underneath the bases. Old candlesticks, of brass or pewter, china or silver, found in Ontario, are usually of English origin. Pressed glass candlesticks, very popular from 1840 on, are more likely to be American.

Oddly enough, very few early Ontario inventories list any great number of candlesticks. William Dickson's inventory mentions only four brass candlesticks and thirty-six candle moulds. The inventory of the James Baby house (1833) lists one pair of plated, round candlesticks, valued at 10*s.*, and one pair of plated, square candlesticks, valued at 12*s.* Presumably the common tin or sheet-iron candlesticks or saucers which must have been in these splendid houses were scarcely worth mentioning. Advertisements, however, were more explicit. In Kingston in 1817, "brass, iron, and japanned candlesticks and elegant plated ditto" were for sale; and japanned, silver-mounted, plated and brass candlesticks were sold in Brockville in 1830. Other advertisements listed similar items. Most brass, silver and glass candlesticks were made and sold in pairs.

Metal wall sconce for candles, of good design but crude craftsmanship. / Niagara Hist. Soc.

Silver candlesticks and the account listing them. They were sold by Savage and Lyman of Montreal to Mr. George Robinson of Milles Roches for £1.12.6 in the year 1853. / U.C.V.

Handsome glass candelabra, the kind imported from England and stocked in the best shops throughout the first half of the nineteenth century. / Catalogue of F. & C. Osler, London

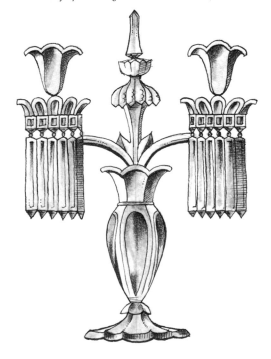

English glass chandelier made in the early Victorian era, similar to those used in Upper Canada. / Catalogue of F. & C. Osler, London

Sinumbra lamp with an Argand burner and an annular oil font, patented 1820. It was used for at least twenty-five years. / Dundurn

Every household contained several cheap tin or sheet-iron candleholders which were made by local tradesmen. Branched tin sconces and chandeliers were made by Canadian tinsmiths but were used, for the most part, in churches, taverns and town halls; private homes had many round or rectangular single or double candle sconces. Glass and heavy cast-brass chandeliers were imported for wealthy people, but those found today in Ontario are usually late "settler's effects" or antique store imports brought in long after the time when they could have been used in Upper Canada. Blacksmiths made iron candelabra, to stand on floors and tables, and trammels which hung from hooks in the ceiling to support candleholders.

A great many brass candlesticks were apparently used in the homes. These had square, round or rectangular bases and baluster-turned stems, and sometimes the stick screwed into the base. Old brass candlesticks are heavy and the metal has a beautiful silky sheen.

Many iron and brass candleholders had a slot in the side of the stem to accommodate a small button which could be moved to adjust the height of the candle as it burned down. Some candlesticks had a spring in the stem which expanded to push the candle up as it burned and lost weight.

Most houses possessing fine candlesticks kept a supply of bobêches, or "receivers," which were shallow upcurving cups of metal or glass, with holes in the middle. These were slipped over the candles to catch drips.

The general style and taste of the period was reflected in the design and ornamentation of the best candlesticks. These were kept, polished and supplied with fresh candles, on mantel or table in the rooms where they were to be used. The common sticks were kept on a shelf in the kitchen or pantry, and the chamber sticks were kept on a table in the hall, ready to be taken upstairs.

Candle lanterns of punched tin, glazed sheet iron and wood were commonly used from the earliest times. Very few lanterns with windows of horn-pane survive, but the horn was advertised in Upper Canada and must have been used before glass was easily available. Having seen some dozens of lanterns in their original homes where they are known to have been used in the nineteenth century, I am constantly surprised by the great variety of types and the fact that they are almost always pleasing in design. Lanterns were chiefly for outdoor use but sometimes hung on a hook from a ceiling beam in the house. The candle lanterns used in the barn had to be taken outside or back to the house for snuffing, so great was the danger from a spark falling in the hay. The kerosene lantern was a great advance, though it too was dangerous.

Throughout the nineteenth century, spills made of old paper rolled into slender tapers were used for lighting candles and lamps from the fireplace. This practice lingered on long after matches became safe and inexpensive. Long slender taper candles were imported from England in the middle of the century, and one taper would light every candle and lamp in the house.

There was a circular metal tinderbox in most households. It contained a flint made of quartz, a piece of iron called the steel, and some tinder. (Tinder was tow or scorched or scraped linen, or any other easily ignited material. Worn-out handkerchiefs were saved for this purpose.) It sometimes took as much as half an hour to ignite the tinder with a spark caused by striking the flint downward on the steel. Inside the lid of the box was an inner cover used for damping out the tinder after it had lit a bit of punk. The punk, a thin piece of wood with a sulphur tip, resembled a large-sized match and it was used in the same way—to light lamps or the kindling on the hearth. Some households had a tinderbox of improved design which contained a steel wheel that was spun with a piece of cord to make it strike the flint. It was easier to use than the earlier tinderbox and produced a flame more quickly.

The first matches made in Canada were produced at Hull by Ezra Butler Eddy who marketed them as early as 1856. These were safety matches which would not ignite without being struck on the side of the match box. Phosphorus matches, Brimstones (which were sulphur-tipped and put up in sheets), and Loco Foco matches (which would strike anywhere) had all been available for some time, but for many people banked fires and tinderboxes were the principal source of flame. Lucifers, as all matches were called, were not sold everywhere in the early days.

Glass lamps (c. 1830s) that employed burning fluids were usually sold in pairs. / Dundurn

To make a candle burn brightly it was necessary to snuff it about every twenty minutes, in order to cut away the charred wick. Snuffers were therefore necessary in all households where candles were burned. A snuffer was made of tin, sheet iron, brass or silver, and looked like a small pair of scissors with a box mounted above the blades. (The box was to catch the clipped wick.) The snuffers were kept either in an open space designed for them in the bottom of chamber or saucer candlesticks or on the trays with which they were usually sold.

Some saucer candlesticks had small cone-shaped extinguishers that were attached to them by a chain or were set on a projection on the saucer rim. Most households also had a long-handled extinguisher, one that was carried around the house to put out candle flames. Another way to avoid burnt fingers was to use a douter, an extinguisher made like a pair of scissors with small flat discs instead of blades. However, candles were probably most often extinguished by wetting the thumb and forefinger with saliva and pressing the wick; all done in a split second.

In 1784, when the first settlers in Upper Canada were drawing lots for their future homes, Aimé Argand of Geneva was patenting in London the first great improvement in lighting. This was a tubular wick, three inches in circumference, fitted between two upright brass cylinders, one inside the other. Argand lamps burned gravity-fed spermaceti oil from a reservoir mounted above the burner. Glass globes protected the flame. This revolutionary lighting device was said to give the light of ten candles.

Above: Examples of good burning-fuel lamps. Note the divergent burners—a necessary precaution since the fluids used were extremely volatile. Such lamps were usually sold in pairs. These belong to 1830-40 period. / U.C.V. Below: Two common burning-feul lamps, one with its extinguisher missing. / U.C.V.

Lamps designed on the Argand principle immediately came into use in England. A few were evidently brought to Canada, for one was listed on an auction bill in York in 1811. They were soon manufactured also in the United States where they were often called mantel lamps. Mantel lamps frequently came in sets of three—two single lamps for the ends of the mantel and a double-burner for the centre. Because of the high cost of both lamp and fuel, the Argand never came within the reach of the ordinary family.

Gradually other less expensive but improved lamps became available. Most of these had a wick like that of a candle and burned either spermaceti or whale oil. Spermaceti oil, the most efficient fuel, was also the most expensive and consequently was used least. In 1810 it cost $1 a gallon, whereas ordinary whale oil was 35 cents. In the 1830s olive oil was advertised as "a superior article for lamps."

Lard oil, a cheap fluid obtained as a by-product of lard-making, came into use in 1820. It could not be burned in ordinary lamps, however, and a special lamp with a broad, flat or double wick was made especially for use with the new fuel. Most lard-oil lamps smoked and household hints recommended soaking the wicks in strong vinegar to prevent this.

The new whale-oil and lard-oil lamps of 1820 to 1840 were made of pewter, Britannia ware, heavy tin, blown glass and pressed glass. All had closed fuel containers. All burned without a chimney. The stopper at the mouth of the lamp was at first made of cork but after 1830 was made of metal and had one or two vertical metal spouts set into it. These held cotton wicks which, after 1830, were usually plaited. The taking apart and cleaning of oil lamps was a slow, messy task but unless it was done the lamps burned badly, giving off both smoke and stench.

Some of the earliest whale-oil lamps were made of blown glass. Pressed

163

glass lamps were introduced about 1825 and some combinations of pressed and blown glass were also made. A pleasing trick of the 1840s was to colour the oil in glass fonts with an infusion of alkanet chips. The chips (which can still be bought) were tied in a piece of thin cotton like a tea-bag and dipped in the oil; a short immersion produced a pink colour, and a long immersion a red. Miss Leslie's *Lady's Receipt Book* for 1846 recommended that lamps coloured with alkanet be used "for ballrooms, or dispersed among the shrubbery at a garden entertainment."

These whale- and lard-oil lamps without chimneys were probably the lamps most commonly used in Ontario before kerosene. Like the primitive grease lamps which preceded them, however, they are not familiar to the amateur collector of antiques, nor are they often found in shops. Some early metal lamps (particularly rare) bear the stamps of their makers, and the names of such firms as James Dixon and Sons (English) and Boardman and Hart (American) appear on lamps made from 1825 to the 1840s.

Peg lamps were spherical oil reservoirs with a stub or peg on the bottom and one- or two-wick tubular burner at the top. They were popular between the 1820s and 1840s because they could be inserted into the sockets of candlesticks, a feature which made them versatile and economical.

The introduction, in the 1840s, of some American and English patent lamps (the Astral, Sinumbra, Solar and Moderator) opened a new era of elegant home lighting for people who had not been able to afford expensive Argand lamps. These four patent lamps, all with winding wicks and most with chimneys, had Argand burners or modifications of them but could burn a cheaper fluid than spermaceti oil. Common whale oil could be burned in Astrals, and whale or sperm oil, (and eventually kerosene) could be burned in Solars.

The Astral was one of the most handsome lamps of all time. It usually had a marble base, brass column and font, tall chimney, and frosted and engraved shade. It was slow to be adopted but became the most popular "best room" lamp of the 1840s and was used well into the 1860s. A pair of "Astrol" lamps were sold at the auction sale of R. Starkweather at Niagara in 1835 and Astrals appeared very frequently in illustrations and paintings of the forties and fifties. Catharine Beecher was still recommending them in her *American Woman's Home* of 1869, although she admitted that the sperm oil which burned best in them was expensive.

The Astral lamp gave an excellent light from its circular wick, and the shallow ring reservoir did not cast a shadow, as the deep font of the Argand had done. The first Astrals contained the ordinary Argand burner but a spiral wick-raiser was added later. The flame was a radiating one.

Astral lamps are seldom seen in Ontario now, and when they are found they have usually been converted, first to kerosene and then to electricity.

Sinumbra ("shadowless") lamps, which were first introduced in 1820, belonged to the class of lamps with annular fonts. The oil reservoirs were large rings surrounding the lamp, and they made a rest for the shade. The base was a tall brass column sometimes as high as two feet, surmounted by the ring font and a large ground-glass shade which served as a chimney. The elegant shapes of Sinumbra lamps became prototypes for table lamps made throughout the eras of kerosene, gas and early electricity. They are consequently very familiar to people born in the early years of this century.

The Solar lamp was widely advertised in Upper Canada during the 1840s and '50s. It differed from the Astral in having, on the burner, a glass or metal cone with a small hole directly over the wick. This drew up the flame and narrowed it. Solars burned well with lard oil, which was cheaper than whale oil, and their construction rendered them practically smokeless. They were equipped with wick-turners, chimneys and shades. They had a heavy base, often marble, and a metal column of classical design. The font and shade were often ground glass, and prisms hung from the shade-rest. On this continent

This tin Betty lamp on a stand has a cloth wick for soaking up the fat or oil. / U.C.V.

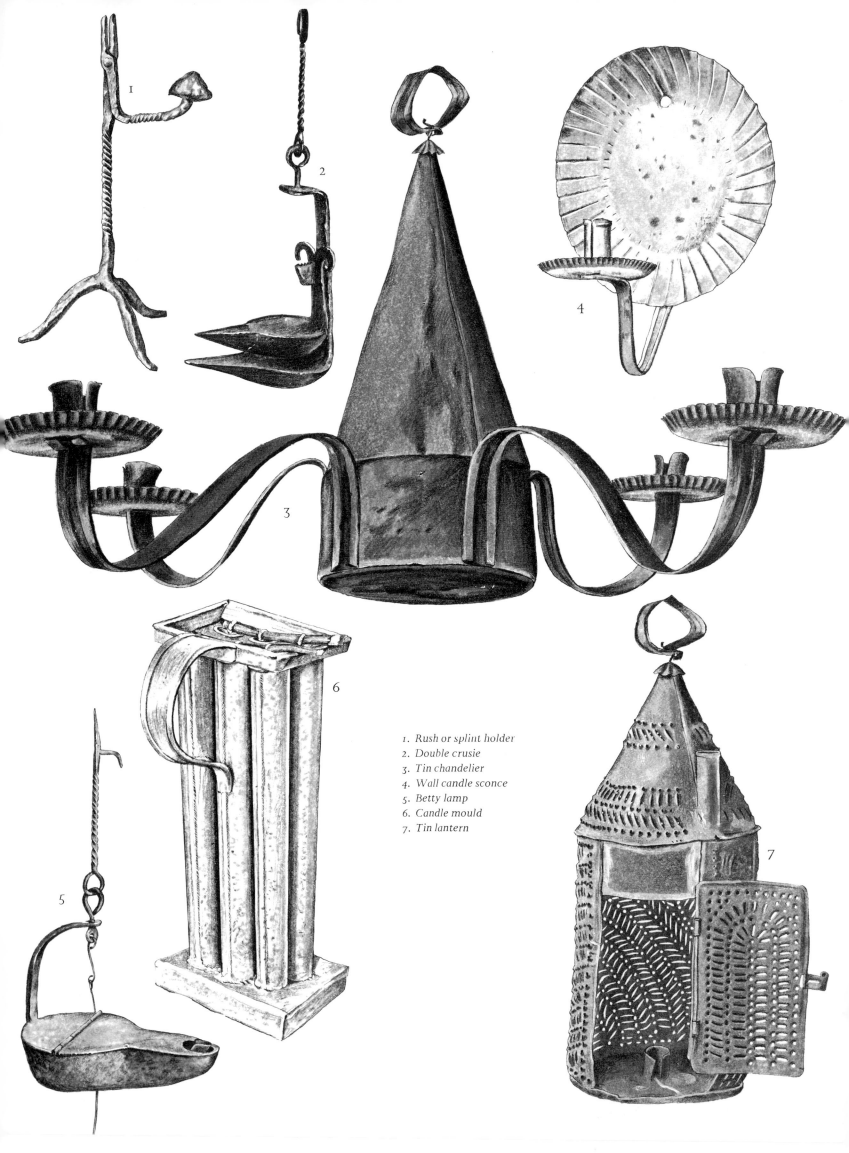

1. Rush or splint holder
2. Double crusie
3. Tin chandelier
4. Wall candle sconce
5. Betty lamp
6. Candle mould
7. Tin lantern

1. Solar lamp, c. 1845
2. Sinumbra lamp, c. 1840
3. Glass peg lamp, c. 1830
4. Pressed glass whale-oil lamp, c. 1830
5. Double-arm Argand lamp, 1820-40 / Dundurn

they were made principally by Cornelius and Company of Philadelphia.

The Moderator was a fashionable lamp suitable for drawing rooms. The flow of whale or sperm oil which it burned was moderated by a spring-and-piston mechanism in the base, which acted as a force pump. There was a turn-button for adjusting the wick and a key for winding the spring on either side of the burner. The oil was contained in a china, glass or metal reservoir shaped like an elaborate urn or vase. A spherical glass globe and narrow glass chimney were positioned over the burner. For beauty and efficiency, Moderators were probably the most desirable of all early oil lamps. But though they were advertised as economical to burn, their initial cost was prohibitive for most people, and few were used here.

New shadeless lamps for ordinary use were introduced in the 1830s and advertised as being greatly superior to those burning whale oil. The search for a brighter flame and a cheaper fuel had resulted in various turpentine-alcohol mixtures, of which the best known was camphene, patented in the United States in 1830. All sorts of minor variations on this mixture were patented later, the most famous being Porter's Patent Portable Burning Fluid (1835), which was advertised extensively in Canada. The new fluids could be used in lamps especially made for them, or in the old whale-oil lamps if they were fitted with new burners. (The new burners differed from the old single and double whale-oil burners in having two spouts rising from the collar, slanted outward from each other as a safety precaution.) The turpentine-alcohol fuels were highly combustible. It was dangerous to blow out the flame and small metal caps were attached to the spouts by chains for extinguishing the lamp as well as for preventing evaporation. These caps are frequently missing from lamps found today, but if the two spouts are divergent it can be assumed that the lamp once burned camphene or one of the other patented burning fluids.

Special lamps, some called camphene lamps, were introduced about 1840. These used an Argand burner and burned turpentine and alcohol in approved proportions. Some, the English Vesta and Paragon lamps, for example, burned turpentine alone. The new lamps were made in a variety of designs, some of them elaborate, with shades and chimneys. But the burning fluids, particularly camphene, had to be handled carefully. It was so risky that many people reverted to using whale oil in the special lamps. Gradually all the turpentine-alcohol fluids, so eagerly adopted at first, were abandoned because of the great danger of explosion. They were the nightmare of the insurance companies. Nevertheless they continued to be sold in limited quantities until kerosene, which was first advertised as being non-explosive, came into use.

Only the best and fanciest of lamps were left in their position for use. All others were removed to the kitchen or pantry where every day they were cleaned, filled, and stored on a shelf. Beside the shelf hung the scissors for trimming wicks, never used for any other purpose. If the pantry was cold the lamp chimneys had to be warmed before the wick was lit; otherwise they would crack and break.

All types of lamps required careful handling. They could not be tended indifferently or carelessly without great inconvenience and danger. In many houses women who left other tasks to servants did their own lamp cleaning and filling. The smoke caused by an untrimmed wick or a dirty font, the excess oil that left smears on the table or stains on the lamp rug which protected it were a household trial. Lamp rugs, which were very generally used, were thick square mats, knitted, crotcheted, or embroidered. They not only absorbed excess oil but protected the tables or lamp stands from scratches when lamps had metal bases or feet. The stands usually had four legs, as these were considered safer for lamps than the old tripod candlestick stands.

Most people used candles to light themselves to bed, especially children, who were adept with candles but still unsure with lamps.

Like candlesticks, early lamps were rarely listed in inventories. There is an often-published drawing by Anne Langton showing the parlour at Blythe

Kerosene lamp, base and shade in apricot and white opaque glass—a fine example of good style during the 1860s. / Upper Canada Village

Kerosene lamp of the late 1860s, the type of lamp most commonly used. / Author's coll.

Farm in 1840 in some detail, yet the house inventory listing even the busts on top of the bookcases and the clock on the mantel does not mention the mantel candlesticks nor the elegant Astral lamp on the table. The inventory of *Alwington* made about 1841 during Lord Sydenham's tenancy, gives the contents of over twenty-five rooms. It lists such homely details as the oilcloth on the hall table, tin covers for the stovepipe holes, and 210 flowerpots, but only the chandelier in the dining room and two bronze candlesticks "in a closet off the hall" are listed as lighting equipment.

Before kerosene was generally available, manufactured gas-lighting was introduced in Ontario. The first public installations on this continent were made in Baltimore in 1817, Boston in 1823, New York in 1828 and in Montreal in 1838. There was both street and house gas-lighting in Toronto in 1841, in Kingston in 1850, in Hamilton in 1851, and in Brockville in 1853. There was, however, a widespread opinion among the population that gas was both unhealthy and dangerous and it caught on slowly. Only 640 houses had gas-lighting in Hamilton in 1857. Its complete acceptance was not general until after 1885 when the Welbach incandescent mantel gave increased brilliance and eliminated most of the hazards of the open flame. On the street where I lived with my grandparents in downtown Toronto about 1908 most houses had gas. One had electricity. And I remember one where deep prejudice restricted the lighting to candles and kerosene.

When Ontario towns and cities installed gas lighting during the 1850s tons of finely cast brass fixtures were imported from Britain, especially from Birmingham. / Dundurn Castle

In ordinary speech kerosene and coal oil seem to have been used interchangeably as names for the illuminating fluid which so changed the lighting of houses from the middle to the end of the nineteenth century. Although petroleum was discovered at Oil Springs in Ontario in 1855, it was not until just after 1860 that the commercial development and marketing of kerosene was established in Canada.

Special lamps using adapted Argand burners with a draught deflector over the wick were quickly put on the market for kerosene burning. When kerosene was accepted by the public, lamps with much larger fonts became usual, thus making it unnecessary to refill the lamp during an evening's use. The safety, comparative lack of odour, and enormously improved lighting quality of kerosene lamps made them popular everywhere. In 1860, kerosene was sold in Canada for $1.25 a gallon, but by 1865 the price had dropped to 40 cents and at some stores to 35 cents.

The first kerosene parlour lamps made in America were copies of the Astral, which had unfortunately deteriorated in design over the years and was being made with gaudily painted flowers on shade and font and loaded with ornament. These were frowned upon by magazines and housekeeping manuals as bad taste but nothing stopped their popularity or sale. Yet the 1860s' kerosene lamps were restrained by comparison with those of the 1880s and '90s.

To describe the varieties of lamps and shades available before the end of the sixties would be impossible. By far the most commonly used were table lamps of pressed glass with a chimney and no shade, and squat, small glass lamps with handles, which were easily carried about. By 1867 most Ontario families had at least one kerosene lamp. Compared to the home lighting of the pioneers, this was like stepping from cellar gloom into sunlight.

How short is the transition that has revolutionized modern living! In my own lifetime I have lived in houses lighted entirely by kerosene and candles, then by gas, and finally by electricity. I saw the customs and habits that were retained from a darker world. My grandfather's easy chair was placed close to a sunny window where he read long after the hour when we casually turn on electric lights today. My grandmother often walked to a window to read a letter or pick up a dropped knitting stitch. The curtain in her bedroom had a pin in it with which it could be quickly pinned back while she did her hair in front of the dressing-glass. She *felt* in cupboards and drawers without even looking. The lamps were not lit till dark.

I loved picking the candle ends from sockets and putting them in a tin box, away from the mice, to be used in a saucer candlestick which stood on a shelf near the cellar door. When I made the descent to the cellar for preserves or apples I always took this little blue candleholder, lighting the candle from a match taken from a tin holder on the door jamb. (Beside the match-holder was a small piece of sandpaper on which to scratch the match.) The candle, held high, made it possible to run down the stairs without tripping over the tray of milk jugs which were put on the steps to cool, but hardly provided adequate light when it was placed on the preserve shelves to lighten the fragrant darkness where the apple barrel was. Good apples were selected by feel, and slightly soft ones were dropped in a basket to be used for sauce.

Once, as children often did, I accidentally set my long hair alight from candle flame. I was quickly dunked under the cistern pump in the sink where gushes of cold cellar-smelling water extinguished me. We were not afraid of fire, but we were always aware of its possibility. We early learned that a blazing lamp must either be smothered or quickly thrown outdoors, or both. We were told of an uncle's bravery in snatching a burning lamp from the midst of a family gathering with his bare hands and running with it to the door where he tossed it into the snow. We had few accidents; the most common was breaking a lamp chimney during the washing and polishing process. My mother once cut a vein doing this and fainted—blood and glass all over the table—to the terror of us all.

In my father's Toronto home we kept coal oil and candles on hand, but we used gas for our lighting. At five o'clock in the winter, the halls, dining room, sitting room, kitchens and most of the bedrooms were lit. The double parlour remained dark, however, unless company was coming. I loved to watch the ritual when the long tapers were taken out of the red and gold box in the pantry, lit with a kitchen match, and taken through the house to light the gas. On company nights there was the most exciting illumination of all. The whole of the back parlour (from which a door opened on a small conservatory) was lit by gas candles fixed at regular intervals to a cornice a foot or so below the ceiling. Each side of the room had its own gas tap in a little door in the wall. These were turned on, then candle after candle was lit by the long taper until the whole ceiling was dancing with the reflection of tiny flames. The front parlour had a fixture with several etched glass globes over gas mantles, and a cool white light seemed to flow from it into the grey-green room, to be reflected with soft beauty in the mantel mirrors.

All bedrooms but the "best" one had ordinary gas jets emitting a blue and yellow forked flame. The long shadowy corridor that led to the bathroom was full of mystery, and the low-turned gas jet in the bathroom where we children washed our hands before dinner lent a ghostly quality to the faces reflected in the mirror above the basin. We were reluctant to turn up the gas for fear it would not turn down again without going out, leaving us blind in the darkness of the big bathroom.

The hissing (sometimes delicate, sometimes shrill) and the popping of the gas jets we took for granted, but my grandmother remarked how much more peaceable it had been with coal oil.

We accepted the lack of uniform light, as we accepted the lack of overall heat. We were aware of light, and we valued it. We were unutterably cosy as we sat round a single kerosene lamp doing homework, shading our eyes from what then seemed like a glare. We accommodated ourselves to the lack of light by habits and behaviour which have now completely gone.

This is the ordinary glass kerosene lamp used everywhere from the 1860s. It varied little in shape and size but, according to design and colour, was priced anywhere from 50¢ to $3.50.

169

Children's furniture & playthings

The first children of the wilderness—all those little Janes, Marys, Tabithas and Phoebes; the Johns, Thomases and Henrys whose names appear on the baptismal records and gravestones of the Loyalists—are without biographers. Theirs was a hard life: cold and hunger, heat and swamp malaria threatened their very existence. The freedom of their childhood was short, perhaps five or seven years, and then the small tasks of pioneering descended on their shoulders. We can imagine what playthings they had: dolls made from cornhusks, chestnuts and rags; pebble marbles; acorn dolls' cups and saucers. Rhymes and stories told by the fireside were their literature.

Very rarely was special furniture allotted to the children. They huddled together in makeshift beds and sat with their parents on benches or stumps. The earliest children's furnishings found today are homemade cradles, high and low chairs and the small footstools which were used for seats. And as these pieces remained very much the same for many years, it is difficult to date them.

Although furniture for children was rarely advertised in the early days, just after 1830 advertisements begin to appear in the newspapers for dolls and toys. Cecil Mortimer, who owned a fancy goods store in Hallowell (now Picton) advertised in 1836 that he sold "Lead toys, Marbles, Musical workmen, Dogs, Rabbits, Squirrels, Dolls, Jews harps, Tumblers, Boats, Horses, Chairs, Whips, and Noah's Arks." He also sold children's books, including a beautifully produced book, *Juvenile Forget-Me-Not* published by Ackermann in London. Perhaps some of these were bought for little Ann Macaulay when she stayed with her aunt and uncle in Picton—a visit recorded in her father's letters which also tell us that she "loved jujubes," and that she was beginning to speak with "quite a Toronto accent." In most journals and letters the interests and pleasures of the young are ignored; only their harrowing illnesses and deaths are described. But Ann Macaulay emerges from her family's unpublished letters as an alternately happy and naughty child, and always as a beloved one.

A homemade child's chair. It was crafted in Glengarry County about the year 1820. / U.C.V.

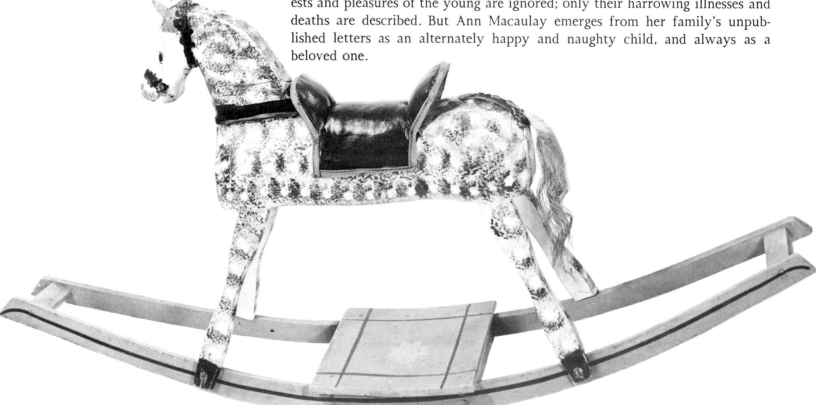

In *My Boy Life*, the story of his childhood, the Reverend John Carroll gives us a vivid child's-eye view of the burning of Newark in 1813. But this account is exceptional. Most men who have written reminiscences of a childhood in Upper Canada simply say over and over again how much more obedient, self-reliant, content and happy were the children of earlier generations—homilies which are still being repeated.

Through the first fifty years of the nineteenth century, children were often subjected to methods of training and treatment which had been carried over from earlier times. Babies were still being fed with the ancient cowhorn nursing bottle. (The glass bottle with long tube and nipple did not become standard until about 1860.) Boys and girls were still dressed like their elders. They continued to wear charms to protect them from harm. (The seventeenth-century custom of giving children coral objects to ensure that the wearer would not be replaced by a changeling was particularly persistent. I myself wore a coral necklace and some children had coral rattles or bracelets.) When children became ill they were subjected to traditional "cures" that must sometimes have killed. And their minor ailments were often alleviated by old practices which were still current when I was a child. For example, wedding rings were rubbed on sties, and raw potatoes on warts.

The almanacs were consulted before a baby was weaned. No baby was ever weaned under the sign of Aries, Gemini or Taurus, but usually under Virgo or Libra. Otherwise his health would be in jeopardy. Great attention was paid to those babies born with a caul, and I remember looking with awe at a girl in my school who was pointed out to me as having had this astonishing distinction.

A child's first piece of furniture was a cradle. The number of early cradles still stored in homes all over Ontario is surprising even when one makes allowance for the fact that it would have taken a desperate need for wood or storage space to make a man chop up the cradle of his ancestors. The style of the cradles varied so little, from the early eighteenth to the mid-nineteenth century, that it is difficult to know just how early are the ancient-looking cradles that one sees today.

There were two kinds of cradles. The earliest but most persistent style was the rocking cradle which stood on the floor. Less common was the swinging cradle, suspended from posts, a style which was being made by as great a cabinetmaker as Sheraton in the eighteenth century. Hooded cradles were also made in the eighteenth century but examples found today are not necessarily older than the plain cradles.

The style of cradle most commonly found in Ontario is a simple box on rockers, with the side boards slightly higher at the head. These were generally made of pine and were therefore light to carry. They were always painted. Small wooden knobs on the side were used to rope the baby in. Other surviving cradles have posts with turned finials at the four corners, a style reminiscent of European cradles. There are also more elaborate cradles, made in maple, cherry and walnut, which show an amazing variation in detail.

Highchairs like this one dating from about 1860 were made and sold almost everywhere. / U.C.V.

Rocking horses, favourite playthings of the nineteenth century, were often made at home but handsome ones, like that shown here, were bought. / Mr. and Mrs. Esmond Butler, Ottawa

This walnut cradle with knobs for tying the baby in at one time belonged to the Bethune family in Dundas. / Dundas Historical Museum

Doll, 24″ tall, brought from England in the 1840s. Its head is wax over papier-mâché and it has brown eyes and brown human hair. The body is hand-sewn and the hands are kid. / Mrs. Roger Greig, Cherry Valley, Ontario

Kaleidoscope viewer containing prisms and bits of coloured glass. When a handle was turned many patterns were formed. / U.C.V.

There were very few non-rocking cribs in the early days. When children left the cradle they slept with their parents or with other children.

Short benches and stools were made for children to use by the fireside. No nineteenth-century book describing children in the home fails to say somewhere, "He seated himself on the stool." This was an attitude of proper respect for the elders. Later stools were often beautifully fashioned and upholstered and one can easily imagine a child coming to love a particular stool as his very own. My grandparents were old-fashioned people and followed the practice of only putting young children to bed when they themselves retired. So I shared with the children of early Upper Canada the experience of sitting on a stool, leaning my head against a comfortable knee, or curling up to sleep on the hearth rug.

Children's chairs were made by chairmakers from an early date. Little ladder-backed chairs with bark seats—with and without arms—were made in the style of larger chairs. Windsor chairs for children were apparently made, but are not often found today. And highchairs of simple style were produced by chairmakers, although the majority of early highchairs that remain are obviously homemade, of hickory, ash or pine.

Children's chairs of the 1840s and '50s were miniatures of the current fashions. We find the popular low-backed late Windsor (often called a captain's chair), complete with paint and decoration; the charming vase-splat with upholstered seat; and the caned rocker—all good chairs of the period and very appealing in these small versions.

Mugs and plates were more usual than toys as gifts for children, and some of those that survive are very early. Name mugs with early dates (before 1820) are usually of fine English porcelain. Many of them are Leeds and Bristol ware and must necessarily have been brought with settlers or sent by Old-Country relatives. Many mugs had both of the child's names, the date of his birth and occasionally the place. Sometimes the inscription would read, "A Present for John," or "A Trifle for Sarah," the words enclosed in beautifully executed painting of leaves in wreaths or garlands. Some of the most attractive of these had a canary-coloured background, with the name in comparatively large letters in silver resist.

Earthenware mugs with transfer-print designs, overpainted in colour and imported from England, were stocked in stores from the 1830s. A little later heavy-based white porcelain name mugs, trimmed with bright gilt, were imported from England, France or Germany. The mugs were produced with a great variety of names, to afford a wide selection. By about 1850 there were local china painters who supplied both names and dates to unlettered mugs.

There once was at least one mug in every farmhouse and they are frequently found today, particularly small earthenware mugs. I have seen dozens of these, made about mid-nineteenth century, but never two alike. There are name mugs and mugs with verses both tender and moral. (The poetry of Ann and Jane Taylor, Benjamin Franklin's Maxims and two series, "The Months" and "The Seasons," were popular.) Mugs showing children skipping rope, fishing, rolling hoops, playing blindman's buff, battledore and shuttlecock, as well as those depicting children at prayers are to be found. Some mugs were lettered as awards for "learning" or "sewing well." Very few are marked with the maker's name, and their origin can only be determined by a good knowledge of the glazes, colours, designs and shapes characteristic of the various potters.

The custom of giving children plates as special presents also became popular. Most gift plates had embossed borders or rims, and rims of the Daisy pattern seem to have been the most common. The centres of the plates sometimes contained names or maxims or verses, but often had cheap but fascinating little transfer-prints of children's activities. Later plates depicted practical jokes and such childish crimes as jam stealing or tying a cat's tail. Other plates pictured cats, dogs and monkeys performing human acts such as drinking tea or sitting in school. Illustrations from *Uncle Tom's Cabin* were a popular subject of the mid-century. Some plates had moulded A.B.C. borders and injunctions to learn in the centres. Unlike the mugs, many plates are marked and show that they were made by J. & G. Meakin, William Adams, H. Aynsley and Co., Ralph Stevenson, Elsmore and Forster, and others.

The first, and in some cases the only, manufactured toys that Ontario children saw in early days were those carried in the pedlar's pack. These are known to have been "Dutch" wooden dolls, skipping ropes, tops, jews'-harps, glass marbles and chapbooks with woodcut illustrations. All these toys and many more were carried as well in small and large shops in villages and towns. By the 1830s store stocks of toys were quite extensive. Horace Billings and Company advertised French and German toys in Brockville in 1831. By 1850 the choice was enormous. Dolls, dolls' carriages and dishes, dolls' houses and furniture, jack-in-the-boxes, whips, Noah's Arks, marbles, hoops, rocking horses and hobby horses, sleds and carts, drums, games of all kinds, blocks, whistles, toy soldiers, pull and squeak toys, musical toys, toy theatres, jigsaw puzzles. Yo-Yos (which date from the eighteenth century), mechanical and musical toys, rattles of carved bone, ivory, wood, silver and coral—all were advertised. Brunton's of London, Ontario advertised in December, 1865: "Dolls, Toy tea sets, work boxes, Punch and Judy, Children's knives and forks, wagons, beads, musical toys, jumping jacks, etc."

Most of these toys came from European factories. Many were made in England but there was a good sprinkling of toys from the Continent as well. American toy factories did not produce much before 1875, and the first Ontario toy maker I have found mentioned was Morris Lintner who made rocking horses in Berlin (Kitchener) in 1871.

Portrait of the granddaughter of James Baby the fur trader—Mary Eliza, born 1835. She is wearing a lucky coral necklace, as did many children. / Black Creek Pioneer Village

Marbles, that universal game, has always been part of every boy's and girl's playtime in Ontario. (A Western Ontario name for marbles is "miggles," and there are other local names, most of them reflecting English or Scottish colloquialisms.) The early marbles were of unevenly shaped clay but some of the later ones, of agate, sulphides, jasper, carnelian and onyx, were very beautiful. Agates were the most highly prized of all. The large alleys, of glass with coloured veins, are often collected today. The game of jacks was originally played with marbles before the little pronged metal "jacks" were available.

Children in early portraits are often shown holding a pull-toy, a top, a whip, a doll or drumsticks, as well as the usual book or orange, posy or pet bird. We also know from early paintings that "playing horse" was a favourite game, and little sets of reins were sold for this. The hobby-horse (which is now so seldom seen that it may be necessary to say that it is a horse's head on a long cane which the child pretends to ride by holding it between his legs) is one of the oldest toys in the western world. Many a father made a hobby-horse or a primitive rocking horse for his child. The manufactured rocking horse had enormously long rockers or was suspended in a frame which allowed it to bounce as well as rock. Even in my childhood there were awe-inspiring rocking horses. They had real pony skin and manes, rich saddles, wide-open eyes and snorting nostrils. The more expensive of the nineteenth-century rocking horses were really works of art. There were also little horses, mounted on wooden platforms and with wooden wheels, which vied with lambs, dogs, cows and even tigers for popularity. They were for little children to pull along the floor and often made uncomfortable bed companions for those who loved them so dearly that they could not be parted with them for an instant.

A homemade doll with a nut head, dating from c. 1850, wearing the original clothes. / U.C.V.

Noah's Arks, usually of German origin, always made of wood and with a folding-back or lifting roof, were sometimes so simple that the animals were nothing more than blocks, sometimes so elaborate that there were hundreds

173

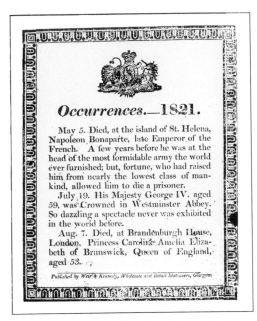

School copybook used by the Farlinger family children, Dundas County, before 1825. / U.C.V.

Jointed wooden doll, called a penny wood in America and a Dutch doll in England. They were available everywhere from 1820 and were often included in a pedlar's wares. / U.C.V.

of carved and painted figures. Noah and Mrs. Noah were always round but the animals were flat. In my childhood it was still a Sunday game, allowable when all boisterousness had been shut down for the day.

Toy soldiers of wood, cardboard, paper and lead, now rare collectors' items, were once so common that damaged ones were very frequently tossed out and new ones bought. They were too uniform in size and make to be treasured and kept.

Dolls' furniture and dishes, on the other hand, seem to have been favourite things to put away in a box for the next generation. The best of the early sets of dishes we see here were transfer-printed Staffordshire, imported from England. Small ewers and wash basins were also sold. Most early dolls' furniture consisted of cradles and chairs, and of course, wagons and sleighs. The few little chests of drawers that survive are usually 1840 or later, and are much valued today.

Dolls' houses, which were called baby-houses till about 1850, were not common, but those we do see are invaluable, as they indicate the kind of rooms and furniture which were considered "ordinary" at the period when they were made.

Benjamin Pollock's toy theatres were imported into Canada but were apparently never as widely sold here as they were in England. A beautiful example which belonged to a Canadian family is in Upper Canada Village.

Jigsaw puzzles were a favourite pastime in late eighteenth-century England and are sometimes found in Ontario, in their common dissected map form. One of the most delightful I have seen is located at Pioneer Village and is called "A New Dissected Map of the United States of North America." The map includes Upper and Lower Canada, New Brunswick, James Bay and Lake Winnipeg. The bottom of the box is inscribed, "Presented to Miss Mary Ann Barker as an encouragement to her in her learning, by her friend D. L. Fairfield, Hallowell [Picton] 1st August, 1832."

A game called Conversation Cards was sold in a little packet in the 1830s, and the popular card game known as Dr. Busby was introduced in 1843. I learned to play Happy Families with a set of cards which was worn and marked by the small fingers of two generations of children before me. Parchesi, advertised as "The Royal game of India," was first put on the market in 1867.

In no century has the cult of the child's doll been so widespread as in the nineteenth. Then the art of doll-making was at its zenith. The rag doll, the easiest and cheapest to produce, was not made commercially until late in the century, but most little girls owned one, made by mother or grandmother. It had a painted face, wool hair, and clothes that matched those of the grown-up female members of the family. Dolls, like children, were dressed as miniature adults.

There were wooden dolls with jointed arms and legs, faces and necks painted white, a blob of red on their cheeks, a tiny pointed piece of wood for a nose. These were called Penny Woods and Peg Dolls in America, and Flanders Babies or Dutch Dolls in England. Their style has never varied. They were first made in Germany but the craft spread to Holland.

Dolls with papier-mâché heads were imported into America early in the nineteenth century. They were made with kid or linen or sometimes canvas bodies, and were stuffed with sawdust. Their arms and legs were of wood and stuck out stiffly. These were followed by dolls with china heads from Austria and Germany and dolls with wax heads from England, but the dolls with papier-mâché heads were popular for a long time. The first papier-mâché doll patent applied for in America was taken out by Ludwig Grenier in 1858.

The production of dolls in factories greatly reduced prices. Most manufactured dolls were, for some time, a luxury that few families could afford, however. Factory-made dolls were sold both with and without clothes. The china-headed ones came from Germany, some with white, some with tinted faces. It is only by knowing the hair styles and other fashion details that dolls in this period can be accurately dated. Heelless ankle boots were in fashion from 1815 to 1840, and linen pantelettes from 1818 to 1858. Hair was usually black. Until the young Queen Victoria captured the public imagination, most dolls' eyes were brown; they then became predominantly blue. The little flat dolls on strings and the puppet-like dolls on a stick were sold everywhere for pennies.

Dolls and dolls' heads of rubber were made and patented by Goodyear in 1851 in America. They were sold in Toronto in the same year by J. W. Skelton who also sold wax and kid dolls. Rubber dolls were made in England in 1859.

Children's paper dolls of the nineteenth century were, and are, very charming. *Godey's Lady's Book* in 1859 included a series of paper doll cut-outs, and there were some lovely little sheets of "Jenny Lind" (with ten costumes) which were sold in the United States in 1850 and were probably also available here.

From time to time I have seen old birdcages which bear witness to the fact that at one time a pet bird was part of every family's life. Sparrows were caught and tamed and lived in little wooden cages which hung on the wall or in the window. Crows were coaxed to stay around the doorway and became so familiar that eyeglasses and trinkets sometimes disappeared in their beaks, never to be seen again. Caged birds, such as canaries and finches, could be bought. And parrots were treasured family pets. There was one called Polly (as they almost all were) in the house of my great-uncle at Redners-ville when I was a child. He was let out of his cage during the day and perched around the summer kitchen from which he waddled down the lane to bring the men to noon dinner calling, "Dinner's ready, Dinner's ready!" My grandmother had known him in her youth and he lived long enough for my own daughter to feed him crackers. Everyone in the family was written to when he died, for they had all known and loved him. At Canadian farm-house sales birdcages like little houses (many of them resembling cages seen in European paintings of the eighteenth century) and empty parrot cages are mute reminders of the days when a bird was one of the most important pets in a child's life. Cats and dogs worked for their living but birds were pure entertainers.

A few fancy goods stores listed toys for sale in the month of December but there was no special emphasis on them as gifts for the holidays. Only the family exchanged gifts and they were never wrapped in fancy trimmings. Mittens and stockings were the common presents for children, as well as skates and sleds, but other items were also advertised: dolls and rocking horses, and—Oh, delight—"miniature violins and guitars of painted tin." The Christmas tree is said to have been introduced into Canada in 1855, and the *Montreal Witness* mentioned Santa Claus in a story of the Christmas season in 1857. The early Christmas tree was trimmed with lozenges, fruit drops in the shapes of strawberries, grapes, apples, pears, lemons and raspberries. There were also little baskets of sugared almonds, rings of coloured barley sugar and fancy cakes hanging on coloured ribbons.

Daguerreotypes of the 1840s and '50s, and small photographs of the '60s have preserved for us the tiny faces which once enjoyed these treats. They are solemn-looking children. The length of time necessary to expose a photographic plate wiped the smiles from their faces and induced a serious demeanour. Even their painted portraits show them as staid and rather important-looking. The laughter and the mischief that must have been there have disappeared beyond memory, but something of their early Canadian childhoods comes back to us when we look at the cradles and highchairs and dolls and hobby-horses which have so long survived them.

Hand-coloured pictures illustrated an 1820s children's story which was sold in a little case. / Mr. and Mrs. Leslie Donaldson, Galt

Child's chair in its original coral red paint with black decorations. Made c. 1860. / U.C.V.

Mugs for children have always been favourite gifts but few have survived as long as this little English porcelain one with the owner's name and birthdate in purple and blue. Behind it is a typical gift plate of the 1840s with a scene in vivid colours. / Author's coll.

175

The homemade chair in Upper Canada was the same in structure and appearance as those made throughout Western Europe and America in the eighteenth and nineteenth centuries. This one is in Upper Canada Village, Ont.

Chairmaking

Eastern Ontario ladder-back chair showing the French influence. It has a woven splint seat. Such chairs were made from about 1830. / U.C.V.

Homemade chairs are the same the world over. Whether they were made in fourteenth-century Europe, seventeenth-century America or early Canada, they all look alike. They have posts and stretchers roughly squared, whittled horizontal spindles and woven seats. They represent the simplest method of chairmaking and any handyman could, and can, produce them. Every once in a while a homemade chair is discovered in a woodshed or an antique dealer's store, but because it so closely resembles every other homemade chair, it is very difficult to be sure of its date or origin.

In Upper Canada such chairs were made, from any suitable wood that came to hand, because they were needed and because there was either no money to buy other chairs or no other chairs available to buy. They were usually rather rickety and uncomfortable, although a slight improvement over the backless bench.

Once I called on some people who lived in Glengarry County in one of the oldest houses I have ever seen, built to be reached by river and not by road. Its new owners had been breaking and burning the contents of attics and woodsheds in an effort to clean up. There I saw the broken pieces of at least a dozen homemade chairs, and managed to retrieve two small baby chairs from the woodpile. The wreckage of enough primitive furniture to fill the house was heaped in the yard. Only once before had I seen actual evidence of the fact that a house had at one time been completely furnished with homemade furniture. That was on an isolated farm in Dundas County, where a large proportion of the furniture had been made by hand in the period styles of 1840-50.

Although few pieces are left today, furniture was homemade everywhere in Ontario in the first fifty years of the nineteenth century. Handymen even made crude adaptations of Windsor and ladder-back chairs and occasionally the results of their work are found today. They are neither particularly good-looking nor important as pieces of furniture, but they are interesting and they help us to appreciate the skill and inventiveness with which the pioneers made what they required.

The English Windsor chair, which came into use as a common piece of furniture following the heavier wainscot styles, was a provincial chair which started its long period of popularity at the beginning of the eighteenth century. Windsors had spindle backs, and most of them had splayed legs braced with stretchers. There was a great variation in these chairs, however, and some English Windsors were made with a cabriole leg that ended in a Dutch foot. During the mid-eighteenth century a Windsor with a shaped and pierced back-splat as well as spindles was introduced.

Ladder-back chair with bold finials. It was made in Prince Edward County and is still in use there. / Mr. & Mrs. R. Greig, Cherry Valley

Windsor chairs were chiefly used in cottages, farmhouses, inns and kitchens, though they are sometimes seen in old paintings as outdoor chairs in relation to a fine house.

The first American Windsors date from about 1725. They were low-backed and heavy, and were called Philadelphia chairs, since they were first made in that city. There were other styles of American Windsors, however; from the mid-eighteenth century there were men who called themselves Windsor chairmakers who made no other type of chair. They developed nine

177

major shapes of Windsor and, though there are some inevitable variations in details, it is still possible to classify the old chairs found today both geographically and in relation to these original styles.

Where the English used elm, ash and yew to make Windsors, the Americans chose maple, birch or beech for the legs, arms and stretchers; hickory, ash or beech for hoops and bows; and pine, whitewood or basswood for seats. The chairs were put together with pegged mortise-and-tenon, or socket, joints. They were both sturdy and attractive, and were used in all rooms of the house. They were also the common chair of the inns and meeting places.

The high-backed American Windsors that emerged in the eighteenth century were the most comfortable chairs available. This was due to the resilient rod-back, saddle-shaped solid wood seat, and sturdy legs. The best of these chairs were not only practical but were also among the most graceful in the world. Thousands were made, with enormous variance in the details of their design. But the finest surviving examples are traditional and can be recognized by anyone.

Windsor chairs, along with ladder- or slat-back chairs, were the first to be made by trained artisans in Upper Canada. There were chairmakers among the earliest settlers and immigrants. And seasonally, particularly on the Niagara frontier and the Upper St. Lawrence shore, chairmakers came across the border, men who had learned their craft in the United States or even in England. Apprenticeship as a maker of spinning wheels had often served to prepare them for chairmaking. There were apparently a great number of men who made *only* chairs (predominantly Windsors and slat-backs), but with the traditional coffin-making and funeral-conducting as an adjunct.

The American Windsor was the prototype of the Windsor made in Canada. Examples of some of the recognized American styles found in Ontario differ in no detail from those made in the States. The American styles with which early Canadian Windsors can be related are: low-back, comb-back, bow-back, arch-back, fan-back and loop-back.

Canadian Windsors were constructed in the same way as the American. They were always made with solid wood seats from 1¾" to 2¼" thick, and there was almost always some attempt at saddling or body shaping. The H-stretcher was present in all early chairs but the brace-back was rare in Ontario.

To some extent, the original Windsor shapes lost their satisfactory proportions with the introduction of simplified "Sheraton," or rod-back forms, and the use of bamboo turnings as embellishments. Chairs in this style appeared as early as 1820 and were very popular in the 1830s. Many are found in Canada and are greatly liked by today's antique collectors. They seem to be a link between the Windsor and the fancy chair, in that many of them were painted and decorated.

At the same time a development occurred which brought us one of the most charming of chairs—the arrow-back Windsor. The arrows, used as spindles, were also borrowed from the designs of Sheraton and his contemporaries. The quality of an arrow-back chair depends so much on the ability of the chairmaker to give the right cant to the legs and the right spring to the arrows that one finds great variations in individual examples. Many arrow-backs were painted red or black over red, but others were promoted into the class of fancy chairs by the addition of stencilling and striping in coloured and metallic paints. Arrow-backs were also made as rockers, with and without arms. (Some early Windsors and rod-back Windsors are also found with rockers, but the rockers have almost always been added later, usually very close to the stretchers, showing that the legs have been shortened to receive them.)

All research as to the types of Windsor chairs made in Upper Canada depends on the chairs that are found and the very few advertisements which

Delicate Windsor chair in a style common 1825-1840. It was first painted a dark red. / U.C.V.

Arch-back Windsor chair, 1785-1820, with characteristic stretchers. / U.C.V.

name the styles offered. The only contemporary illustrations seen are conventional American woodcuts used as trademarks in chairmakers' advertisements.

Daniel Tiers of York, advertising in 1802, specifically mentioned fan-back and brace-back chairs. He also stated that he was expecting a shipment of "Common Chairs from below." (These were probably ladder-back chairs from Lower Canada.) In 1817 Chester Hatch of Kingston advertised that he made "Windsor bamboo chairs" (a comparatively late development of the Windsor) and "slat-back chairs." Undoubtedly there were many other early chairmakers who produced Windsors and slat-backs but who did not take the trouble to advertise in their local newspapers.

The fact that the Windsor was still popular in the 1830s, and after, is also indicated by advertisements. H. Billings & Co., Brockville, announced in 1832 that they had "received for sale several dozen Windsor chairs, first quality, assorted pattern." W. Curtis & Co., also of Brockville, advertised in 1834: "Windsor chairs of a superfine quality kept constantly on hand." Thomas Bain was still making Windsor chairs in Hamilton in 1850, as well as "Grecian, French, and Fancy chairs."

Most early inventories list Windsor chairs. The one drawn up at the death of John Walden Myers in Belleville in 1821 included ten Windsors valued at £2.10s. Daniel Haight's auction sale at Adolphustown in 1829 listed six Windsors at 45s. the lot. When Andrew Hurd took inventory at Augusta in

From left: Bow-back Windsor chair, c. 1800,
originally painted a light blue. / U.C.V.
Armchair in bow-back style, 1770-1820. / U.C.V.
Late low-back Windsor chair, 1840-80. / Mr.
and Mrs. Blake McKendry, Sharbot Lake, Ontario
Arrow-back Windsor armchair. Versions of this
comfortable chair were made from 1825 to 1865. /
Mr. & Mrs. L. Donaldson, Galt, Ontario

1839 he listed six Windsor chairs valued at 3s.9d. each. All inventories differentiate between Windsors and what are called common or kitchen chairs, which are presumed to be ladder- or slat-back chairs in some variation.

We have other evidence of the prevalence and value of Windsor chairs. Robert Maitland Roy of Chippewa lost six black Windsor chairs valued at $5 during the Rebellion of 1837. Joseph Pickering in his *Inquiries of an Immigrant*, published in 1832, said that common chairs cost "a quarter dollar each" and painted Windsors "two dollars each." In 1846 Robert Smith of Chatham advertised that he sold "good Windsor chairs per set from $3.00 to $3.50," and added: "They are of my own manufacture, not imported from Detroit."

Generally speaking, the early Windsors found here are of good design and fine construction and it was not until the middle of the nineteenth century that delicacy ended and coarse, heavy and sometimes ungainly Windsors appeared. The early chairs were usually painted green or black but chairs painted blue-grey, yellow-ochre, sand or red have been seen.

English-style Windsor chairs are not found in Ontario farmhouses, though at least two travellers to the Canadas mention having seen "common English chairs" arriving with immigrants at an early date. (They point out the folly of their having been brought to a country where such good and cheap chairs were to be had.) Very few of these chairs appear to have survived, however, and they were not copied here. There must have been English artisan immigrants accustomed to making the very best kind of Windsor chair, as good as those made at High Wycombe. But if they produced any of them here they have all disappeared. A few Windsor chairs in the somewhat rustic English style with typical pierced splat and rods in the back were brought in as settlers' effects in the later years of the nineteenth century, but have never been very popular here, even as antiques, and they certainly had no place in the farm home. Almost as rare are the American writing-arm Windsors, a thoroughly practical style which in Canada only appeared in its last evolution, as the quick-lunch or classroom chair. The early low-backed Philadelphia style of Windsor was probably not made here.

All types of early Canadian Windsor chairs were used by all classes of people in Upper Canada. For most people they were an acceptable chair for any room in the house; for the rich they provided kitchen and bedroom chairs of unexcelled practicality. The old Windsors found today are still strong and beautiful.

Slat-backs were made in Europe from the end of the fifteenth century and in England from the beginning of the seventeenth. They are frequently to be seen in European and English paintings and engraved illustrations from the eighteenth century on. Slat-backs in simple styles were used everywhere in the English countryside. Fine houses had sophisticated versions, with arched slats (carved and pierced), turned posts and legs, and rush seats.

The American and Canadian slat-backs are based on the English design rather than the European. Elaborate examples were made in the United States, though the designs there differed recognizably from the English. Definitely shaped slats and ring-ball-and-vase turnings on posts and legs were not uncommon. Such chairs are not to be found in Ontario, however; by the beginning of the nineteenth century, when the slat-back was commonly made here, it had been much simplified. (Only in counties near the Quebec border does one find shaped-slat chairs and these derived their design from French-Canadian styles.)

Slat-back chairs were the common chairs of Upper Canada for the first fifty years of the nineteenth century. They were produced in great quantities and sold, generally in sets of six or twelve, at about fifty cents apiece. Usually they were made of hickory or maple, though birch, beech and ash were also employed.

The materials used for seats depended on the locality in which the chairs were made. Wood splint and elm bark were most frequently used but rush was also used to some extent. The splints were narrow strips of wood pounded when wet and separated into layers to be woven, basket-fashion. They often showed a wood grain. Elm bark strips (usually wider than splints) were cut in spring, stripped, soaked, pounded, and then woven in the same way as the splint seats. Both materials had a certain resilience. Elm bark had the advantage of being handsome. It looked like leather (it was a warm brown colour) and responded, to a certain extent, to oiling, as leather does. Sometimes elm bark was twisted into a rope and then laced on the seats.

Indian people were expert at making chair seats and were frequently employed for this purpose. When replacements are required for elm bark seats today they are usually made by Indians.

Slat-back chairs were of mortise-and-tenon construction. There were from three to six horizontal slats, usually made of green wood which swelled to a tight fit, locking the tenons into the mortise holes. The extraordinary durability of these chairs is proven by the fact that one can still tilt back in a century-old ladder-back without loosening its joints. They were always painted, which concealed the diversity of woods used, and they were usually red or green. The Eastern Ontario version, which borrowed the shape of its slats from Quebec chairs, was most frequently painted blue or grey.

The earliest of slat-back chairs have well-shaped finials on the back posts

Opposite page: The earliest houses almost invariably contained a comfortable comb-back Windsor with slanted back, whether well made, as the one on the left or more crudely put together, as that on the right. Shadowy in the background is the common all-purpose chair that succeeded them. / Upper Canada Village

The early rod-back chair, serviceable and cheap, became the prototype for most kitchen chairs produced throughout the 1800s. / U.C.V.

Empire-style chairs, all with vase-splats,
c. 1835-55. Left: a maple parlour chair.
Right: a maple side chair, one of a set of
nine. Lower: late kitchen chair. / All U.C.V.

in a great variety of shapes. Occasionally a flattened mushroom shape is used and repeated as a hand rest on the arms. Later chairs show a vestigial point at the top of the back post. Slat-back rockers are not unusual, but on some the rockers were added at a later date.

Ladder-back chairs made in American Shaker colonies were imported into Canada—to what extent it is not yet known. Some examples have been found, most of them made after 1850 when power machinery was introduced into Shaker workshops. Cheaply-made American chairs, both Windsor and slat-back, were probably always imported to some extent from the Northern United States, since shipping from that area was economical. However, the larger wholesalers in Montreal supplied many small dealers with cheap chairs of their own manufacture.

Around 1900 an oversized version of the ladder-back chair was made, both plain and with rockers, especially for verandah and garden use. Originally painted green, these chairs were used very extensively, and they still abound in the province. At the same time a vogue developed for high-backed and low-seated ladder-backs with turnings and slats done in American eighteenth-century style. These were often painted in combinations of vermilion and black (as were the early chairs they imitated), and they were referred to as Colonial chairs. They were used as hall chairs and occasionally

184

in dining rooms. Unfortunately, these late chairs often confuse the amateur collector because of their resemblance to earlier chairs.

The typical kitchen chair has rounded legs and posts (the back posts projecting above the top-rail), four or five round spindles in the back, and a thick wood seat. Such a chair was made as early as 1860 and has really only been supplanted in the last ten years by chairs of metal. A variation of this style is a chair with a cross-slat joined by spindles to the seat.

The low-backed, heavy, late Windsor chair, commonly called a captain's chair or barroom chair, was made as early as the 1840s. It had a continuous back-and-arm, shaped like a horse-collar. This was joined to the seat with seven (or eight, or nine) spindles, a single turning on each. The captain's chair was the last of the derivations to be made and sold under the name of Windsor. The early examples of it had pine seats and maple or birch legs, stretchers, arms and spindles. Later examples, dating from about 1880, employed other combinations of woods. Though all early captain's chairs were painted, some of the late ones were varnished.

The name "captain's chair" is much more generally used here than the American term "firehouse Windsor." It is certain, though, that the low-backed late Windsor, as we know it here, was used in firehouses as well as in lodge meeting rooms, bars, hotel sitting rooms and town halls. It probably also appeared at the head of every farm dining table in the country between 1850 and 1900.

By the mid-nineteenth century Ontario had a great many small chair factories, all turning out some late expressions of the original Windsors and slat-backs. These chairs were sold very cheaply in furniture and general stores everywhere. They were soundly made and are already beginning to be classified as antiques.

Armchair in Sheraton style, one of a dining set. / Mr. & Mrs. Blake McKendry, Sharbot Lake

While most simple early chairs were painted, those that were decorated and sold as "Fancy Chairs" contributed an unpretentious style which in gaiety and charm has never been surpassed in domestic furniture. Their enormous popularity and use extended through the first half of the nineteenth century. In that time they changed, in design, from adaptations of Sheraton styles to Empire to Victorian. The imagination and skill that went into the decoration of these chairs were rarely employed for other pieces of furniture.

Very few people in Canada are interested in, or collect, furniture which is simply painted in contrasting colours. Nor are they intrigued by the brilliantly or sombrely grained pieces which imitate fine woods. These are so much disregarded that even dealers often take a knife to the perfect surface of such furniture and scrape away the carefully applied graining, leaving a small exposed piece of basswood, ash or pine to encourage collectors of stripped furniture to buy. But they stop short in contemplating the decorated chair with its staggering variety of design, its bold use of colour, gilt and bronze, and its air of being a special, one-of-a-kind creation.

Painted chairs, with decoration visible and intact, are not common. They do exist, however, and chairs still bearing freehand designs or stencilled decoration are frequently found in Ontario. They appear so often, in fact, that one could wish for a province-wide stripping of late paint to bring about a resurrection of the colour and gaiety which these chairs added to the domestic scene from 1800 to 1850.

Some clues to the age of decorated chairs are found in the shape of the chair itself as well as in the style of ornamentation. Side chairs which were generally sold in sets of six or a dozen were considered the most suitable chairs for decoration. These included chairs with plain back-rails and shaped centre-rails; chairs with rows of narrow centre-rails joined by balls, spindles

Pillow-back chair in traditional style 1835-1850. / Mr. & Mrs. Homer Talcott, Bloomfield

or other devices; arrow-backs; pillow-backs; vase-splats; and Regency-style chairs. Ornamentation was also applied to Victorian side chairs with shaped back-rails and four or five spindles joining a lower cross-rail. They have no style name but survive by the thousands, their cane seats often now replaced with plywood or upholstering. They were the common cheap parlour or sitting-room chair of the late fifties and early sixties. Windsor armchairs and rockers, short and long benches, and rocker benches were also decorated, and most Boston-style rockers, whatever their finish today, once bore some form of decoration on their back-rails.

Like the fancy chairs made in New York and Baltimore, our best early fancy chairs show the influence of Sheraton and other English designers, and of the Directoire period in France. A chair with a design completely unrelated to American fancy chairs is very rarely seen in Ontario. The Sheraton type of fancy chair of 1800-20, most often found here, has a rush seat. Any cane-seated early chairs seen in Ontario seem to be rather more English than American, and are probably early imports, or "settler's effects." A solid wood seat was rarely used at this date.

The back-rails on the early chairs were generally narrow and were sometimes formed of two or three rungs, or two rungs connected by short, turned spindles. The centre-cross-rail was often composed of three slender horizontal rungs connected by balls or fret designs.

Legs were straight, with simple turnings; the back legs were slightly canted. The front stretcher was often flattened to take decoration, or had a

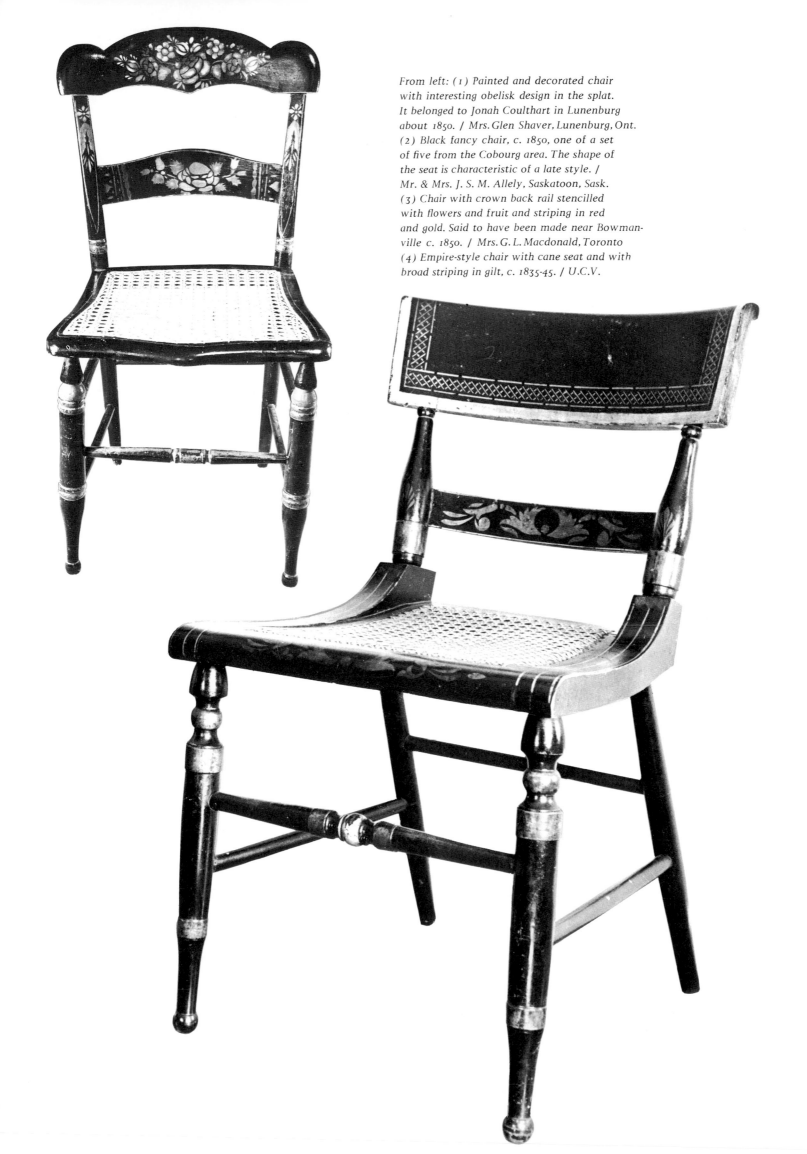

From left: (1) Painted and decorated chair with interesting obelisk design in the splat. It belonged to Jonah Coulthart in Lunenburg about 1850. / Mrs. Glen Shaver, Lunenburg, Ont. (2) Black fancy chair, c. 1850, one of a set of five from the Cobourg area. The shape of the seat is characteristic of a late style. / Mr. & Mrs. J. S. M. Allely, Saskatoon, Sask. (3) Chair with crown back rail stencilled with flowers and fruit and striping in red and gold. Said to have been made near Bowmanville c. 1850. / Mrs. G. L. Macdonald, Toronto (4) Empire-style chair with cane seat and with broad striping in gilt, c. 1835-45. / U.C.V.

round, oval or rectangular centrepiece for this purpose. Legs were sometimes reeded, and bamboo turnings throughout the frame were not uncommon. Some chairs had a controlled sweeping line of back posts, seat-rail, and slightly out-curved leg (which ended in a spade foot)—a shape very familiar as a Duncan Phyfe design.

The earliest decorated chairs found in Ontario were made for rich houses, and may have been imported from England or the United States. With one exception there seems to have been no advertising before 1820 by chairmakers claiming to be able to produce decorated chairs. The exception is an advertisement by C. Hatch & Co. in Kingston, in 1817. The stock of this "chair shop" is listed as:

Elegant broad top, fall back
Fancy, and Windsor Bamboo
Slat back
Fancy
Waterloo
Commen [*sic*]
Rocking, and Children's

Two chairs of a set of six made about 1815, with painted landscape on the back rails. Heirlooms of the Strange family of Kingston, they are identical with chairs in the Peabody Museum, Salem. / Miss Mildred Jones, Kingston

Professional painters like Greno and Sawyer in Kingston probably undertook chair decoration, however. They advertised in 1811 that they sold "fashionable chairs" and repaired and repainted old ones.

It is difficult to trace the history of decorated chairs in Ontario. Not all chairmakers advertised. Very few early fancy chairs found in Canada bear makers' names, places or dates. The chairs which do survive as possessions of old families are rarely accompanied by dated family histories of purchase and changing ownership. Consequently, the extent of their production here can only be conjectured.

The earliest background paints for fancy chairs were light; white, cream, oyster, pale blue and green, greyed blue and green, terra cotta and yellow ochre were usual. Early chairs with imitations of wood grains are sometimes seen. (They differ in appearance from later chairs with simulated mahogany and rosewood backgrounds, however. In the early chairs the imitation is more accurate and less stylized.) Most chairs imitating wood grains were brown, though occasionally they were black.

The first decoration began as painted imitation of inlay, ormolu and carving, and was usually done in gold leaf. The work was accomplished by

Left: Exceptionally well decorated chair from a set of six, c. 1825-30. Feathers, coronet and circles in bronze and colours are painted on a green background. It came from an old home in Belleville. / Upper Canada Village

Parlour chairs made around the year 1830. The simulated walnut background and decoration in gilt, imitating brass stringing, display a deliberate attempt to give the impression of a fine Regency chair. / Author's collection

189

Fancy chair, c. 1840—black with red and gilt rim and painted rush seat. It is now in the McFarland house. / Niagara Parks Com.

Fancy chair with elaborate stencil in bronze and colours over creamy yellow paint, c. 1835. It was formerly owned by the Ruttan family in Prince Edward County. / Marysburgh Museum

meticulous hand-painting and not by stencilling. There were swags, flowers, feathers, urns, wreaths, fruit and ribbons in the designs. The tiny balls which appeared between the cross-rails, and the ball-turnings on legs were usually gilded. Striping was often done with a "pencil" dipped in umber, Spanish brown or Venetian red.

By 1820, the rich man's "Fancies" had become, by popular demand, much cheaper and more generally available. Originally the price of these chairs was between $5 and $7 apiece, but the simplification of design, the use of some stencilling, and the larger sale for the chairs brought them down to $1 or $2. The making was no longer the exclusive work of the fashionable chairmakers and cabinetmakers. About 1825 the aggressive Lambert Hitchcock established a factory in Barkhamsted, Connecticut (which became Hitchcock-ville) and so began a mass production of his charming "Fancies," the vogue for which persisted for about twenty-five years. Hitchcock's name has become, for many, a synonym for fancy chairs.

Hitchcock made arrow-back and slat-back chairs in their traditional shapes, as well as rockers and bench rockers. His basic design for chairs and rockers was simple: a seat wider in front than back; turned, straight legs; a wide back-rail or pillow-back; a cross-rail wider or narrower than the top (both rails decorated). Back posts were simply a continuation of the legs. The front of the seats was usually finished with a flat rolled piece of wood bearing decoration or some gilt. The seats were at first made of rush, later of cane, and sometimes they were of solid wood.

In the period in which Hitchcock worked (1818-52), the art of stencilling, which he had employed from the first was developed, perfected, and degenerated.

The first product of Hitchcock's factory were chair parts. These were shipped all over the continent and some may have come here. His chairs are important to Canada, however, not because many are found here—they are not—but because they were undoubtedly the inspiration of most competent chairmakers in the United States and Upper Canada.

Other makers did not confine themselves to Hitchcock's chair designs, though. A cutout cross-rail in an enormous variety of shapes (of which the "turtle" was a popular design) began to be one of the chief attractions of the best period of the decorated chair. The vase-splat; the wide cross-rail with spindles relating it to the seat; and the back-rail with rounded shoulders and what looks like two large bites out of the bottom edge are all to be found. The manner of their graining, striping, stencilling and gilding varies so much that it is difficult to sort them into classes.

After 1820 the backgrounds of most fancy chairs were painted black. This was especially so for the most elaborately stencilled chairs, but some rockers and some very simply striped or lined chairs were finished in a greenish sand or ochre and striped in blues and reds and bright yellow. White chairs also occur. The black chairs were usually given a filler coat of whatever red earth pigment the chairmaker had on hand, and then were overpainted. Cheap chairs imitated the gold-leaf striping of the better ones with stripes of vivid yellow. On the earliest chairs, the turning on rung or post was gilded all the way around, but on later chairs it was only brushed on the surfaces immediately visible. This is one feature which is useful in dating chairs.

Graining in imitation of rosewood and mahogany was common and sometimes this was so boldly and attractively done that only a contrasting line at the turnings and at the edges of the back-rail was added for decoration. Further ornamentation would indeed have been gilding the lily. Most chairs were veined or grained when their black top coat was still tacky. This was done by drawing a brush or feather over the surface, revealing the red beneath. The effect was also sometimes achieved by stencilling.

Stencilled chairs. Left: chair with black background decorated in red, yellow and green with pink striping, c. 1835-45. Right above: one of a set of nicely shaped arrow-back chairs with fine original stencils in colours and gilt, Belleville, c. 1825-30. Right below: dark green armchair with yellow decoration and striping, c. 1825-30. / Upper Canada Village

Left to right: (1) Decorated rocker from Camden East in fine condition. It has black paint over red ground, yellow and green striping and rings; red, green and silver stencilling; silver feathers on arrows. / Dr. & Mrs. H. C. Burleigh, Bath (2) Painted rocker, c. 1840, with decoration in black and dark green on a yellow ground. / National Museum of Canada (3) Putty-coloured rocker trimmed in blue, yellow and red, c. 1840s, from the Napanee area. / Upper Canada Village (4) Decorated arrowback rocker, c. 1835, with ochre ground. There is brown decoration on the arrows; black, brown and blue decoration elsewhere. / Also National Museum of Canada

The stencilled designs found on back- and cross-rails of some surviving chairs are magnificent. Fruit and flowers and their containers—cornucopias, urns and baskets—are the most common, but painted landscapes also appear.

Fancy chairs were made in such an assortment of shapes and with such a variety of decoration that only a very interested observer can classify them by name of style or date.

Most fancy chairs of the 1820-40 period had one thing in common: they were graceful and delicate in shape. They looked fragile even when they were quite strongly made. Chairs in the so-called Empire or Late Empire shapes are exceptions to this rule. These chairs, which were made from about 1835 to 1840, have sturdy black frames and cane or wood seats. They are heavily gilded and the back-rails are often broadly outlined in gilt. In the United States they seem always to be referred to as Southern chairs but they are sometimes found in Canada. One of their chief characteristics is an upward curve from the seat-rail to the back posts, a feature which gives them a heavy look.

193

Good arrow-back side chair, c. 1820, which came from the Alpheus Jones house in Prescott. It has decoration, largely in green and black, on a yellow ground. / Canadian Gov't Exhib. Com.

Yellow side chair with black decoration, one of a set of four said to have been made at Merickville. / Canadian Industries Limited

Opposite page: The factory of G. P. Walter and Company, Bowmanville, in 1863, as it appeared in a periodical of the time. The chair was made at the Walter factory and the name of the manufacturer is impressed, as shown, on the back rail. / McMaster University Library

After 1840 the decoration on chairs was modified. The shape of the vase-splat chair which became popular about this time dictated new designs for the stencils. Gold leaf was used less often. Orange-red was commonly used, in combination with a somewhat diluted gold or silver. Chairs were often heavily grained, and were boldly stencilled and striped.

The decorating of chairs continued well into the mid-Victorian period. The tricks of the trade were simply adapted to changing shapes. A cheap chair, with an unshaped solid wood seat and with ordinary rods as spindles in the back, began to flood the market after 1850. Its style was that which has survived to our own day as the common kitchen chair—found everywhere until the advent of the chrome suite. These chairs were often stencilled in a comparatively crude manner, no attempt being made to create a harmonious arrangement. The stencilling was applied to back-rails without discrimination—merely to fill a space. They are the least desirable of all stencilled chairs.

The best fancy chairs of the mid-Victorian period were usually painted by hand in a romantic style of decoration similar to that found in the lush pictures then being painted on papier-mâché boxes and tea trays. It was a tender, allusive manner of painting and the shading of naturalistic flowers and leaves was very effectively done. This type of decoration was also applied to coffee and tea canisters, safes, sleighs, signs, coal hods, and almost everything that could be decorated. Sentiment rather than design was the keynote of the last period of furniture decoration.

Some rocking chairs were also decorated, particularly those of the Boston type. Rockers of the slat-back variety, that have simple decoration on back- and cross-rail, are usually especially attractive. Boston rockers were generally highly decorated, with flowers, fruit and landscape designs on the back-rails. A roll at the front of the seat was often decorated, and the turnings on legs, stretchers and spindles were striped with gilt or colour. The maple or cherry arms were left without paint, however, and have been polished by the hands and arms of several generations of owners—which gives the rocker an odd appearance.

Decorated rockers occur in various styles: slat-back, arrow-back, Windsor, and—a style that is occasionally found in Ontario—Pennsylvania German. The colours used as background paints were red, yellow, black, green and sand. All rockers were striped, and coarse graining in traditional or unusual techniques was common. Occasionally the impress of the end of a corncob was used to make a pattern. In other cases umber pigment was dissolved in vinegar and painted on a rocker which was then spotted all over with the marks of a roll of putty. (Red streaks were applied over black, and vice versa.) Because a rocker was for use and not for show, few are found today with all their decoration intact.

In my experience, almost every type of chair made for adults was at some time reproduced in a size suitable for children. Although I have seen a great number, I have found very few alike, except perhaps in the captain's chair shape. Children's chairs were not all made to order, as some people suppose; chairmakers offered them for sale in advertisements. A decorated chair made for a child is a rarity to be treasured.

In many homes fancy chairs were used in the parlour; in others they appeared in bedrooms and even in kitchens. They could be bought very cheaply, were sturdy in use, and gave colour and style to a room. The flickering light from candles and lamps caught glints from varnished colours accentuated with bronze and gilt. The fact that fancy chairs were not comfortable for relaxed sitting was unimportant to generations that believed sitting up straight was good for body and spirit.

BOWMANVILLE CABINET FACTORY.

THE Bowmanville cabinet factory is situated in the town of Bowmanville, county of Durham, and was started by the present proprietors about eighteen months since, and already ranks as one of the best in the Province. All kinds of cabinet furniture are made at the establishment, from the cheaper to the higher class.

The firm have been honored by making a large quantity of furniture for the residence of N. G. Reynolds, Esq., Trafalgar Castle, Whitby. As also the counters and fittings to the Ontario Banks in Toronto.

Their principle business however, is in the manufacture of cane-seat chairs, which have hitherto been imported in large quantities, from the United States; they make a greater variety of this class of goods than is made elsewhere in Canada, and fully compete with the American manufactures; their prices for this class of goods are as low as they are sold for in the United States, thereby saving the import duty of 20 per cent to the dealers who buy from this firm. There is on an average, seventy hands employed in this factory, a portion of whom are girls, who have been introduced to plait the cane in the chair seats and backs.

The girls work at their own houses, the work being sent out to them, and brought back when finished.

The proprietors themselves being practical working men, the works are carried on under their own immediate supervision, and the system

G. P. WALTER & CO.
Bowmanville, C.W.

of labour is such that all the hands employed work to advantage. In the chair department each man has his part to do; a chair having to pass through six different hands before being completed. In the three story building the wood work is done, the first floor being devoted to cutting out the stuff, &c., here are found planors, turning lathes, saws of various kinds, &c.

On the second floor the cabinet work is made. The third floor is used solely for making cane seat chairs; here a great variety of machinery is employed to great advantage, all of which is of the best description. All chairs before leaving this room are stamped with the name of the firm.

The machinery is driven by steam power, the rooms, dry house, glue pots, &c., being heated by the exhaust steam from the engine.

The two story building is used for finishing and chair painting. The other buildings are used as storehouse office, &c., &c.

By special arrangement with the Grand Trunk Railway Company, they are enabled to send their goods at a low rate of freight.

As we like to see our Canadian Manufactures encouraged we would recommend any furniture dealer about purchasing goods to try G. P. Walter & Co.

Cabinetmaking

The first Loyalists to reach Upper Canada came, for the most part, with empty hands. Their land and houses had been confiscated by the new American republic. Because their movable possessions would have complicated the hazardous journey, most of them had been divided among members of the family remaining in the States. Practical and resourceful families had brought tools rather than furniture.

Once established in a cabin on his lot, the Loyalist must have experienced some gratification in providing furniture for his family from trees felled in the work of clearing. He was an experienced hand with an axe and quite capable of making something useful out of whatever was at hand. From split basswood he made benches, tables and shelves. Stumps often provided seats, and spruce boughs served as beds.

Some Old-Country settlers brought their furniture with them at great inconvenience and expense, only to have it arrive half-broken, and to find that in any established centre they could have bought furniture quite cheaply. Many volumes of instruction and advice to immigrants were published and eagerly read, but the reiterated caution against bringing furniture from Britain was often ignored. A letter from "An Emigrant in Upper Canada to a Friend in Glasgow" published in London in 1818, said, "It will be unnecessary to bring chairs, bedsteads or tables," but advised the prospective immigrant to bring nails, hammers, handsaws and chisels. Robert Lamond in his *Narrative of the Rise and Progress of Emigration from the Counties of Lanark and Renfrew to the New Settlements in Upper Canada* (Glasgow, 1821) said:

> Complaints have been made in the most severe terms, of the very great trouble and expense thrown upon the government, and also, of the serious injury the settlers have done themselves, by bringing out large quantities of old and useless luggage. The government have estimated the expense of conveying them to the place of settlement at £2 per head, whereas, in consequence of this, it has actually cost £8; as they had been obliged to transport for them old and worm-eaten boxes and chests, and these mostly empty, together with old wash-tubs, and other articles of furniture which might be purchased for half the expense of transportation.

Settlers continued to bring their furniture, however. As late as 1832 George Henry was appalled at the waste this entailed. In *The Emigrant's Guide: or Canada As It Is*, while describing the beach at Toronto after the arrival of a steamship, he said:

> You will see, probably, a few old chairs not worth half a dollar each, which have been brought nearly, or quite, five thousand miles; with old bedsteads and other pieces of common furniture that could have been disposed of at home for nearly as much as the new articles would cost here, for wood is very cheap in most parts of the Province; very good common chairs quite new, are to be bought for four or five shillings each, and sometimes less; but the people at home imagine there are no persons here who can manufacture these kind of things.

Much of the furniture the Old-Country immigrants had found impossible to leave behind did not survive the sea voyage and the journey by open cart over remote roads that were rutted and mired. So these settlers too were forced to replace their essential furniture with pieces made by their own hands. Much less experienced in make-do carpentry than the settlers from the American colonies and equipped with inadequate tools, they nevertheless

Opposite page: A cabinetmaking shop typical of those once found in every village. / U.C.V.

Bow-front cupboard of exceptional design. It was recently discovered in a house in Prince Edward County that had long been vacant and is now in process of restoration. The cornice is missing and the feet have been restored. It is made of pine and was originally painted red. / Mr. and Mrs. Roy Stevens, Waupoos, Ont.

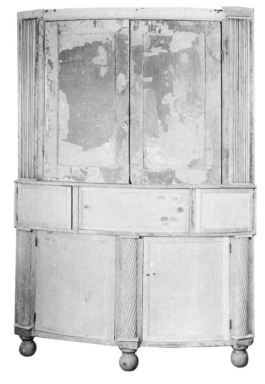

managed, with the kindly help and advice of their neighbours, to produce what they required. Benches, stools, a table made from a board nailed to a stump, split boards for shelves, a bed made with poles attached to the wall sufficed to furnish their first cabins.

A few settlers, who had had some training in furniture-making and who owned tools, made furniture not only for themselves but also for their neighbours. When a sawmill was established in a community these men naturally gravitated to that vicinity and set up workshops there, as did the blacksmith from whom they got nails and hinges. The shop owners quite often called themselves chairmakers and certainly they made a great many common chairs—of pine, basswood, hickory, maple, ash, elm and birch. (Those which survive show clearly the influence of American styles, a fact which suggests that most of the makers came from the United States.) There were some men in large settlements like Kingston, Brockville and York who made and imported nothing but chairs (the most common Windsor and slat-back type) which they sold at 50 cents to $1. Chairs could be had in exchange for ashes or potash, lumber, or any farm produce. A chair could be obtained from a pedlar's wagon in return for old pewter or perhaps a night's lodging.

The woodworkers made other furniture besides chairs, however: bedsteads, chests, cupboards, desks, dish-dressers, tables and, always, coffins. But they did very little upholstering; wood, splint and elm-bark made the seats of chairs which were eventually softened by the use of loose cushions.

The furniture the woodworkers made cannot be said to have had a style but it did reflect the accepted forms of the period. Many crude chairs were made in the general shape of the American Windsor and the slat-back chairs of the eighteenth century, and bedposts and headboards were simplifications of Sheraton designs. The dish-dressers followed the pattern of those that had been in use in the Old Country for at least a century. All the furniture was made according to the woodworker's own conception, however; he had probably never seen a book of designs in his life, only pieces of furniture which were themselves adaptations of the original styles. The traces of Sheraton and Hepplewhite sometimes discernible in the early furniture of Upper Canada are usually three or four times removed from their source.

Though the simple, practical pieces of furniture needed for daily living continued to be made in small woodworking shops for many years, the making of fine furniture gradually came into its own as an industry. Some of the men who had started woodworking in a small way developed their businesses, employed journeymen cabinetmakers and painters, and became full-fledged cabinetmakers. Other shops were opened by itinerant cabinetmakers from the United States who were tempted to remain in Canada because land was available for little or nothing.

We know few names of cabinetmakers in Upper Canada before 1812, and almost nothing of their personal histories. Directories were not yet common. Most furniture was not labelled. Consequently the work of many of these craftsmen is largely unrecorded.

Advertisements give us some information, however. Some cabinetmakers, newly arrived at a settlement and just starting up in business, advertised their names and addresses in the papers. Such a man was Abia B. Sayre who throughout one whole year, 1810, stated in the Kingston *Gazette* that he made clock cases, sideboards, desks, bookcases, bureaus, dining tables, and bedsteads. At the end of the year he stopped advertising, probably because by that time he was well known. There was little competition and established men did not need to advertise.

Public records and private papers of the years before 1816 have yielded a few names. In Kingston there were Chester Hatch and Son, 1815; Abia Sayre, 1810; William Baker, 1812; Samuel How, 1811; and Greno and Sawyer, 1811. In Brockville there was Richard Leech, 1812. And at York there were Daniel Tiers, 1802; Elijah Dexter, 1815; and Harvey Gilbert, 1815. John Benson is

Opposite page, clockwise from the top left: Cherry chest in Hepplewhite style, c. 1829, an example of the early cabinetmakers' version of English taste. / Black Creek Pioneer Village

Cabinet-made chest with cherry frame, knobs and pilasters, maple drawer fronts and side panels. (Prince Edward Co., c. 1830) / Dundurn

Among the finest early custom-made pieces of furniture were desks like this, 1820-30, with contrasting woods. The drawers are of curly maple. / Mr. & Mrs. Walter Beevor, Carrying Place

Chippendale-style looking-glass with fretwork frame. (Prince Edward Co., 1780-1800.) / U.C.V.

Pair of maple candlestands, 1820-30. / U.C.V.

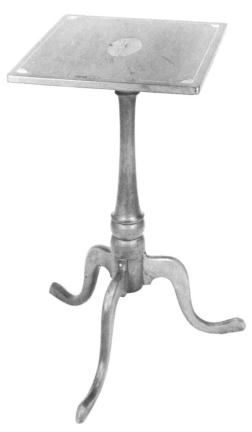

Tripod candlestand, cherry inlaid with sumach. The top is 16" square and it is 28¼" high. It was made in Prince Edward Co. / Author's coll.

Opposite page, clockwise from top: Table with cherry frame and pine top, Prince Edward Co., c. 1800. / Fine walnut tilt-top table, 1800-1825. / Sofa frame with roping for springs, formerly owned by the Foran family, Glengarry Co., c. 1830. / Cherry tea table in Pembroke style, Prince Edward Co. / (The last courtesy Mr. Earl Collier, South Bay; others U.C.V.)

recorded as a cabinetmaker in the little village of Dover which burned in 1814. Further research will bring a few more names to light but we shall probably never know the extent of the earliest and simplest cabinetmaking. Many men combined furniture-making with the joiner's art and other trades, and almost all owned some land and cultivated it. After a few years at the woodworking trade many must have returned to the land or taken up other pursuits.

It was not until after 1825 that cabinet-shops were well established in many centres. They sold to increasingly affluent families in the expanding population. Among the newcomers were men like John Keith, born in Scotland in 1809 and described by John R. Connons in a book entitled *Elora*. Keith arrived in Elora about 1834, where he commenced to make "window sash, water pails, wash tubs and churns, spinning wheels, threshing mills, lanterns, clock cases, cradles and coffins." This versatility was characteristic of the growing number of woodworkers in the province. In the same party of 1834 pioneers was John Gordon, a "master cabinetmaker" from Aberdeen. There was plenty of demand for both skills.

While local cabinetmakers were well patronized by all classes, however, some well-to-do people continued to order special pieces from the Old Country. And, ignoring patriotism, they sometimes bought across the border where furniture was good, prices low, and transportation easy. A suspiciously well-written letter in the *Canadian Freeman* at York in 1827 accused the prominent families of that town of buying in New York, Buffalo and Rochester:

> There is one cabinetmaker in Buffalo, a Mr. Staats, and I really believe that he carries more money annually out of this Province, for articles in his line, than is received by half of all those in the trade within its limits. He supplies, as I hear, the Receiver-General, Attorney General, the Archdeacon of York, the Boultons, etc. etc. etc.

The letter was followed by scathing editorial comment.

Furniture was bought one piece at a time by country people: a cupboard, a desk, a bedstead, a comfortable chair. In towns whole rooms might be furnished at one time, but although there would be a general look of "new style" about the furniture, it did not necessarily match. Each piece was selected for its quality and the design which most appealed to the buyer (whose taste might be of either English or American origin). The purchase of furniture was usually a male prerogative, though the preference of a wife or mother was sometimes expressed. Only the very conservative farm families preferred old shapes and styles when newer ones were offered. The ownership of old or old-style furniture had no value or prestige, and the only reasons for keeping it were sentiment, thrift, or lack of money.

The cabinetmaker's place of business was more a workshop than a salesroom, but common wants such as bedsteads, chairs, candlestands and dressing-glasses might be made ahead and kept on hand. The pieces most commonly custom-made were sideboards, cupboards, secretary-bookcases, chests of drawers, dining and serving tables and bedsteads.

Adam Fergusson, a Scottish traveller, was one of the few visitors to Upper Canada who showed an interest in the furniture. In his *Practical Notes Made During a Tour in Canada and a Portion of the United States*, published in 1831, he listed representative prices of furniture in Upper Canada:

Handsome sideboard, two doors, and five drawers	£15/0/0
Secretary or Writing table	10/0/0
Sofas	£12 to 15/0/0
Dining tables, three to a set	7/0/0
Bureaus, six drawers	5/0/0
Bureaus, six drawers, plain	4/0/0
Bureaus with four drawers	3/0/0
Breakfast tables	1/5/0
Black walnut chairs, hair-bottoms, each	
[i.e. stuffed with horsehair]	1/15/0

Opposite, from top: (1) Mahogany sofa in the American style, upholstered in contemporary chintz. / U.C.V. (2) Regency-style walnut sofa, country version, c. 1830. Mr. & Mrs. Roger Greig. Cherry Valley (3) Maple sofa of the 1840s. / Mr. Paul Godfrey, Port Hope

Common Windsor chairs, each	/5/0
Drawing-room table, claw feet	7/10/0
Drawing-room table, plain	4/10/0
Bedsteads, high posts	2/0/0
Tent bedsteads	1/10/0
Dressing-table and washstand	1/10/0
Double washstand	1/10/0
Light washstand	/12/0 Odd
Ladies' work table	1/10/0

Two-drawer walnut table with carved legs, in American Empire style, dating from 1830-35. / Miss Ann Farwell of Cherry Valley, Ontario

China cabinet or bookcase that was made in Prince Edward County for the Asa Weller family whose fine house still stands at the Carrying Place. The heavy cornice and the turned feet indicate that it was made after 1830. / Mr. & Mrs. B. Napier Simpson, Thornhill

He described this furniture as "handsomely and substantially finished and went on to say, "The native woods such as bird's eye maple, black walnut, birch, elm, oak, cherry, etc. supply excellent and beautiful materials."

From an early date some upholstering was done. Fabrics suitable for upholstery and curtaining were advertised from the end of the eighteenth century. "Furniture prints, furniture and printed calicoes, cotton checks, china blue furniture, moreens, figured and embossed furniture calicoes, chintz and haircloth" were all listed before 1812. (Furniture was the word commonly used for a covering or a fitting. Thus bed furniture meant all the fabric used for curtains and covers on a bed; furniture prints referred to fabric suitable for curtains and upholstery but not for clothing; bureau furniture meant the knobs or pulls, escutcheons and locks for a desk or a chest of drawers.) A certain amount of furnishing fabric was stocked in most general stores in Upper Canada. If something special was wanted an order was dispatched to London in the fall for delivery the following spring. But some people preferred to buy fabrics in Montreal where extensive stocks were carried. Colonel Stone, a wealthy landowner in the vicinity of Gananoque, bought, from Sanford's in Montreal in 1809, two pieces of "furnishing calico" totalling fifty-seven yards. Tassels and fringes were sold at Niagara in 1798 and through the first ten years of the nineteenth century many types of trimmings were available.

Furniture hardware was also widely sold. Before 1817 an advertisement listed: "bureau trimmings; bedcaps, screws, and keys; wood bed casters, brass drawer handles, brass case locks, iron ditto, clock-case trimmings, commode knobs and bed caps, drawer locks in sets; brass butt hinges; brass sofa and bed casters; chest locks, brass locks, brass nails, brass locks with knobs." Brass and lacquered tacks were sold at Niagara in 1798. Upholstery was put on chairs with brass-headed nails until about 1830 when ordinary tacks, covered with narrow, machine-made gimp, began to be used.

In early years, the designs of furniture in Ontario probably showed an equal influence of British and American styles. The English influence was evident in the furniture used in the large towns. This was particularly the case in garrison towns where British officers and their families lived in luxury, compared to the backwoods settlers. Much furniture had been brought from Britain by people of some means and had been left here when they returned or moved on. Some of it had been specially ordered from England for fine houses. And some of it apparently came from Quebec, since there are records of cabinet-made pieces being ordered from Montreal. (The Quebec furniture imported into Ontario at this time was made in English establishments and showed little, if any, French sources of design.)

Auction sales of fine furniture in places like Kingston and Niagara gave cabinetmakers the opportunity to see, acquire and copy furniture likely to be popular with the growing community. Much furniture used in the towns, however, would have been beyond the reach of the average settler—items advertised for sale in Kingston: "guilt [sic] and painted tea-boards" and "elegant bedsteads" for example. Though a typical Kingston advertisement of 1828 addressed itself to "the Inhabitants, Gentlemen of the Army and Navy . . .," it was the latter group who did most of the buying.

From about 1815, new cabinet-made furniture reflected the handsome English Regency style which continued to be popular in Upper Canada until the 1840s. In England the Regency period of furnishing began before 1811 and continued until after the coronation of George IV in 1820, after which it gradually became less popular.

The simple beauty of the Regency style of furniture made in Upper Canada must have been seen to advantage in the half-empty rooms of early houses where curtains were often only brilliantly-coloured, fringed swags on cornices. It is probable, however, that no *pure* Regency furniture was made in Ontario, for beyond the designers' shops in England the style was everywhere tinged with suggestions of Hepplewhite and Sheraton. Moreover, cabinetmakers worked more often from memory than from pattern books. Surviving pieces can be attributed to the period but not always to the place of origin because much unlabelled English provincial furniture came into Ontario throughout the early nineteenth century and can easily be mistaken for locally-made pieces, which also lack labels.

Whereas in England furniture was chiefly made of mahogany, with brass trim, inlaid and applied, in Canada it was more often of walnut. The lists of furniture in the 1812 war claims record as much if not more native walnut than cherry or maple in good furniture, proving that it was, even at that early date, well established as a good furniture wood. In the drawers of Canadian tables the secondary wood was usually pine, in the English oak. More wooden knobs and fewer brass knobs and pulls were used here than in England.

Ontario furniture made in the period between 1820 and 1840 is of great interest to collectors today. Its styles have remained continually pleasing, its workmanship is excellent, and some individuality of design is found.

Most of this furniture was made in the Regency or Early Empire styles, for though these designs were becoming less popular in fashionable centres like London, Philadelphia and New York, they were still commonly accepted in Upper Canada. Indeed, many people who could not afford such "good" furniture when it first appeared were now better off and hastened to buy. (This pattern of delayed style buying continued in later years.)

New designs were introduced in this period, however, notably the American versions of the French Empire styles. Furniture in these modes began to appear in the homes of the well-to-do in Upper Canada in the 1830s. Columned sideboards, chests of drawers, secretaries and French bedsteads were all advertised, and the new pedestal card tables were in use.

Numerous advertisements listed "Grecian chairs," a term which included most chairs with inward-curving front legs (called sabre legs) and back legs that were square, with a backward cant. In profile these chairs resembled the Greek chair called a klismos.

Trafalgar chairs were also frequently mentioned in advertisements at this time. These were chairs produced in honour of Nelson's great victory. They had cross-rails, cresting and other trim made in nautical shapes (rope, dolphins or anchors) and they were painted and gilded in the same vein. In shape they were comparable to the Grecian chairs and it seems that eventually the name "Trafalgar" came to be used here as an alternative to "Grecian."

Other furniture in the French Empire style included French and sleigh beds which had headboards and footboards of equal height, often made with an outward curve. Since the bedding on these beds tucked into shaped sideboards, the old dust frill disappeared.

It was during this period that scrolls began to be used as supports for the now overhanging top portions of sideboards, cabinets and bureaus, and for the arms of sofas and the feet of pedestals.

It was during this period, too, that Canadian advertisements first began to describe furniture in some detail and to refer to the various styles by name.

Opposite page, clockwise from the top left:
(1) Butternut cupboard with drawers, 1840-50, Glengarry County. / Miss Marion MacRae, Toronto
(2) Hallstand with crotch-grained mahogany veneer, made about 1850. / Upper Canada Village
(3) Desk of cherry and maple, with drop front (c. 1840), in the McFarland house near Queenston.
(4) Mahogany parlour table, c. 1840, also in the McFarland house. / Both Niagara Parks Com.

Parlour tables. Top: maple table in the 1840s style. Centre: table crudely made of various woods but imitating high style. Lower: home-made table fashioned in the same high style.

Burl walnut dressing-glass in Gothic style,
1830-50. Such glasses were used on draped
dressing tables and fine chests. / U.C.V.

In 1840 a book was published which influenced the making and acquisition of furniture in Upper Canada. This was *The Cabinetmaker's Assistant* by John Hall, an architect and draughtsman in Baltimore. It contained a number of drawings of furniture referred to as "the most modern style of cabinet furniture." Actually many of the designs depicted were inspired by the earlier style of French Empire furniture and the New York furniture-making establishment of Joseph Meeks and Sons had been making similar furniture in the French style since 1830. (The cabinet work produced by Meeks was especially influential because the firm distributed widely a large lithographed sheet illustrating forty of their designs. Orders for these pieces of furniture could be filled immediately and shipped anywhere.) But Hall's book appeared at a time when small furniture factories were beginning to use power machinery, when transportation was becoming simpler and cheaper, and when industry (through wages) was creating a new buying public. Hall's chunky styles, which were pictured in magazines and advertised at varying prices, captured the fancy of upper and middle classes alike.

An extraordinary number of pieces of the new furniture were made, all with certain features characteristic of the designs: Massive scrolls served as supports or ornaments. Heavy claw or paw feet appeared on sofas, chests and tables. Marble tops were used on tables. Crotch-grain mahogany, walnut and rosewood veneers were usual.

The furniture made to Hall's designs was at the height of its popularity between 1840 and 1850. Chronologically it can be included in the Victorian period but it appeared in Ontario homes long before the French Antique style of furniture which we associate with the name. Perhaps it might best be referred to as Early Victorian.

The bold and heavy styles of the new furniture required a new setting. Colours became more vivid; aniline dyes in undreamed of brilliance were developed. (Yellow and scarlet were favourite colours, also pale green and turquoise blue.) Pattern was everywhere—in carpets, over-curtaining, upholstery and wallpaper—and large-scale designs for the wallpaper and carpets were particularly fashionable. Curtaining was heavy. Drapes in the "best" rooms of the house contained three times as many yards of damask, velvet, moreen and brocatelle as formerly. Undercurtains of muslin, mull, or machine-woven cotton lace shrouded the windows. Pictures were larger to balance the furniture. The delicate water-colours and embroidered pictures went to the attic and were replaced by enormous gilt-framed oils and engravings.

At this time many people felt the need of some guidance in the correct furnishing and decoration of their homes. This need was filled by such writers as Thomas Webster and A. J. Downing. An 1845 American Revised edition of Webster's *Encyclopedia of Domestic Economy*, first published in London in 1844, was the first widely-read illustrated compendium of information about every aspect of domestic life, including furniture. Its illustrations showed all modern articles for furnishing, including pots and pans. (It is interesting to note that Webster accepted the what-not as replacing the étagère, defining the word as "a whimsical appellation for a very convenient stand of several stories.") While the book did nothing to innovate style, it presented an accepted standard of furnishing in a manner which left no doubt in the reader's mind as to what was required in a respectable house. It was consequently influential.

Canadian architects were influenced by the eclectic styles of Andrew Jackson Downing whose *Country Houses*, published in 1850, often inspired the styles of important "villas" built on the outskirts or at some distance from the growing towns—houses which are now either demolished or enveloped in business sections of cities. Downing had firm ideas regarding furniture; he felt that it should suit the architectural style of a house. He maintained that not only furniture but also the use of colour, graining techniques and garden-

Above: Sofa, armchairs and side chairs in a set of parlour furniture made by James Reid of the city of Hamilton for the Hon. Thomas Bain on the occasion of his marriage in Dundas in 1872. Suites in this style were fashionable from 1860 to 1880. / Dundas Historical Society Museum

Left: Drop-front desk in crotch-grain mahogany veneer—a style very popular throughout the 1850-60 period. / Mrs. Irene Arnould, Ottawa

Above: Walnut sofa over 80″ long, with piecrust moulding along the front. It bears an Abram Southard label and dates from about 1855. / Mr. and Mrs. C. L. Sanders, Ottawa, Ont. Below: Walnut sofa with medallion back, 1855-70, one of three known labelled Southard sofas having only small differences in carving. / Mrs. S. Nourse, Miss N. McDonald, Picton

Above left: This dressing-glass of walnut veneer and whitewood carries the label of Abram Southard, cabinetmaker of Picton. It was made in the year 1850. / Author's coll.
Above right: Southard's label, which is found on a great many fine pieces of furniture still in use in Ontario, advertises a wide assortment of merchandise, from books to sofas.

Southard painted pine lift-top desk, labelled,
c. 1850. / Mr. & Mrs. W. Beevor, Carrying Place

Whitewood washstand with Southard label in
the drawer, from the 1860s. / Author's coll.

ing should enhance the original plans and he wrote about all these things. His book had some direct, and a great deal of indirect influence here. His ideas were accepted as authority in the United States and were disseminated through other books and periodicals which borrowed his ideas without credits or scruples.

This was the beginning of a time when much fine early furniture was abandoned, first by the fashionable and eventually by the majority. Fancy chairs were painted over and used in bedrooms and kitchens. High-post beds were dismantled and put up on rafters in woodshed and attic. In the kitchens new cupboard-sideboards in which the dishes were concealed took the place of the old dish-dresser, commencing a popularity that lasted until the 1880s. Spinets and pianofortes were exchanged for stubby-looking cottage pianos. The finish on delicate desks and tables suffered from neglect. Only the large, heavy pieces such as chests of drawers and cupboards were too cumbersome to be put away. The furnishing of most homes gradually became "Victorian" and remained in that style till at least the end of the century.

In the fifty years since the turn of the century, Upper Canada, (now Canada West) had seen the change from homemade furniture to inexpensive, factory-produced furniture in the latest styles. Before 1846 less than 200 makers of furniture were recorded, although there may have been many whose names are lost. Between 1857 and 1869 nearly 1500 were recorded. Some of these workers were employees rather than owners of establishments but they all earned their living making furniture. They advertised themselves as cabinetmakers, chairmakers, bedstead makers, looking-glass and picture-frame makers. Upholsterers were also numerous. Many Old-Country artisans who had come in the immigrations of the 1840s lent some English influence to the furniture they made. (The most popular furniture, however, was identical with that made in the United States, though its arrangement and use in the home might differ.)

There were several cabinetmakers in every sizeable town. Even in villages chairmakers and general woodworkers continued to make the homely furniture, the spinning wheels and other woodenware required in the home. The diary of J. O'Brien Scully of Wellington, Prince Edward County, noted that in 1844 the population of 387 in 70 dwelling houses supported a chair factory, two painters and three cabinetmakers. Of course the people in the surrounding area also made use of their services.

In the 1850s many of the furniture makers had adopted new techniques, mostly of American invention, and many had steam power. All employed the circular saw, and some the band- and fret-saw machinery that was developed in the 1850s.

Early furniture advertisements used the adjectives "useful" and "handsome"; later ones used "elegant" or "latest." But by the 1850s furniture was often referred to as belonging to an historic epoch. The revivals of styles mentioned were Gothic, Elizabethan, Renaissance and Louis XIV or Louis XV. (The last two styles were popularly called French Antique and rococo, respectively.)

Some intimations of the Gothic style may be seen in Canadian furniture—in the doors (glazed or unglazed) of cupboards and secretary-desks, and in the ecclesiastical-looking side chairs used in parlour and hall.

The Elizabethan style degenerated here into spool turning which formed and decorated much of the inexpensive furniture of the 1850s. (Spool turning rarely resembles spools but is an overall term used to describe ball, ball-and-ring, urn, knob-and-vase, sausage and button turning. It is turned in lengths on a power lathe and is cut as needed.) Spool turning was extensively used as trim on the solid ends of beds and couches, but it also formed the legs of tables, spindles of chairs, and the frames of what-nots and towel racks. Maple and black walnut produced the best of the spool furniture, but birch, stained to look like mahogany or walnut, was also commonly used.

Renaissance furniture was ponderous. It was largely reserved for the houses of the rich but details of the style were reflected in the furniture of modest homes—in headboards of beds and backboards of sideboards, both of which were encrusted with carved ornament.

The French styles, which came to be labelled French Antique or rococo, are not remembered as French but only as the common style of the mid-Victorian period. Chairs, tables, desks, dressing tables, sofas, bureaus, and every small object sold at the time shared the characteristics of the period. None of the "antique" styles of furniture really resembled its prototype. The mark of the Victorian era was on all of it. Perhaps the most persistent manifestations of the rococo style were the parlour suite and the balloon-back chair, both of which remained in favour for many years. Such fully up-holstered furniture—sofas, lounges, chairs and ottomans—introduced a new standard of comfort.

About 1850 American factories began to produce sets of what they called cottage furniture, which was inexpensive and charming. The beds, dressers, washstands, tables, chairs (one side, one rocker), towel racks and zommos (night stands) which constituted a full set, were in the current style. Pieces could be bought separately but a small set cost only about $25. All pieces were finished with enamel paint in colours of pale green, grey, blue, and even pink. Stencils and hand-painted flowers, objects and scenes frequently decorated the drawers of the bureau, washstand, zommo and headboard. A lining brush was used to outline shapes and provide little arabesques in corners in thin lines of bright yellow, dark blue, and other contrasting colours.

Cottage furniture was often advertised in Canada by the furniture factories. A typical advertisement was that of the New York Enamelled Furniture and Chair Factory on King Street, Hamilton, in 1853:

> All kinds of chairs, plain and ornamental, wholesale and retail at low price.
> Old ones re-seated, repaired and repainted in any style. Also enamelled chamber
> sets in the most elegant styles with or without marble tops, on hand or made
> to order.

Very few cottage sets remain intact today; fifty years of wear made it necessary to overpaint most of them.

In 1860 there were many houses in the province furnished in a style comparable to that of the rich houses in England and the United States. Increased travel had broadened taste, and a wealth of furnishings was available. There were many furniture showrooms, and even manufacturers like Jacques and Hay of Toronto and James Reid of Hamilton, who made "bespoke" furniture, had approximately 220 men employed in producing furniture, pianos, picture frames and allied furnishings during the ten-year period from 1857 to 1867.

Yet such furniture was not within the reach of everyone. As late as 1854, Catharine Parr Traill was meeting a genuine need in publishing *The Female Emigrant's Guide* in which she gave advice on furnishing a log house:

> Let us see now what can be done toward making your log parlour comfort-
> able at small cost. A dozen of painted Canadian chairs such as are in common
> use here will cost you £2.10s. You can get plainer ones for 2/9 or 3 shillings
> a chair; of course you may get very excellent articles if you give a higher
> price; but we are not going to buy drawing room furniture. You can buy
> rocking chairs, small, at 7/6, large, with elbows, 15/. You can cushion them
> yourself. A good drugget which I would advise you to bring with you, or
> Scotch carpet, will cover your rough floor; when you spread straw or hay
> over the boards this will save your carpet from cutting. A stained pine table
> may be had for 12s. or 15s. Walnut or cherry wood costs more; but the pine,
> with a nice cover will answer at first. For a flowered mohair you must give
> 5 or 6 dollars. A piece of chintz, of suitable pattern, will cost you 16s., the

Much furniture changed hands at auction sales which were held continuously in early days.

Arrow-back chair that bears Southard's label. / Mr. and Mrs. Edwin Robinson, Picton, Ontario

piece of 28 yards. This will curtain your windows, and a common pine sofa, stuffed with wool, (though many use fine hay for the back and sides) can be bought cheap if covered by your own hands. If your husband or older sons are at all skilled in the use of tools, they can make, out of common pine boards, the framework of couches or sofas, which look, when covered and stuffed, as well as what a cabinet maker will charge several pounds for.

A common box or two stuffed so as to form a cushion on the top, and finished with a flounce of chintz, will fill the recess of your windows. A set of book-shelves stained with Spanish brown to hold your library, a set of corner shelves, fitted into the angles of the room, one above the other, diminishing in size, forms a useful receptacle for any little ornamental matters, or a few flowers in the summer, and gives a pleasant finish and air of taste to the room.

The prosperity and increased population of the 1860s stimulated the buying of furniture and there was scarcely a house which did not have a parlour set, a melodeon, piano or organ. Prices were higher but so were wages. Families were large and houses were big; there was no hesitation in buying enormous pieces of furniture which, once they were in place, could not be budged even for housecleaning. For many people the prospect of ever moving from their homes was an unlikely one. Married children often came home to live (sometimes occupying a separate wing of the house) and they brought even more furniture into the house.

Furniture buying was still done locally; the mail order companies were not yet competing. The town cabinetmaker supplied rich and poor. He was known to everyone and took it for granted that much of his stock would be sold on credit or by exchange of goods. His horse and wagon, or those of the buyer, made deliveries. I was fortunate enough to gain an insight into the transactions of one such cabinetmaker through two strange chances.

In 1956, Homer Talcott, a Prince Edward County man, sent a pedestal table to a local cabinetmaker to have the pedestal cut down to coffee table height. Inside the pedestal a small glass bottle capped with sealing wax was found. (It had been attached to the wood by fine leather straps.) Inside was a paper with a message written in pencil:

Picton. May 29 A.D. 1863.
This was written in the morning of the 29th of May A.D. 1863 and put in this bottle to be preserved till some future generation and it is marked up inside of a centre table pillar which is made by Alexander Fredrick Yarwood in Abram M. Southard's cabinet shop. Please preserve the document and if you chance to know Alexander Fredrick Yarwood, David Charles Ferguson, Volenay Wallace Root or Aaron John Wight please send this document to either one of these persons and oblige.

Yours,

David C. Ferguson

I heard about this find and was interested. Ten years later I acquired a shabby old account book without binding or fly leaves, evidently that of a cabinetmaker. It had been used during the years between June 1859 and May 1864. Because the customers' surnames were familiar to me, I could recognize the book as belonging to a man who had worked in Prince Edward County. But there was no indication of the owner's name. However, on the back pages were the names of apprentices and employees, their dates of employment, and their wages. And among them were Yarwood, Ferguson, Root and Wight. This established the accounts as those of Abram M. Southard, the most prominent cabinetmaker of this period in the town of Picton.

The Southard family are said to have come to Prince Edward County from Long Island in 1812. They had been lumbermen in New York State. Southard had been, through the early 1850s, a partner with James Gillespie, an established cabinetmaker in Picton, but in 1854 had bought a lot and set up his own business. The location referred to in his labels was "Main Street, near the corner of Little Lake Road," which is now the junction of Main Street and the Cherry Valley Road. The population of Picton at the time was 2,000 and that of the surrounding country was 21,000. The townsfolk consisted of retired farmers, professional people, mill owners, shopkeepers, and a few "gentlemen" with incomes from investments. Other cash incomes were small. It was a static community, with little industrial growth in sight. The most aggressive of the younger generation had left or were planning to leave for the cities, the Canadian West, or the United States. Southard had competitors: there were two cabinetmakers in Picton and several craftsmen in the surrounding villages.

Despite these handicaps the firm apparently prospered. It employed from three to eight workers, usually one or two journeymen, the rest trained hands and apprentices. Southard paid a painter, Nelson Derbyshire, "to ornament furniture." John Demain, a journeyman, was paid $312 a year in 1861 and '62. Volenay Walter Root received $70 in 1860 but in 1865 he was paid $24 a month on the understanding he would board himself. Apprentices were hired for three or four years at $25 or $30, "all found," for the first year, rising to $60 and $85 at the end of the term. Southard seems to have boarded his apprentices and furnished their tools. He also debited himself for some of their clothing.

The figures in Southard's account book suggest that his income in 1860 was only $2,500, of which only $700 was in cash, the remainder in supplies, commodities and services credited. The book lists "sewing a suit for myself" [work done by a customer] $2.25; two days' digging potatoes at $1.60; 12 pounds salmon at 5¢ a pound; one cord of wood $2; one hundred pounds of wheat flour $2; 150 pounds cornmeal $2.25; 114 pounds maple sugar $11.40. Many accounts were settled by the supplying of walnut, butternut, basswood and pine boards. By 1866 Brock's Directory credited Southard with an income of $4,000 per annum.

Southard bought chairs, some of them rush-seated, from J. M. Wright of Oswego, New York, whose firm had made rockers, Grecian and fancy chairs since before 1840. For one lot he paid $276.91. DeGraff and Taylor of New York City, manufacturers of French Antique furniture in rosewood and walnut, billed him for $290. His freight bills for this period were paid to schooner captains. S. Muckleston and Company of Kingston supplied him with hair stuffing, haircloth for upholstery, and looking-glass plates.

In 1860 Southard bought wood turnings from Canadian factories. These items were: 71 sets "lounge stuff and parts"; 83 sets table legs at 20¢ each; 89 sets washstand legs (14 basswood, 8 walnut); 91 sets washstand stretchers; 91 sets bedposts and 225 cottage bed spindles; 7 sets cradle posts at 20¢ each and 9 dozen cradle spindles; 32 sets of stand legs.

Included in the shop's 1860 sales were: 20 bedsteads; 4 cradles; 3 cribs; 2 couches; 9 bureaus (walnut, mahogany, and pine); 160 chairs of which 47 had cane seat or backs; 9 lounges; 6 sofas; 10 writing desks; 5 candlestands; 108 picture frames; 54 pictures (lithographs and engravings); 3 what-nots; 1 high-post bedstead; 4 Boston rockers; and 1 Grecian cane-back rocker. There were also children's chairs, both low and high, portable desks, tea-boards, work boxes, shaving-boxes, footstools, window "cornishes" and porcelain-topped picture nails, a set of bentwood chairs, a marble-topped centre table, towel racks and a "shawl stand."

Additional services Southard performed were cutting wood type, fixing clocks, fitting window cornices, painting and repairing all types of furniture, carving ornaments for other cabinetmakers' sofas, making plateholders, repairing a stereopticon for the town photographer, and varnishing oil paintings.

Furniture prices were in line with the low wages and living costs of the time. Among the most expensive items made in the shop from 1859 to 1863 were:

Walnut chest of drawers with Southard's label, 1850-60. / Mrs. J. S. Stenning, Bloomfield, Ont.

Walnut secretary	$28.00
Set of Walnut leg'd dining tables	$25.00
Walnut sofa and centre table	$43.00
6 walnut chairs and hall table	$38.00
Sideboard	$24.00
6 walnut haircloth chairs	$28.00
Mahogany tête à tête	$40.00

Items of "common furniture" (so written in the accounts) ranged from $3 to $4 each. A cradle was billed at $3; a low common bedstead at $3.75; a walnut table at $4; 6 walnut cane chairs at $2 each; 1 "misses" Boston rocker at $1.75; a small coffin at $3; a sewing chair at $1.50; and a pine breakfast table at $3.

Southard's furniture label is a familiar one in Prince Edward County. It is found on furniture of the 1850s and '60s and later. I have a set of dining chairs of an earlier style on which a small card with the name "A. Southard" was tacked to the inside back of the seat frame. His label-advertisements show quite clearly that his warehouse and store carried an extensive stock of made-up furniture, pictures and supplies. His last label is seen in an old book *The Backwoods Preacher* which he sold about 1878. It reads, "A. Southard, Books and Stationery, Toys and Fancy Goods, Organs, Sheet Music, Furniture, etc." Few people remember the Southards today, though a great many own furniture with his label. An old relative of mine recalls that Abram and his wife sat in front of her family in church and that Mrs. Southard was the last woman in Picton to wear ringlets on either side of her face under an old-fashioned bonnet, a style which first came into fashion in the 1840s.

By the 1860s farm and middle-class families who had been in Ontario for some time had adequate furnishings. Some of these they had acquired themselves over a long period of time, some they had inherited. Further purchases were usually for single items or for a one-time replacement of parlour or dining-room furniture in the newest style. (This is reflected in Southard's accounts.) Worn-out or broken furniture could be repaired cheaply and even repainted at a cabinetmaker's. Young families starting housekeeping bought some new furniture but could augment it with purchases from auction sales and "furniture brokers" who were the second-hand furniture dealers of their day. So, by the time they had reached middle age, most home-owners had a mixture of old and new furnishings with which they settled down comfortably for the rest of their lives.

Before the First World War, I was familiar with houses in small towns and on farms where the furniture and some of the wallpapers, carpets and curtains were at least fifty years old. There was no social pressure of any kind to persuade the families who owned such furnishings to add to them or to alter their style of living. If the owners grew tired of the unchanging décor they did not complain. There were favourite rooms, favourite chairs and favourite dishes. These were loved from familiarity and sentiment and there was time to enjoy them. The houses were well managed and were equipped for visitors with well-stocked linen closets and bountiful pantries. Life was comfortable and pleasant, both for the occupants and for the visitors, partly *because* there were few changes in furnishings or household arrangements. There was an atmosphere of order and stability.

In the last twenty years the collecting of furniture from the old homes in Ontario has been rapidly increasing. It has been partly stimulated by the same trend in the United States, and partly by a communal wish to make a visible show of having a past. The old furniture is once more sold and auctioned and finds its way into new rooms where, in a refurbished state, it is deeply appreciated. Whole rooms are furnished with old Ontario furniture. If anything is missing it may be the serenity which once pervaded the rooms from which it came.

Russell's furniture store, Port Hope, c. 1865. / Late Mr. Albert Schultz, Jr., Port Hope

Plants of Upper Canada

The flowers, shrubs, vines and herbs listed below were available in the Northern United States and presumably in Upper Canada before 1860. Most of this plant material was familiar to gardeners here and obtainable before 1840. Plants not procurable before 1840 are marked with an asterisk. (*)

All these listed plant names were mentioned in contemporary sources: books on life in Upper Canada, advertisements, nurserymen's catalogues, and books on gardening in the Northern United States which were sold in Canada.

Some native plants which grew wild in Upper Canada are included because they were cultivated in gardens or gathered for use in the kitchen. I have not included the immense variety of orchard trees and hothouse and window-sill plants which were certainly here but were not really part of garden making.

Some of the old names are those which were popularly, though sometimes incorrectly, used by our early gardeners. The botanical names are those used in old gardening books where the spelling varied considerably.

MODERN NAME	OLD NAME	COLOUR	BOTANICAL NAME
		– A –	
Achillea	Maudlin, Sneezewort, Shirt-buttons, Goose Tongue	white	A. Ptarmica
Adonis, Autumn	Flos Adonis	crimson	A. Autumnalis
Ageratum (*)	Ageratum	blue	A. Mexicanum
Almond, Flowering	Flowering Almond	pink	Prunus Gladulosa
Amaranthus	Amaranthus, Joseph's Coat	variegated	A. Tricolor
Amaryllis	Amaryllis, Jacobean Lily	red	A. Belladonna
Antirrhinum	Snapdragon	white to purplish red	A. Majus
Artichoke (Jerusalem)	Artichoke, Canada Potato	yellow	Helianthus Tuberosos
Aster (China) (*)	China Aster	blue, violet, white	Collistephus Chinensis Germanicus
		– B –	
Bachelor's Buttons	Bachelor's Buttons	white, pink, blue	Centaurea Cyanus
Balloon Flower	Balloon Flower	blue	Platycodon Mariesii
Basil	Sweet Basil	white, purple	Ocimum Basilicum
Bedstraw	Lady's Bedstraw	yellow	Galium Verum
Bellflower	Chimney Bellflower	purple-blue	Campanula Pyramidalis
Bergamot	Bergamot	lavender	Monardus Fistulosa
Bladder Senna	Bladder Senna	yellow	Colutea Arborescens
Bleeding Heart (*)	Bleeding Heart	rose	Dicentra Spectabilis
Boneset	Boneset, Thoroughwort	white	Eupatorium Perfoliatum
Bouncing Bet	Bouncing Bet, Soapwort	pale pink	Saponaria Officinalis
Burnet	Garden Burnet	crimson	Sanguisorba Minor
Buttercup, double	Ranunculus Bachelor's Buttons	yellow	Ranunculus acris fl. pl.
		– C –	
Cacalia	Flora's Paint Brush, Tassel Flower	red	Emilia Sagittata
Calceolaria	Calceolaria	red, yellow spotted	C. Rugosa Integrifolia
Camomile	Camomile, Anthemis	white	Anthemis Nobilis
Candy Tuft	Candy Tuft, Candy Tuff	white, purplish	Iberis Amara, Iberis Umbellata
Canterbury Bells	Canterbury Bells	blue and white	Campanula Medium, Persicifolia
Cardinal Flower	Cardinal's Flower, Indian Pink	crimson	Lobelia Cardinalis
Carnation	Carnation, Gilliflower, Pink	rose, white, variegated	Dianthus Caryophyllus
Carolina allspice	Sweet shrub, Strawberry Bush	reddish	Calycanthus Floridus
Carraway	Carraway	white	Carum Carvi
Cassia, Maryland	Maryland Cassia, Senna	bright yellow	C. Marilandiea
Catnip	Catnip, Catmint	insignificant purplish	Nepeta Cataria

Celosia	Celosia, Purple Amaranth, Cockscomb	various colours	C. Argentea Cristala
Chicory	Chicory, Succory	light green	Cichorium Intybus
Chives	Chives	purple	Alium Schoenoprasum
Chrysanthemum	Chrysanthemum	yellow	C. Indicum
Clarkia	Clarkia	lilac, purple	C. Eleganus, C. Pulchella
Clary	Clary, Clear-eye	bluish-white	Salvia Sclarea
Clematis	Traveler's Joy, Old Man's Beard, Withywind	white	C. Vitalba
Clematis, Herb	Clematis	violet-blue	C. Integrifolia
Clematis (Wild)	Virgin's Bower, Woodvine, Love Vine, Climbing Fumitory, Mountain Fringe Alleghany Vine	white	C. Virginiana
Cleome	Cleome	pink, white, rose-purple	C. Spinosa, C. Pungens
Clethra	Clethra, Sweet Pepperbush		C. Almifolia
Cobaea	Cobaea, Cup and saucer vine, Mexican Ivy	violet, greenish-purple	C. Scandens
Coleus	Coleus, Foliage Plant	insignificant white, purple	C. Blumei
Collinsia	Collinsia	lilac, purple	C. Bicolour
Columbine	Columbine	white, blue, purple, yellow and red	Aquilegia Vulgaris, C. Canadensis
Coreopsis	Drummond's Coreopsis	yellow	C. Tinctoria, C. Drummond
Costmary	Sweet Mary, Lavender, Mint Geranium	yellow	Chrysanthemum Balsamita
Crocus	Crocus	purple, lilac, yellow, white	Crocus Vernus, Susianus, Byzantinus
Crocus (Autumn)	Meadow Saffron, Naked Boys	purple	Colchicum Autumnale
Crown Imperial	Crown Imperial, Caesar's Crown	orange, yellow, light red, pale rose	Fritillaria Imperialis
Cucumber (Wild)	Wild Cucumber, Wild Balsam Apple	white	Echinocystis
Currant (Flowering)	Fragrant Currant, Missouri Currant, Buffalo Currant	flower—yellow, fruit—nearly black	Ribes Aureum
Cypress Spurge	Spurge, Cemetery Flower	yellowish	Euphorbia Cyparissias
Cypress Vine (*)	Cypress Vine	crimson, white	Quamoclit Pennata

– D –

Daffodil	Daffodil, Smoke Pipes	yellow, white	Narcissus, Pseudo-Narcissus
Dahlia (*)	Dahlia	many colours	Dahlia Variabilis Pinnata The honeycomb or quilled variety are called "Shows" and "Fancies" in seedsmen's nomenclature.
Daisy	Crown Daisy	yellowish-white	Chrysanthemum Coronarium
Daisy	English Daisy	pink, white	Bellis Perennis
Daphne	Daphne, Mezereon	purple, white, pink	D. Mezereum
Didiscus	Didiscus	blue	D. Coeruleus
Dill	Dill	green, yellow	Anethum Graveolens
Dutchman's Pipe	Dutchman's Pipe, Birthwort	yellowish-brown	Aristolochia Sipho

Feverfew

– E –

Elecampane	Elecampane	yellow	Inula Helenium
Everlastings	Everlastings, Immortelles, Goldy-locks, Straw Flowers	yellow	Helichrysum Arenarium

– F –

Fennel	Fennel	yellow	Foeniculum Vulgare
Feverfew	Feverfew, Featherfew	white	Chrysanthemum Parthenium
Filipendula	Filipendula	pinkish-purple, white	F. Purpurea

Solomon's seal, violets, iris, fern, and rose bushes under an old apple tree.

Forget-Me-Not	Forget-Me-Not	blue	Myosotis Palustris
Four O'clocks	Four O'clocks, Marvel of Peru	red and yellow	Mirabilis Jalapa
Foxglove	Foxglove	white, yellow, purple	Digitalis Purpurea
Fuchsia (*)	Fuchsia	crimson, white, rose, purple	F. Hybrida, F. Procumbens

– G –

Gas Plant	Dittany, Fraxinella	white, rosy purple	Dictamnus Albus, Rubra
Geranium	Geranium	purple, pink, red, white	Pelargonium, Var: scarlet, blush, horseshoe, silver-edged rose scented, strawberry leaved, sweet scented, oak leaved, Martha or Lady Washington, balm scented, myrtle leaved
Gilia	Gilia	blue, variegated	G. Capitata, G. Tricolour
Globe Flower	Globe Flower	yellow	Trollius Europeus
Globe Fower (Great)	Globe Thistle	pale blue	Echinops Exaltus
Globe Flower (Lesser)	Globe Thistle	blue	Echinops Sphaerocephalus
Gomphrena	Globe Amaranth	red, pink, white, yellow	Gomphrena Globosa
Grape Hyacinth	Grape Hyacinth, Grape Flower	blue	Muscary Botryoides
Grove Love	Grove Love	white-purple spots	Nemophila Maculata

– H –

High Bush, Cranberry	High Bush Cranberry, Cranberry Tree, Mountain Viburnum	flower—white, berries —scarlet	Viburnum Opulus, Var: Americanum
Hollyhock	Hollyhock—single and double	red, pink, white	Althea Rosea, Var: Black Antwerp, Double yellow, Double Chinese
Honesty	Honesty, Moneywort, Moonwort, Silver Pennies, White Satin	pinkish-purple	Luneria Annua, biennis
Honeysuckle	Honeysuckle, Twin flower, Woodbine	yellowish	Lonicera Periclymenum, Lonicera Etruscan
Hop Vine	Hop Vine	pale yellow	Humulus Lupulus
Horehound	Horehound	greenish	Marrubium Vulgare
Horse Radish	Horse Radish	white	Roripa Armoracia
Hyacinth	Hyacinth	various colours	Hyacinthus, Var: Passe tout blue, Prince Henri de Prussia blue, La Rosse blue, Duc de Berri yellow, Phoenix red, La Fidelle red, Rose Sarre red, Rose Surpassant pink, Nannette white, Prince Wm. Frederick white, Don Gratuit white, Belle ferme white.
Hydrangea	Hydrangea	white	H. Quercifolia, H. Florists
Hyssop	Hyssop	blue, pink, white	Hyssopus Officinalus

– I –

Impatiens	Impatiens, Patience, Sultana, Busy Lizzie	pink, rose, scarlet, purple, white, yellow	I. Balsamina
Iris	Flower de Luce, Sword Lily	purple, yellow, white-lavender, blue	I. Persica, I. Xyphium, I. Xyphioides, I. Florentina, I. Pumila, I. Germanica
Ivy	English Ivy	green	Hedera Helix

– J –

Jacobaea	Jacobaea, Tansy Ragwort	purple, yellow	Senecio Jacobaea
Japonica	Japan Apple	rosy red	Chaenomeles Speciosa
Job's Tears	Job's Tears	white	Coix Lacryma-jobi
Joe Pye Weed	Joe Pye Weed	rose	Eupatorium Purpureum
Johnny-jump-up	Johnny-jump-up	purple variegated	Viola Tricolour
Jonquil	Jonquil	yellow	Narcissus Jonquilla

– K –

Kerria (*)	Kerria	yellow	K. Japonica

218

Kochia	Kochia, Belvedere, Summer Cypress	green turning red	K. Scoparia

– L –

Larkspur	Larkspur	blue	Delphinium Ajacis
Lemon Lily	Lemon Lily, Liricon Fancy	yellow	Hemerocallis Flava
Lilac	Lilac, Laylock	purple, white	Syringa Vulgaris
Lilac (Persian)	Persian Lilac	purple	Syringa Persica
Lily (Day)	Japanese Lily	white, blush, spotted rose, red, carmine pink	Lilium Speciosum
Lily (Madonna)	Madonna Lily, Annunciation Lily	white	Lilium Candidum
Lily (Martagon)	Mountain Lily	white to pale purple	Lilium Martagon
Lily, Orange	Orange Lily	orange	Hemerocallis Fulva
Lily (Turk's Cap)	Turk's Cap Lily	orange	Lilium Superbum
Lily of the Valley	Lily of the Valley, May Lilies	white	Convallaria Majalis
Linaria	Linaria	purple	L. Reticulata
Linaria	Toad Flax	yellow, orange	L. Vulgaris
Live Forever	Live Forever, orpine	purple	Sedum Telephium
Loasa	Loasa	yellow with red and white	L. Tricolour
Lobelia	Lobelia	blue	L. Syphilitica
Lovage	Lovage	greenish	Levisitcum Officinalis
Love-in-a-mist	Love-in-a-mist, Devil-in-the-bush, Fennel Flower	blue, white	Nigella Damascena
Love Lies Bleeding	Love Lies Bleeding, Tassel Flower	red foliage; green, yellow or red flowers	Amaranthus Caudatis
Lungwort	Lungwort, Soldiers and Sailors, Joseph and Mary	reddish-violet	Pulmonaria Officinalis
Lupine	Lupine	blue, yellow, white	Lupinus, Luteus, Hirsutus, Albus

– M –

Maiden-Hair	Maiden-Hair	green	Thalictrum, Adiantifolium
Mallow	Mallow	pink	Lavatera Trimestris
Maltese Cross	Maltese Cross, Catchfly, Jerusalem Cross, Scarlet Cross	scarlet	Lychnis Chalcedonica
Marigold	Pot Marigold	yellow and orange	Calendula Officinalis
Marigold (African)	Marigold	lemon yellow to deep orange	Tagetas Erecta
Marigold (French)	Marigold	yellow and red, pink, red	Tagetas Patula
Marjoram, sweet	Sweet Marjoram	white	Marjorama Hortensis
Matrimony Vine	Matrimony Vine	purple	Lycium Europeum
Mignonette	Mignonette	yellow, green, white	Reseda Odorata, Reseda Alba
Mignonette (Wild)	Yellow Weed	green, yellow	Reseda Luteola
Mimulus	Mimulus, Monkey Flower, Musk	spotted yellow	Mimulus Luteus
Mint	Mint	purplish	Mentha
Mint, Apple	Mint, Apple	purplish	Mentha Rotundifolia
Mint, Peppermint	Mint, Peppermint	purplish	Mentha Piperita
Mint, Pennyroyal	Mint, Pennyroyal	purplish	Mentha Pulegium
Mint, Spearmint	Mint, Spearmint	purplish	Mentha Viridis
Mock Orange	White Pipe Tree	white	Philadelphus Coronarius
Monarda	Bee Balm, Oswego Tea	red	Monarda Didyma
Monkshood	Monkshood, Aconite, Wolfsbane, Cupids Car	blue	Aconitum Napellus
Morning Glory	Morning Glory (Blue Bindweed)	blue	Convolvulus Mauritanicus
Morning Glory (Climbing)	Morning Glory	various colours	Convolvulus Major
Morning Glory (Dwarf)	Morning Glory	blue with white star at centre	Convolvulus Tricolor
Myrtle	Periwinkle	purple	Vinca Minor
Myrtle, wax	Candle Berry Myrtle	white	Myrica Cerifera

– N –

Narcissus	Poet's Narcissus	white	N. Poeticus

Double red rose most commonly found in farm gardens.

Nasturtium	Nasturtium, Indian Cresse, Yellow Lark-sheels	yellow	Tropaeolum Majus
New Jersey Tea	New Jersey Tea, Red Root	white	Ceanothus Americanus

– O –

Oxalis	Oxalis, Wood Sorrel	purple	O. Violacea

– P –

Pansy	Heart's Ease, Ladies Delights	purple, yellow, white, blue	Viola Tricolor
Penny Royal (Mock)	Mock Penny Royal	pinkish-purple	Hedeoma Pulegioides
Peony	Piny	crimson, purple, white, red-striped with white; all double	Paeonia, Var: Officinalis (Ancient), Festiva Maxima (1851), Boule de Neige (1862)
Peppergrass	Peppergrass	green	Lepidium Virginicum
Perrenial Pea	Everlasting Pea	violet, purple	Lathyrus Latïfolius
Persicaria	Persicaria, Lady's Thumb	red	Polygonum
Petunia	Petunia	purple, white	P. Violacea, P. Nyctagina Flora
Pheasant's Eye	Pheasant's Eye	red	Adonis Annua
Phlox	Phlox	red, pink, violet, blue, white, variegated	P. Drummondi, P. Paniculata
Phlox (Wild)	Wild Phlox	blue	Phlox Divaricata Canadensis
Pinks	Pinks, Painted Ladies, Star or Snow Pinks	pink, white, kind of carnation type	Dianthus Plumarius
Plantain Lily	Plantain Lily, Funkia, Hosta	insignificant purple	Hosta
Plume Poppy	Plume Poppy	pinkish white	Bocconia Cordata
Poppy	Corn Poppy	red, purple, white	Papaver Rheoas
Poppy	Poppy	white, pink, red, purple	Papaver Somniferum
Primula	Primrose	lilac, crimson, rose, yellow	Primula Polyantha
Prince's Feather	Prince's Feather, Princess Feather	red	Amaranthus Hydridus Var: Hypochondriacus
Proboscis	Unicorn Plant, Devil's Claw		Proboscidea Jussieni

– R –

Ribbon Grass	Gardener's Garters	green, white	Phalaris Arundinacea Picta
Rose, Blush	Maiden's Blush	pale pink	Rosa Alba
Rose, Centifolia	Provence Rose, Cabbage Rose	pink	Rosa Centifolia
Rose, Cinnamon	Cinnamon	deep pink	Rosa Cinnamonea
Rose, Damask	Damask	pale pink, red	Rosa Damascena
Rose, Eglantine	Sweet Briar	pale pink	Rosa Eglanteria
Rose, Gallica	Rosa Mundi	deep pink, crimson	Rosa Gallica
Rose, Moss	Moss Rose	pink, red	Rosa Centifolia Muscosa
Rose, Musk	Musk Rose	white	Rosa Moschata
Rose Bay, striped	Rose Bay	pink	Epilobium Augusti Folium
Rose Campion	Rose Campion, Flower of Bristol, Dusty Miller, Mullein Pink, Nonsuch	crimson	Lychnis Coronaria
Rose of Sharon	Rose of Sharon, Shrub Althea	red, purple, violet	Hibiscus Syriacus
Royal Fern	Royal Fern	green	Osmunda Regalis
Rudbeckia	Coneflower, Black-eyed Susan, Golden Glow	purple, yellow	R. Bicolor Superba, R. Hirta, R. Laciniata, Var: Hortensia
Rue	Rue	yellow	Ruta Graveolens

– S –

Sage	Sage	grey-green	Salvia Officinalus
Salpiglossis (*)	Salpiglossis, Painted Tongue	variegated	S. Sinuata
Savoury	Sweet Savoury, Summer Savoury	lavender, white	Satureja Hortensis

Pink "Salet" moss rose, 1854, with sweet William.

The old pink rose, usually Maiden's Blush, most commonly found in farm gardens.

Scabiosa	Fading Beauty, Mourning Bride, Sweet Scabious	white, red	S. Atropurpurea
Scarlet Runner	Scarlet Creeper	red	Phaseolus Coccineos
Schizanthus	Schizanthus, Fringe Flower	rose, purple	S. Pinnatus
Scilla	Squills	blue	S. Festalis, Hispanica, Autumnalis, Italica
Scurvy Grass	Scurvy Grass	white, green	Cochlearia Officinalis
Silene	Campion, Catchfly, None-So-Pretty	light or deep pink	S. Armeria, S. Tenorei, S. Pendula
Snail Flower	Snail Flower, Corkscrew Flower, Snail Bean	red, blue	Phaseolus Caracalla
Snake Root	Snake Root, Black Cohosh	white	Cimicifuga Racemosa
Snapdragon	Snapdragon, Snout Flower	white, variegated, purple, red, yellow	Antirrhinum Majus
Snowball	Guelder Rose	white	Viburnum Opulus Sterile
Snowdrop	Snowdrop	white	Galanthus Nivalis
Solomon's Seal	Solomon's Seal	greenish-white	Polygonatum Biflorum
Sophora	Sophora, Pagoda Tree	white, blue	S. Japonica
Southernwood	Southernwood, Lad's Love	yellowish white	Artemisia Abrotanum
Spindle Bush	Red-berried Spindle Tree		Euonymus Europaeus
Star of Bethlehem	Star of Bethlehem	white	Ornithogalum Umbellatum
Strawberry Bush	Strawberry Tree	yellowish or reddish green	Euonymus Americanus
Stocks	Stock Gilliflower, Ten Week Stocks	white, rose, crimson, purple, mixed	Matthiola Incana
Sunflower	Sunflower	yellow	Helianthus Annuus
Sun Love	Sun Love	blue	Heliophila Araboides
Sweet Alyssum (*)	Sweet Alyssum, Sweet Alison, Snowdrift, Madwort, Gold Dust	white, yellow	Lobularia Maritima and Saxatile
Sweet Pea	Sweet Pea	various colours	Lathryus Odoratus
Sweet Rocket	Damask Violet, Dame's Violet, Eve Weed	purple, mauve, white	Hesperis Matronalis
Sweet Sultan	Sweet Sultan	white and purple	Centaurea Moschata
Sweet William	Sweet William, Bunch pink	white, pink, red variegated	Dianthus Barbatus

– T –

Tansy	Tansy, Bitter Buttons	yellow	Tanacetum Vulgare
Tarragon	Tarragon	white, green	Artemisia Dranunculus
Thyme	Thyme	rosy lilac	Thymus Serpyllum
Tomato	Love Apples	red, yellow	Lycopersicum Esculentum
Tradescantia	Tradescantia, Spiderwort, Widows Tears	blue	T. Virginiana
Trumpet Vine	Trumpet Vine, Trumpet Creeper	orange	Tecoma Radicans
Tulip	Tulip	white, red, yellow variously marked	Tulipa

– U – and – V –

Valerian	Valerian, Garden Heliotrope	white, red	Valeriana Officinalia Var: Alba & Ruba
Venus' Looking Glass	Venus' Looking Glass	deep blue, white	Specularia, Speculum-Veneris
Verbena	Verbena, Vervain	pink, red, yellow, white	V. Hortensis
Violet	Sweet Violet	blue, purple	Viola Odorata
Virginia Creeper	Virginia Creeper	green turning red	Parthenocissus Quinquefolia

– W – and – X –

Wormwood	Wormwood	green, yellow	Artemisia Absinthium

– Y – and – Z –

Zinnia (*)	Zinnia	scarlet, yellow, orange, green-white, pink, rose	Z. Elegans
Single 1861	Youth		
Double 1865	Old Age		

Valerian

Selected reading

The reader who is interested in nineteenth-century social and domestic life, whether generally or in Canada, will find no end to the number of books which can contribute to an understanding of the subject. Listed here are some which I have found especially valuable. Many are now out of print but can be had from second-hand book dealers or seen in reference libraries.

I have excluded all fiction and political history and have not listed cookbooks, even if Canadian, unless they contain housekeeping principles and practices. Most of the works from which I have quoted in this book are listed.

Old newspapers containing advertisements, which can be seen in archival collections, are invaluable sources of information. The magazines listed can be found in second-hand stores or in some libraries as annually-bound volumes. They are particularly useful for their fine engraved illustrations for fiction and articles on domestic subjects because they show room interiors with furnishings as they were at that time. The fashion plates also often include furnishings and draperies in the latest style of the period.

GENERAL

Bishop, J. Leander, *A History of American Manufactures*. Philadelphia, Edward Young, 1861. Two vols.

Canniff, William, *History of the Settlement of Upper Canada, with special reference to the Bay of Quinte*. Toronto, Dudley and Burns, 1869.

Carroll, Rev. John, D.D., *My Boy Life*. Toronto, William Briggs, 1882.

Christmas, Rev. H., *Pictures of Canadian Life, the Emigrant Churchman in Canada, by a pioneer of the wilderness*. London, R. Bentley, 1849.

Connon, John R., *The Early History of Elora and Vicinity*. Elora, The Elora Express and Fergus News Record, 1930.

Cooley, A. J., *Encyclopaedia of Six Thousand Receipts*. New York, Appleton, 1845; and subsequent editions.

Copleston, Mrs. Edward, *Canada, Why We Live In It and Why We Like It*. London, Parker and Son and Bourn, 1861.

Downing, A. J., *Architecture of Country Houses*. New York, Appleton, 1850.

Dunlop, William, *Statistical Sketches of Upper Canada; for the use of emigrants*. London, John Murray, 1832; Toronto, McClelland & Stewart, 1967.

Fergusson, Adam, *Practical Notes made during a tour in Canada and a portion of the United States in MDCCCXXXI*. Edinburgh, W. Blackwood, 1833. Second edition with added notes made during a second visit to Canada in MDCCCXXXIII. London, T. Cadell, 1834.

Firth, Edith G., *The Town of York, a Collection of Documents of Early Toronto*. Toronto, The Champlain Society for the Government of Ontario, University of Toronto Press, 1962 and 1966. Two vols.—Vol. 1, 1793-1815; Vol. 2, 1815-1834.

Fowler, Thomas, *Journal of a Tour through British America to the Falls of Niagara*. Aberdeen, Lewis Smith, 1832.

Guillet, Edwin G., *Early Life in Upper Canada*. Toronto, The Ontario Publishing Company, 1933; and subsequent editions.

Haight, Canniff, *Country Life in Canada Fifty Years Ago*. Toronto, Hunter Rose, 1885.

Hind, Henry Y., *Eighty Years' Progress of British North America*. Toronto, L. Stebbins, 1863.

Howison, John, *Canada in the Years 1832,* *1833, and 1834*. Dublin, 1835.

Howison, John, *Sketches of Upper Canada ...* Edinburgh, Oliver and Boyd, 1821; New York, Johnson Reprint Corp., 1965.

Kingston, W. H. G., *Western Wanderings, or a Pleasure Tour of the Canadas*. London, Chapman and Hall, 1856.

Lamond, Robert, *Narrative of the Rise and Progress of Emigration from the Counties of Lanark and Renfrew to the New Settlements in Upper Canada. . . .* Glasgow, 1821; San Francisco, California State Library Reprint, 1941.

Langton, H. H., ed., *A Gentlewoman in Upper Canada: The Journals of Anne Langton*. Toronto, Clarke Irwin, 1950; paperback, 1964.

Langton, John, *Early Days in Upper Canada: Letters of John Langton from the backwoods of Upper Canada and the Audit Office of the Province of Canada*, ed. by W. A. Langton, Toronto, Macmillan, 1926.

Loudon, J. C., *An Encyclopaedia of Cottage, Farm and Villa Architecture and Furniture*. London, Longmans, 1833; and subsequent editions.

MacRae, Marion and Adamson, A., *The Ancestral Roof*. Toronto, Clarke Irwin, 1963.

Moodie, Susanna, *Life in the Clearings versus the Bush*. London, Richard Bentley, 1853; and subsequent editions.

Moodie, Susanna, *Roughing It in the Bush; or Forest Life in Canada*. London, Richard Bentley, 1852; and subsequent editions.

Need, Thomas, *Six Years in the Bush; or Extracts from the journal of a settler in Upper Canada, 1832-1838*. London, Simpkin, Marshall and Company, 1838.

Pickering, Joseph, *Inquiries of an emigrant ...* London, E. Wilson, 1832.

Scherck, Michael Gonder, *Pen Pictures of Early Pioneer Life in Upper Canada, by a "Canuck"*. Toronto, William Briggs, 1905.

Sellar, Robert, *A Scotsman in Upper Canada: The Narrative of Gordon Sellar*, (published in 1915 as *True Makers of Canada*). Toronto, Clarke Irwin, 1969.

Smith, W. H., *Canada Past, Present and Future*. Toronto, Thomas Maclear, 1851.

DOMESTIC LIFE

Abrahamson, Una, *God Bless Our Home; Domestic Life in 19th Century Canada*. Toronto, Burns and MacEachern, 1966.

Anonymous, *The Cook Not Mad; or Rational Cookery: being a Collection of original and selected Receipts, · · ·* Kingston. James Macfarlane, 1831.

Anonymous, *Family and Housekeeper's Guide: A manual of Household Management*. Auburn, N.Y., Auburn Publishing Co., 1859.

Anonymous, *Ladies' Indispensible Assistant*, copyright E. Hutchinson, also F. J. Dow. New York, 1850.

Brett, K. B., *Ontario Handwoven Textiles*. Toronto, Royal Ontario Museum, 1956.

Beecher, Catharine E., *A Treatise on Domestic Economy*. New York, Harper, 1842.

Beecher, Catharine E. and Stowe, Harriet Beecher, *The American Woman's Home*. New York, J. B. Ford, 1869.

Child, Mrs., *The American Frugal Housewife*. Boston, Carter Hendee, 1835.

Copley, Esther, *The Housekeeper's Guide*. London, Jackson and Walford, 1834.

Cummings, A. L. (compiler), *Bed Hangings; a treatise on fabrics and style in the curtaining of beds*. Boston, Society for the Preservation of New England Antiquities, 1961.

Earle, Alice Morse, *Home Life in Colonial Days*. New York, Macmillan, 1898.

Gould, Mary Earle, *The Early American House*. Rutland, Vermont, Charles E. Tuttle, 1965.

Leslie, Miss (Eliza), *The Behaviour Book*. Philadelphia, A. Hart, 1853.

Leslie, Miss (Eliza), *The House Book, a manual of Domestic Economy for Town and Country*. Philadelphia, Carey and Hart, 1840; and subsequent editions.

Leslie, Miss (Eliza), *The Lady's Receipt Book*. Philadelphia, A. Hart, 1850.

Married Lady, A, *The Improved Housewife*, copyright A. L. Webster. Hartford, Connecticut, 1843.

Rawson, Marion Nicholl, *Candle Days*. New York, Century, 1927.

Roy, L. M. A., *The Candle Book*. Brattleboro, Vermont, Stephen Daye Press, 1927.

Spencer, Audrey, *Spinning and Weaving at Upper Canada Village*. Toronto, Ryerson, 1964.

Traill, Mrs. C. P., *The Female Emigrant's Guide, and Hints on Canadian Housekeeping*. Sold by Maclear and Co., Toronto, 1854. Later editions published under title: *The Canadian Settler's Guide*, printed at the office of "The Old Countryman," Toronto, 1855, and (enlarged) 1857.

Tunis, Edwin, *Colonial Living*. Cleveland and New York, World Publishing, 1957.

Webster, Thomas, *Encyclopaedia of Domestic Economy*. London, Longmans, 1844; New York, Harper, 1845.

Willich, A. P. M., *Domestic Encyclopaedia*. London, Murray and Highley, 1802; and subsequent editions.

FURNITURE AND FURNISHINGS

Anonymous, *Art Recreations*. Boston, J. E. Tilton, 1859.

Candee, Richard M., *Housepaints in Colonial America: Their materials, manufacture and application*. New York, Chromatic Publishing, 1969.

Christensen, Erwin O., *The Index of American Design*. New York, Macmillan, 1950.

Collard, Elizabeth, *Nineteenth Century Pottery and Porcelain in Canada*. Montreal, McGill University Press, 1967.

Comstock, Helen, *American Furniture*. New York, Studio Book, Viking Press, 1962.

Dreppard, Carl W., *A Dictionary of American Antiques*. Garden City, N.Y., Doubleday, 1952.

Dreppard, Carl W., *Handbook of Antique Chairs*. Garden City, N.Y., Doubleday, 1948.

Dreppard, Carl W., *Victorian, the Cinderella of Antiques*. Garden City, N.Y., Doubleday, 1950.

Earle, Alice Morse, *China Collecting in America*. London, Lawrence and Bullen, 1892.

Edwards, Ralph, and Ramsey, L. G., eds., *The Connoisseur Period Guides to the Houses, Decoration, Furnishings and Chattels of the Classic Periods. The Late Georgian Period 1760-1810*, (1956). *The Regency Period, 1810-1830*, (1958). *The Early Victorian Period, 1830-1860*, (1958). London, The Connoisseur.

Elville, E. M., *English and Irish Glass, 1750-1950*. London, Country Life, 1953.

Entwisle, E. A., *A Literary History of Wallpaper*. London, Batsford, 1960.

Entwisle, E. A., *Wallpapers of the Victorian Era*. Leigh-on-Sea, F. Lewis, 1964.

Fastnedge, Ralph, *Sheraton Furniture*. London, Faber and Faber, 1962.

Finley, Ruth E., *Old Patchwork Quilts and the Women who Made Them*. Philadelphia and London, Lippincott, 1929.

Godden, Geoffrey A., *British Pottery and Porcelain*. London, Arthur Barker, 1963.

Godden, Geoffrey A., *Victorian Porcelain*. London, Herbert Jenkins, 1961.

Gould, Mary Earle, *Antique Tin and Toleware*. Rutland, Vermont, Charles E. Tuttle, 1957.

Gould, Mary Earle, *Early American Woodenware and other Kitchen Utensils*. Rutland, Vermont, Charles E. Tuttle, 1962.

Hall, John, *The Cabinetmakers Assistant*. Baltimore, 1840.

Hayward, A. H., *Colonial Lighting*. Boston, B. J. Brimmer Co., 1923; New York, Dover Publications, 1962.

Hughes, G. Bernard, *English and Scottish Earthenware*. London, Lutterworth, 1961.

Hughes, G. Bernard, *Victorian Pottery and Porcelain*. London, Country Life, 1959.

Hughes, G. Bernard and Therle, *After the Regency, a Guide to Late Georgian and Early Victorian Collecting*. London, Lutterworth, 1952.

Jefferys, C. W. (assisted by McLean, T. W.), *Picture Gallery of Canadian History*. Toronto, Ryerson, 1942; and subsequent editions. Three vols.

Jourdain, Margaret, (revised by Fastnedge, Ralph), *Regency Furniture*. London, Country Life, 1965.

Kent, William Winroth, *The Hooked Rug*. New York, Dodd Meade, 1930; New York, Tudor, 1941.

Kettell, Russell Hawes, *The Pine Furniture of Early New England*. New York, Dover Publications, 1929; and subsequent editions.

Kovel, R. M. and T. H., *American Country Furniture*. New York, Crown Publishers, 1965.

Langdon, J. E., *Canadian Silversmiths, 1700-1900*. Lunenburg, Vermont, privately printed

by Stinehour Press, 1966.

Lea, Zilla Rider, *The Ornamented Chair: Its development in America, 1700-1890*. Rutland, Vermont, Charles E. Tuttle, 1960.

Lee, Ruth Webb, *Early American Pressed Glass*. Pittsford, N.Y., The Author, 1931; and subsequent editions.

Lichten, Frances, *Decorative Art of Victoria's Era*. New York, Scribners, 1950.

Little, Frances, *Early American Textiles*. New York, Century, 1931.

Little, Nina Fletcher, *American Decorative Wall Painting 1700-1850*. Old Sturbridge Village, Sturbridge, Mass., in co-operation with Studio Publications, New York, 1952.

McKearin, George S. and Helen, *American Glass*. New York, Crown, 1941.

Miller, Edgar G., *The Standard Book of American Antique Furniture*. New York, Greystone Press, 1937; and subsequent editions.

Minhinnick, Jeanne, *The Early Furniture in Upper Canada Village*. Toronto, Ryerson, 1964.

Musgrave, Clifford, *Regency Furniture*. London, Faber and Faber, 1961.

Ormsbee, Thomas H., *Field Guide to American Victorian Furniture*. Boston, Little Brown, 1952; and subsequent editions.

Ormsbee, Thomas H., *Field Guide to Early American Furniture*. Boston, Little Brown, 1951; and subsequent editions.

Otto, Celia Jackson, *American 19th Century Furniture*. New York, Viking Press, 1965.

Palardy, Jean, (trans. by McLean, Eric), *The Early Furniture of French Canada*. Toronto, Macmillan, 1963.

Potter, M. and A., *Interiors: A record of some of the changes in interior design and furniture of the English home from medieval times to the present day*. London, Jarrolds, 1957.

Russell, Loris, *A Heritage of Light*. Toronto, University of Toronto Press, 1968.

Spendlove, F. St.G., *Collector's Luck*. Toronto, Ryerson, 1960.

Stevens, Gerald, *The Canadian Collector*. Toronto, Ryerson, 1957.

Stevens, Gerald, *Canadian Glass*. Toronto, Ryerson, 1967.

Stevens, Gerald, *Early Ontario Furniture*. Toronto, Royal Ontario Museum and University of Toronto Press, 1965.

Stevens, Gerald, *Early Ontario Glass*. Toronto, University of Toronto Press and Royal Ontario Museum, 1965.

Stevens, Gerald, *In a Canadian Attic*. Toronto, Ryerson, 1963.

Symonds, R. W. and Whinery, B. B., *Victorian Furniture*. London, Country Life, 1962.

Thorn, C. Jordan, *Handbook of Old Pottery and Porcelain Marks*. New York, Tudor, 1947; and subsequent editions.

Wakefield, Hugh, *Nineteenth Century British Glass*. London, Faber and Faber, 1961.

Waring, Janet. *Early American Wall Stencils*. New York, William R. Scott, 1937.

GARDENING

Beadle, D. W., *Canadian Fruit, Flower and Kitchen Gardener*. Toronto, J. Campbell and Son, 1872.

Breck, Joseph, *The Flower Garden*. Boston, John P. Jewett, 1851.

Buist, Robert, *American Flower Garden Directory*. New York, A. O. Moore, 1859.

Coats, Alice M., *Flowers and their Histories*. London, A. & C. Black, 1956.

Coats, Alice M., *Garden Shrubs and their Histories*. London, Vista Books, 1963.

Downing, A. J., *Treatise on the Theory and Practice of Landscape Gardening adapted to North America*. New York, Wiley and Putnam, 1860.

Earle, Alice Morse, *Old Time Gardens*. New York, Macmillan, 1901.

Jack, Mrs. Annie L., *The Canadian Garden*. Toronto, Musson, 1903.

Kemp, E., *How to Lay out a Garden*. New York, Wiley and Halsted, 1858.

Lady, A, *Every Lady's Guide to Her Own Greenhouse*. London, W. S. Orr, 1851.

Lockwood, Alice G., *Gardens of Colony and State*. New York, Charles Scribners, 1931-34. Two vols.

Loudon, J. C., *The Encyclopaedia of Gardening*. London, Longmans, 1822.

Loudon, J. C., *The Gardener's Magazine*. London, Longmans, published from 1826 to 1843.

Loudon, Mrs. Jane, *The Ladies' Companion to the Flower Garden*. London, William Smith, 1842.

Parker, Asa, *The Canadian Gardener*. Aylmer, Quebec, Thomas Watson, 1851.

Provancher, L'Abbé L., *Le Verger, le Potager et le parterre dans la province de Québec*. Quebec, C. Darveau, 1874.

Rohde, Eleanour S., *The Scented Garden*. Boston and New York, Hale, Cushman and Flint, 1936.

Rohde, Eleanour S., *Story of the Garden, with a chapter on American gardens by Mrs. Francis King*. Boston and New York, Hale, Cushman and Flint, 1936.

Tabor, Grace, *Old Fashioned Gardening*. New York, McBride, Nast and Co., 1913.

Traill, Mrs. C. P., *Studies of Plant Life in Canada*. Ottawa, Woodburn, 1885.

Good Words	London, 1860-1911
Belgravia	London, 1866-1899
London Society	London, 1862-1898
The Quiver	London, also New York edition, 1861-1866
Sunday at Home	London, 1854-1878
Household Words	London, 1850-1858
All the Year Round	London, 1859-1895
Leisure Hour Monthly	London, 1852-1899
Once a Week	London, 1859-1880
Punch	London, 1841-
Sunday Magazine	London, 1854-1906
Godey's Magazine	Philadelphia, 1830-1898
Graham's American Monthly Magazine	Philadelphia, 1826-1848
Peterson's Magazine	Philadelphia and New York, 1842-1898

Glossary

Alkanet Chips
Dried roots of a plant which yield a brilliant red dye material.

Ambrotype
An improvement of the daguerreotype in which the photographic image was produced on glass by the "wet plate" process. Popular throughout America from 1850 to 1865.

Arch-back
The arched top rail of a Windsor chair which curves forward at each side to form the arms.

Backboard
A common term for the gallery at the rear of the top surface of a chest of drawers, sideboard, wash-stand, etc.

Back gallery
A metal or wood railing on the edge of a shelf, sideboard, or table top.

Back splat
The central vertical member in the back of a chair.

Balloon-back chairs
Dining and drawing room chairs, c. 1850 and later, in which the general outline of the back resembled the shape of a balloon.

Banc-lit
A box-like bench with sides and back: the seat pulled forward to let down and form a bed. Synonymous with bunk, box and settle bed.

Bandbox
Originally any box which held small dress articles such as ribbands. In the nineteenth century, an oval or round box of split or sawed wood or cardboard, decorated or covered with wallpaper. For holding bonnets, hats, etc.

Basalt
A smooth, unglazed black stone ware introduced by Josiah Wedgwood in the eighteenth century and continuously made since then.

Battledore and shuttlecock
An ancient game still played in the nineteenth century, consisting of tossing the shuttlecock (a cork base surrounded by feathers) with parchment racquets.

Bedding out
The planting of nursery-grown flowers in a garden bed.

Bee skepe
Also pronounced "skip"; a straw beehive.

Berlin needlework
Worsted embroidery done with fine wool in brilliant colours imported from Berlin, Germany, in the nineteenth century.

Bevel
Edge of a sheet of wood or glass cut to an oblique angle.

Blanket rail
A decoratively turned rail joining the two posts at the foot of a bed. Used instead of a footboard.

Bosses
On furniture; small oval or round applied ornaments in metal or wood.

Bow-back
An eighteenth-century Windsor chair design, with a hooped or curved back continuing in a forward sweep down to the arms or chair seat.

Boston-style rocker
A rocking chair based on the Windsor style, usually painted and decorated and with a roll-front seat; chiefly factory-produced and sold everywhere from the mid-nineteenth century.

Brace-back
A Windsor chair in which two metal or wood braces extend from seat to back rail as a triangular support.

Bracket foot
Two pieces of wood joined at an angle to make the foot on a piece of cased furniture.

Brocatelle
A nineteenth-century silk fabric resembling damask, with a pattern which appears to be embossed.

Calendered
Fabrics glazed by passing them between hollow heated cylinders.

Camlet and camleteen
Eighteenth-century woolen upholstery fabrics made in a variety of weaves.

Candle rod
The rod from which wicks were suspended in the process of candle-dipping.

Captain's chair
A low-back Windsor chair, also known as a bar-room or firehouse Windsor.

Cased glass
Glass articles covered with a glass overlay in contrasting colour which is cut to reveal the inner surface in a decorative pattern.

Carcass
The frame of any piece of cased furniture.

Castor or cruet stand
A frame, usually silver or other metal, to hold stoppered bottles and shakers containing oil, vinegar, salt, pepper and other condiments for the table.

Caul
The inner membrane enclosing the foetus before birth, especially the portions which sometimes envelop the head of a child at birth. Popularly supposed to protect against drowning.

Celadon green
A pale grey-green colour famous in Chinese porcelain and popular in eighteenth-century decorative painting.

Centre-rail
Same as cross-rail; the horizontal member joining the two side posts on the back of a chair.

Chair rail
A wood moulding or narrow board fastened to the wall about 30 inches above the floor to prevent damage to the plaster by the back rails of chairs.

Chamber or bed-chamber
Common term for bedroom in the nineteenth century.

Chamfered
In furniture, a right-angled corner cut away to form a bevel.

Chapbooks
Small, unbound pamphlets or books of popular tales and ballads, including the first stories published especially for children; sold in the streets by "chapmen" in the late eighteenth and early nineteenth century.

Cheval glass
A full-length adjustable swinging mirror suspended in a frame.

Chimney glass
A mirror designed to be hung over a fireplace.

Chimney-pot ends
Modern collector's term for a backboard with crested panels at each end, on the back of Empire period sideboards and chests of drawers, c. 1825-50.

Chromo-lithographs
Popular, cheap pictures reproduced by the lithographic process in colours, from 1860.

Comb-back
A Windsor chair in which a comb-shaped group of spindles extend above the centre back.

Commode
A low chest of drawers or a night stand containing a chamber pot.

Common chairs
A term constantly used in chairmakers' advertisements in Upper Canada to denote slat- or ladder-back chairs as opposed to Windsor chairs.

Console table
A table affixed to the wall by brackets or supported by a pair of front legs.

Crocket
A small ornament in the form of leaves or buds derived from Gothic architecture and used in the ornamentation of nineteenth-century furniture in the Gothic taste.

Crotch-grained wood
A veneer cut at the crotch of a tree, with a feather-like or curly grain.

Distemper colouring
Opaque water colours used in nineteenth-century wall painting.

Dog-irons
Another name for fire-dogs or andirons, used in pairs to support burning wood in a fireplace.

Dormer
A small window set in the roof timbering.

Drugget
A term applied to several varieties of cheap carpet.

Duck's nest (grate)
A half-round iron grate for burning coal or wood, seen in marble mantelpieces of the 1850s and '60s.

Dumb stove
A cylinder of sheet metal inserted between stovepipes to radiate extra heat.

Dunce-cap
A metal heat chamber shaped like a dunce's cap, placed on top of a Franklin stove; alternately an urn filled with water placed in this position as a humidifier.

Dundee stove
Box stoves imported in quantity to Upper Canada from Dundee, Scotland.

Dutch foot
A pad or spoon-shaped foot on a curved or cabriole furniture leg.

Eaves
Projection of a roof over a wall face.

Emery
In domestic use, a stick coated with crystalline corundum mixed with oxides of iron and silica, used for sharpening needles; also a bag traditionally made to resemble a strawberry, filled with ground particles of same.

Empire style
Originating in France under Napoleon as a classic revival style of art, architecture and decoration, with massive, lavishly trimmed furniture. In England, Thomas Sheraton and Thomas Hope were the leading exponents of the style, which also influenced the designs of Duncan Phyfe in America.

Fan-back
Windsor chair with spindles that diverge as they rise from the seat to produce a fan-shaped back.

Festoons
Short draperies applied to window curtains or bed valances.

Finial
A terminal ornament on parts of furniture such as chair and bed posts, ends of curtain rods, etc.

Fish drainer
Perforated ceramic tray with large centre hole, used on top of ordinary platter to serve fish which has been cooked in water.

Flock paper
Wallpaper with a design painted with adhesive gum onto which powdered wool or felt is blown, producing a suede-like surface.

French, or New French, style
The term used to describe Louis XV revival furniture styles in mid-nineteenth-century America.

French bed
Early nineteenth-century bed with high curving scrolled head and foot boards of equal height.

Front (The)
The waterfront area along the Niagara River and the north shore of the St. Lawrence River and Lake Ontario, where the first settlements in Upper Canada were established.

Fustic
A yellow dye made from West Indian mulberry wood.

Gentleman's chair
An armchair in the Louis XV revival style, usually part of a drawing room suite, c. 1860.

Gesso
A prepared surface of plaster as a ground for painting; a work of art in plaster.

Gimp
Fancy silk, linen or wool tape used to cover tacks in upholstering.

Gothic style
In furniture, an adaptation in the seventeenth, eighteenth and nineteenth centuries of some of the design elements of medieval Gothic forms.

Granite ware
Alternative name for ironstone pottery.

Grecian chairs
An all-embracing term for an enormous variety of chairs in the Greek revival style from about 1790 to 1850.

Grisaille
Painting or printing in monochrome greys or beiges which gives the effect of a sculptured relief.

Half-tester
A canopy over the head section of a bed.

Hanging griddles
Griddles with a bale or hoop handle for suspending from fireplace trammel.

Harateen
A woolen fabric of the eighteenth and early nineteenth century, now obsolete.

Hepplewhite style
English furniture in the classic tradition designed by George Hepplewhite whose "Cabinetmaker and Upholsterer's Guide," published 1788, influenced designs everywhere.

Hob grate
A type of English grate, the basket of which is flanked by two box-like shelves.

Horn pane
A thin, semi-transparent sheet of horn which preceded the use of glass in lanterns.

Horsehair
Or haircloth—an upholstery fabric made of horsehair in black and various colours.

H-stretcher
A rung joining two stretchers between the front and back legs of a chair thus forming the letter H.

Ironstone
Hard white pottery, also known as granite-ware, extensively made and used in the nineteenth century.

Jacquard
Revolutionary weaving process developed in France by J. M. Jacquard in 1801. The loom he invented produced coverlets in multi-coloured tapestry, pictorial and damask patterns and was adapted about 1825 by the carpet industry.

Japanned articles
Sheet iron, tin, pewter, papier-mâché and wooden articles coated with a quick-drying, oil-based colour varnish.

Keystoned arch
An architectural device in which a wedge shape is inserted at the top of the curve of an arch.

Lady's chair
An upholstered chair with vestigial arms, in the Louis XV revival style, c. 1860.

Linsey-woolsey
A wool and linen fabric, chiefly used for summer blankets and winter sheets.

Loop-back
Same as hoop-back. Windsor chair with a hooped or loop shaped back.

Louis XV style
A revival of the French style which began under Louis Philippe and influenced furniture design in America between 1840 and 1860.

Low-back
A Windsor chair in which the back rail is raised, with or without a comb, only slightly higher than the arms. Sometimes called a bar-room, captain's, or firehouse Windsor.

Lug
Handle or extension on objects such as washtubs by which they are lifted.

Lustre
A glass chandelier, candelabrum, or vase, hung with prismatic crystal drops or pendants.

Moreen
A commonly used eighteenth- and nineteenth-century wool upholstery fabric.

Mortise-and-tenon
A method of joining two pieces of wood by inserting a projecting tenon into a corresponding incised (mortised) opening.

Mull
Fine transparent cotton fabric used for curtaining.

Muntin bars
The dividing bars in window frames in which glass panes are mounted.

Ormolu
Gilded bronze used in the decoration of furniture.

Ox-gall
The gall of an ox, extensively used in household cleaning and washing in the nineteenth century.

Palliasse
A thin straw mattress.

Papier-mâché
Pulped paper, moulded into furniture, boxes, trays, etc. and having a decorated japanned finish.

Parian
A nineteenth-century porcelain resembling Parian marble, used chiefly for jugs, vases, and statuettes.

Pearlash
The common name for impure carbonate of potash, sold commercially as saleratus. It preceded baking-powder.

Pier glass
A wall mirror usually hung between windows above a pier table.

Pier table
A small table originally used between two windows in formal rooms, with a pier mirror hung above it.

Pilaster
A cabinetmaking element comprising a base, column, shaft and capital, also a flat upright member used to support an overhanging surface such as a shelf or drawer.

Pillow-back
Modern term for a chair in which a slightly canted pillow-shaped section is inserted in

the back rail.

Pillow sham
A single sheet of fabric, usually embroidered, laid over each pillow when the bed is made up for the day.

Pintle
A pin or bolt on which another part turns or is suspended.

Plenum chamber
An enclosed space around a stove from which heat is distributed by pipes.

Plinth
The base of a pedestal, column or pilaster.

Porringer
A small flat-bottomed dish for soup or porridge, used chiefly by children.

Potpourri
A mixture of dried petals of different flowers and spices; kept in a bag or jar for its perfume.

Prie-dieu
A low armless chair with a high back having an upholstered shelf on the back rail on which a person kneeling in prayer rested his arms.

Queensware
A name applied in the eighteenth century to lightweight cream-coloured pottery made by Josiah Wedgwood.

Rebated (rabbeted) joints
Two wood surfaces planed or notched to fit together.

Redware
Pottery made from a red clay.

Reeded
Continuous, closely set beading in parallel lines; opposite of fluting.

Regency style
Name applied to English architecture and furnishings developed during the period when George IV was Prince Regent, (1810-20) and popular for some years later; concurrent with French Directoire and Empire styles which were based on Greek, Roman and Egyptian motifs.

Register wheel
A perforated cast-iron plate in floor or wall which could be closed and opened to control the flow of heat.

Revolving gridiron
Circular gridiron pivoted at its centre to a long handle, used for broiling meat in the fireplace.

Ring-and-ball turnings
Alternate ball- and ring-shaped turnings on furniture legs, posts, spindles and stretchers.

Rococo style
Originally rock and shell motifs used in the eighteenth century, and revived in mid-nineteenth-century furniture decoration.

Rod-back
Any chair of which the back is formed with round rods.

Sabre legs
Chair legs shaped like a sabre or scimitar with a pronounced concave curve.

Sander
A box with perforated top from which sand was sprinkled to dry ink writing. Used till the mid-nineteenth century when blotting paper was introduced.

Scroll painting
Outline of a scroll used in decorative painting of furniture.

Settle
A high-backed bench usually placed at right angles to a fireplace.

Shakers
An American religious sect living in celibate communities in rural areas. During the nineteenth century they made and sold furniture of exceptional simplicity and beauty.

Sheraton style
Furniture showing the influence of designs in the "Cabinetmaker and Upholsterer's Drawing Book" by Thomas Sheraton, published in London, 1791 to 1794.

Sleigh bed
American adaptation of the French bed having head and foot boards of equal height.

Slip room
A small bedroom formed by partitioning a larger room.

Spade foot
Enlarged square or tapered end of a chair leg.

Spermaceti
Fatty substance from the head of the sperm whale; used in making candles and as a lamp fuel.

Splayed legs
Outward-slanting legs on chairs, benches, tables, etc.

Squab
A loosely stuffed cushion, used on chairs, benches and stools.

Stearic acid
A purified fatty acid which was used as an additive in candlemaking to produce a clear, smokeless flame.

Stone china
Tableware made by the Spode pottery in England during the nineteenth century. It was cheap, attractive and durable.

Stoneware
Pottery fired at high temperature, producing grey and brown utensils with a hard non-porous glaze.

Strapwork
A repeated interlaced design of narrow strips used on chair backs or applied to cased furniture (dressers, etc.) and as a design in decorative painting.

Stretchers
Cross pieces which connect, brace and strengthen the legs of furniture.

Stringing
A narrow strip of veneer or metal used as a decorative inlaid border.

Swag
Fabric draped in a loose horizontal fold and gathered at each end, usually as a window decoration.

Tabernacle mirror
Late eighteenth-, early nineteenth-century mirror frame, usually gilded, with a row of balls under a cornice and a decorated panel over the mirror area.

Tester
A framework for bed hangings consisting of four laths attached to the top of the posts on a high-post bed.

Tick
A linen or cotton case or cover containing feather or other mattress and pillow fillings.

Trafalgar chairs
Chairs with designs incorporating nautical motifs celebrating Nelson's victory at Trafalgar, 1815.

Trammel
A notched iron rod hung on the crane in a fireplace on which pots could be suspended at different heights.

Trundle (or truckle) bed
A small bed on castors. It rolled under a full-size bed when not in use.

Turn-spit
A person, often a child, delegated to turn the spit before the fire; also a mechanical jack used for the same purpose.

Vase splat
A vase-shaped vertical centre section of a chair back joining the seat and back rail.

Venetian carpet
A common, plain-textured carpet, usually striped, in which the woolen warp conceals the hemp, cotton or woolen woof; used chiefly for bedrooms and stairs in the nineteenth century.

Wainscot
A wooden lining applied as panelling to interior walls; also an early English chair style with a solid wood panelled back.

What-not
An ornamental open shelf on which bric-a-brac is displayed.

Writing-arm Windsor
Chair fitted with a broad flat arm to serve as a writing surface, sometimes with a drawer underneath.

Zommo
A furniture trade term for a small bedside stand to contain a chamber pot.

Index